Uprising

the October Rebellion in Ecuador

Uprising
the October Rebellion in Ecuador

Leonidas Iza, Andrés Tapia, and Andrés Madrid

Resistance Books, London and The International Institute for Education and Research, Amsterdam

Resistance Books
resistancebooks.org
info@resistancebooks.org

The International Institute for Education and Research
iire.org
iire@iire.org

Published 2023 by Resistance Books and the International Institute for Education and Research
First published as *Estallido: La Rebelión de Octubre en Ecuador* in Spanish August 2020 by Ediciones Red Kapari (Quito, Ecuador)

Copyright
Translation © Resistance Books.
Original text in Spanish © Leonidas Iza, Andrés Tapia, and Andrés Madrid

Design
Michael Wallace and Gareth Lindsay
Cover montage by Tony Balseca

Typefaces
Karrik by Jean-Baptiste Morizot and Lucas Le Bihan
Cardo by David Perry

Photos
Daniel Andrade, Luis Herrera R., Vinicio Cóndor, Andrés León, Kevin Armendáriz, Santiago Fernández, Fernanda Gallardo, Alex Villacís, Andrés Loor, Efraín Castellanos, Patricio Hidalgo, Alex Muñoz Terán, Axel Naranjo, Emilio Narváez, Nuno Alfonso, Charlotte Christa Schöneberg Merizalde, Víctor Romero, Hamilton López, David Díaz Arcos, Bryan Garcés, Alejandro Ramírez Anderson, Karen Toro, Fluxus Foto, Cooperativa Audiovisual, Kapucha Comunicación and CONFENIAE Comunicaciones

Uprising: the October Rebellion in Ecuador is issue 74 of the *Notebooks for Study and Research* published by the International Institute for Research and Education

ISBN: 978-0-902869-23-3 pbk
E-ISBN: 978-0-902869-22-6 e-pub

Acknowledgements

The publishers are honoured that the authors Leonidas Iza, Andrés Tapia, and Andrés Madrid have granted Resistance Books and the IIRE the permission to produce the English edition of their book *Estallido: La Rebelión de Octubre en Ecuador*. We are publishing this book as an act of solidarity with the heroic struggle of the Indigenous and campesino movement of Ecuador. We hope this English edition of the book will fulfil the aims of the authors which are to educate a new generation of Indigenous and urban activists and that it is read by those on the front lines of many more, connected struggles, around the world.

The publishers are grateful for the work of translation by Mike Gonzalez, Iain Bruce, Terry Conway, and that of Diana Almeida and Felipe Kohler as a collaboration by the Crisis Magazine editorial team. Jim Ryan proof-read the manuscript, Fred Leplat organised the production, and Michael Wallace and Gareth Lindsay designed the book. Without their contribution, it would not have been possible to publish *Uprising: the October Rebellion in Ecuador*.

Contents

Acknowledgements	V
About the authors	X
Preface to the English edition, *Michael Löwy*	1
Preface to the second Spanish edition, *Leonidas Iza, Andrés Tapia, and Andrés Madrid*	5
Back to October: Preface to the first Spanish edition, *Hernán Ouviña*	7
Introduction	23

I. IMMINENCE: BACKGROUND, ACCUMULATED EXPERIENCE AND RUPTURE — 31

1	A slow-cooked insurrection	31
1.1	Capitalist development in Ecuador: accumulation and crisis	33
1.2	Economic dependence on the world market	34
1.3	Foreign debt: the fatal result of the untouched economic structure	37
1.4	The pressure of the crisis on the working class	40
1.5	Extractivism as an imperialist symptom	43
1.6	Deregulatory state intervention	46
1.7	Twins and rivals: Keynesian and neoliberal 'solutions' to the crisis	49
2	The crisis of legitimacy of the political system	50
3	The spectre of class struggle is haunting Ecuador	56
3.1	Recovery and the return to a critical period, 2007–2016	58
3.2	The period of 'calm': 2017–2018	61
3.3	Mobilization growth in 2019	63
4	Virtue and chance: the collapse of 'dialogue' with the government and the X factor	64

II. AWAKENING: DETERMINATION, STRUGGLE AND RESISTANCE — 75

1	Popular uprising and escalating repression	76
1.1	Start of the national outbreak, 3–6 October	78
1.2	The taking of Quito: the country burns from north to south, 7–10 October	80
1.3	'Curfew and resistance', 11–13 October	84
1.4	Negotiation with burning barricades, 13–14 October	86

2	The leading role of the Ecuadorean Indigenous movement	88
2.1	'We have not come alone; we are accompanied by the people'	90
2.2	Changes in the character and ways of working of the anti-capitalists	93
3	October's actors: pessimism of reason and optimism of the will	96
3.1	Growth of the proletariat and weakness of the trade union movement	97
3.2	Urban uprising and solidarity links between city and countryside	103
3.3	Warmi taki: the struggle of women in the rebellion	105
3.4	Youth: politicization and generational renewal	109
3.5	Range of peasant and Indigenous organizations	112
3.6	Institutional left, liberal performance and the society of the spectacle	114
3.7	The ruling classes: a sick, defeated lineage	118
4	The state: from consensual network to coercive machine	121
4.1	Strengthening the chain of command and the conception of total warfare	124
4.2	Aggravated use of force	127
4.3	Re-equipment and operational modernization	131
4.4	Improving the pay of officers and lower ranks	132
4.5	The state of emergency: more frequent and habitual than exceptional	133
5	Control of official discourse: if business loses, do we all lose?	138
5.1	'Tell them to stay in the wilderness': the media corporations	141
6	Stories that silenced the noise of the official media	147
	III. IMPACT: LESSONS, DEBATES AND PERSPECTIVES	175
1	The memory of history and new forms of struggle	176
1.1	The Community, Indigenous and People's Guards	178
1.2	Street struggle, popular inventiveness and grassroots power	182
1.3	The Indigenous 'state of emergency', popular justice and the wave of occupations	185
1.4	People's solidarity and support for provisions	190
1.5	Symbolic uprising and the myth of October	196
1.6	Lumpenbourgeois Culture And The Excesses Of Popular Rage	202
2	Problems of the rebellion	205
2.1	A repressive apparatus renovated in the boom	205
2.2	The decadent and opportunistic ethos of the party system	206
2.3	Political short-termism, democratic illusions and the absence of any perspective for power	209

3	The question of violence	210
3.1	The state's violent response to protest	211
3.2	The paradox of violence: between the Manual of Good Manners and dignity	213
3.3	Arthur Fleck, popular anger and an unbearable situation	217
4	Pending tasks and prospects for emancipation	220
4.1	Unity of the anti-capitalist left	221
4.2	Expanding the social and organizational network	224
4.3	Preventive counterrevolution and McCarthyist politics	226
4.4	Confronting the actually existing power	228
	EPILOGUE: OUR DAY-TO-DAY OCTOBER	243
Bibliography		247
Appendix: Platform for the 'Campaign of Escalating Struggle'		257
1	Dialogue only between equals	257
2	The Campaign of Escalating Struggle and the people's demands	262
3	Unity in action and its consequences	266
You, poem dedicated to María Paula Romo, in the heat of the repression of the Uprising of October 2019		267
About the publishers		276

About the authors

Leonidas Iza is President of the Confederation of Indigenous Nationalities of Ecuador (CONAIE), and is the best-known of a new generation of Indigenous leaders in Ecuador. He emerged as one of the central leaders of the October uprising, when he was President of the Cotopaxi Indigenous and Campesino Movement.

Andrés Tapia is Head of Communications at the Confederation of Indigenous Nationalities of Ecuadorean Amazonia CONFENIAE and Director of La Voz de la Confeniae Radio. Member of the Kichwa Nationality of Pastaza.

Andrés Madrid teaches at the Central University of Ecuador. He is the author of *In search of the spark on the prairie. The revolutionary subject in the thought of the left intellectuality in Ecuador.*

In memory of mama Rosa Elvira
and father José María.
To father Samuel Román.
To comrade Pedro Guasango Morales.
To the men and women fighters of October,
human beings, full of the world.

In memory of the comrades
assassinated by capital and state terrorism
(2009–2019):

Abelardo Vega Caisaguano
Ángel Raúl Chilpe
Bosco Vicente Wusum Chaoanki
Édgar Yucailla Álvarez
Edison Cosios Andrade
Edison Mosquera Amagua
Francisco Quiñonez Montaño
Freddy Taish Tiwiram
Gabriel Angulo Bone
Iván Muela Racines
José Daniel Chaluisa Cusco
José Isidro Tendetza
José Rodrigo Chaluisa
Marco Humberto Oto Rivera
Segundo Inocencio Tucumbi Vega
Silvia Mera Navarrete

Thousands of people transform
one by one,
cold cobblestones into living barricades.
The breath of the fallen
blurs the dying idols.

The insurrection has awakened!
The voices burst out
amidst the music of drums and burning rubber.

It is the dawn of the eternal October
turned into months, into years,
in burning human effort.

For the power, unbelievable!

To articulate what is past does not mean to recognize 'how it really was'. It means to take control of a memory as it flashes in a moment of danger

Walter Benjamin

Preface to the English edition
Michael Löwy

The CONAIE (*Confederacion de las Naciones Indigenas de Ecuador*) is one of the most important Indigenous movements in Latin America. Its present leader, Leonidas Iza, co-author of this book with Andres Tapia and Andres Madrid, represents the best traditions of struggle, anti-capitalist resistance and insurgent uprising of this movement. Unlike some of its previous leaders, he is a revolutionary socialist who has made no concessions to the ruling class and its political representatives.

The year 2019 saw an unusual, maybe unprecedented, wave of social 'explosions' or movements of mass protest, before the Coronavirus pandemic closed down most of the world. Some had distinct political targets, as in Algiers, Khartoum, Hong Kong or San Juan earlier in the year. Others shared a clear, anti-neoliberal content, as in Beirut, Baghdad or Port-au-Prince. Most were above all movements of young people, and developed outside the structures of established political parties and movements.

The October uprising in Ecuador, however, was the first of several in Latin America that took on an almost insurrectional quality – to be followed by the huge rebellion in Chile, the mass resistance to the coup in Bolivia and the national strike in Colombia. All these experiences were different, of course. But Ecuador's October had a very precisely defined objective – the revocation of Decree 883 that raised the price of fuel. And it ended in a clear, if limited, victory. Understanding what happened in Ecuador in October 2019 and learning its lessons therefore has a much wider relevance.

Chapter 1 of the book examines the conditions that gave rise to the October uprising. It looks at how neoliberal policies were developed, and the struggles against these by the Indigenous and other social movements. Chapter 2 describes what happened in October 2019, and in particular the different forms of struggle, some of them quite new, that were deployed by the movement. Chapter 3 tries to draw out some of the lessons left by the uprising and identify the challenges ahead.

The core of the book is the story of the remarkable insurgent movement against the neoliberal policies of the Lenin Moreno government in 2019 – cooked up by the International Monetary Fund, i.e., by US imperialism. Elected with the support of Rafael Correa, Moreno very quickly operated a 180 degree turn, abandoned any 'progressive' pretensions, and took increasingly repressive and reactionary positions. His previous mentor, Correa, was obliged to go into exile in order to escape arrest, and Julian Assange, who had taken refuge in the Ecuadorean Embassy in London, was delivered by Moreno to the British police. The neoliberal IMF package of 2019 was the spark which ignited the October uprising, an extraordinary movement of strikes, demonstrations, barricades and popular insurgency, led by the CONAIE but supported by the unions, students, women, leftists and the popular classes. So powerful, so massive and so combative was the uprising that the Moreno government was forced to renounce its infamous 'package'. Iza and his comrades describe in detail in this text how this insurgency unfolded, taking the ruling elite by surprise, and winning an astonishing victory.

As we saw, the first chapter of the book gives a brief account of CONAIE's struggles of the last decades against the policies of successive governments. There are few movements in Latin America with such a capacity to mobilize, in defence of the Indigenous populations, but also of the whole Ecuadorean people. What is somewhat lacking in this account is the *ecological dimension* of the Indigenous and peasant mobilizations. We know, from various interviews, that Iza and his co-authors have a keen interest in the ecological issue, but this is not reflected in the book. In fact, the defence of Pachamama and the promotion of *sumak kawsay*, 'living well', are essential components of the Indigenous movement in Ecuador, as elsewhere in Latin America.

In particular, the struggles against extractive industries, in defence of territory (Ley de Tierras), and in defence of water resources (Ley de Agua), have been central pillars of CONAIE's activity for decades. All of this legacy was implicit in the October uprising. But it wasn't explicit, because the specific target of the mobilization was Decree 883 and the increase in fuel prices.

As the authors show, the Indigenous communal traditions, based on non-monetary exchanges and mutual help, have a 'proto-socialist' character and could be considered as 'the starting point for imagining the organization of a new society, based on people's power, beyond the nation state and capitalist modernity – an idea already suggested in the writings of the great Peruvian Marxist, José Carlos Mariategui.

In some cases, the specific demands of the Indigenous movement can converge with global demands around cutting carbon emissions. This was the case with some of the mobilizations around COP26 in Glasgow in 2021, in which Leonidas Iza and his comrades played an active part. A striking earlier example of this (also not mentioned in the book) was the Yasuni ITT Initiative. The Yasuni National Park is a vast area of the Amazonian forest in Ecuador – some one million hectares – with an extraordinary concentration of biodiversity but with large quantities of oil under the ground. The Indigenous communities living in the area, with the support of CONAIE and of the ecological movement, made an original proposal: Ecuador should leave the oil in the soil, and in exchange receive from the rich countries the equivalent of half the value of the fossil energy (some 3.6 billion dollars). This would be an important global contribution to reducing CO_2 emissions, responsible for climate change, and an example which could have been followed by other countries. When Rafael Correa was elected in 2007, he accepted the proposal and started international negotiations. However, in 2013, arguing that only a small percentage of the money had been pledged by a few countries, he dropped the plan, and decided to open the field for the oil companies, in spite of widespread popular opposition. This extractivist orientation, with very negative social and ecological consequences, and a repressive policy against the Indigenous movement, led to serious conflicts between CONAIE and the Rafael Correa government.

*

In the 2021 elections, which took place after this book was published, the left was divided between the partisans of former President Correa, who supported the candidate Andres Arauz, and CONAIE's political wing, the Pachakutik Party, who supported Yaku Perez – a tragic division for which both sides had their share of responsibility. In the second round, when Arauz confronted Guillermo Lasso, the neoliberal right-wing candidate of the traditional bourgeois oligarchy, CONAIE decided to call for an 'ideological null vote'. As Leonidas Iza recognized, in an interview given to the site *Noticias de America Latina*, this was a mistake, which permitted the victory, in the second round, of Guillermo Lasso.

Under the leadership of Leonidas Iza and his comrades, the CONAIE has launched, in 2022, impressive mobilizations against the neoliberal and anti-popular measures of Lasso. For the authors of this remarkable book, to defeat neoliberalism is only the first step; their motto, as stated in the concluding sentence, is inspired by Rosa Luxemburg and José Carlos Mariategui: *Indoamerican Communism or Barbarism.* ★

Michael Löwy is a French-Brazilian Marxist sociologist and philosopher. His works in English include *Marxism in Latin America from 1909 to the Present* and *The war of gods: Religion and Politics in Latin America.*

Preface to the second Spanish edition

Leonidas Iza, Andrés Tapia, and Andrés Madrid

The first edition of *Estallido* had an overwhelming response: the edition sold out completely. The book's most significant repercussion is that it opened debates about the lessons of the October rebellion and understanding what was at stake in Ecuador and the region.

This is the main reason for the present second edition, which has been reviewed and corrected to stand as a central document for all those seeking to understand this critical historical moment. A second reason is to enable the reader to contrast our interpretation of these events with the narrative offered by the mainstream media in the service of power.

History is a constant source of debate; all present struggles rely on the memories of past struggles. The fierce arguments and discussions to which the memory and significance of the October rebellion in Ecuador has given rise have underlined the need to diffuse more widely the ideas emerging from the mass social organizations and ensure that the narrative of this part of history is not left exclusively to those in power. *Estallido* has established a connection with the popular movement because its narrative embraces the experiences of millions of people. This link has permitted different social organisations, committed intellectuals and the militant anti-capitalist left to produce critical and proactive analyses and points of view. These have enriched the debate and opened new collective horizons.

As we write these lines, the strategic positions of actually existing power have become bogged down in outbursts of classism and racism devoid of any scientific rigour. For those in power the production of ideas is restricted to their research centres; all other ideas must be inoffensive, conformist and punished if they are not. If we, as peoples and diverse nationalities, think and write, we are always derided and condemned. *Those who do not question power serve its purposes.*

Hegemonic thought has always denounced any structural or systemic critique, because it reproduces the common sense of liberalism and the parochial phantasmagoria of the oligarchy. Capitalist power classifies the organized working class as 'terrorists' or 'bandits', to discredit the almost 90 percent of society who participated actively in the October rebellion, proof of the irrationality and the intellectual laziness of its intellectual representatives.

The dispute over meaning and representation has political, symbolic and ethical dimensions. To ensure that the history of October is not forgotten, it must be written by the working class. Fear, slander and madness are alien to the working class; they are constitutive elements of bourgeois power. By contrast, critique, love and 'being just too human' are the embodiment of a different world: the melting pot where socialized humanity and all other forms of natural life are merged.

We hope that this second Spanish edition of *Estallido* will enable links between the working class, the only class to produce wealth, that it will deepen the search for a balance with *Pachamama* and contribute to overcoming exploitation, patriarchy and 'adult centrism'. We trust that *Estallido* will contribute to the defence of our great avenues, our endless high plains, our sacred valleys, our mother ocean and our enigmatic rain forests. ★

The authors
Ecuador, Land of the Upright Sun, August 2021

Back to October: Preface to the first Spanish edition
Hernán Ouviña

I

Thirty years ago, in June 1990, Ecuador experienced an Indigenous uprising unprecedented in the country's recent history. It marked the beginning of a cycle of popular rebellions against neoliberalism on a continental and even global scale. Known as the *Inti Raymi* uprising, it shook the entire Andean region and the rest of Latin America; underlining what Peruvian historian Alberto Flores Galindo called, with a trace of irony, the discovery of the obvious: the importance of those who make up the majority in our history.

The white, Spanish-speaking, urban and bourgeois republics, authentic 'skeletal states', were built to mirror Europe, turning their backs on the melting pot of nations and peoples that existed prior to the bloody process of colonization suffered in recent centuries. Their deepest structures, groaning under the weight of the extreme commodification and increasing precariousness of life, were facing increasingly intransigent challenges. A deafening roar rose up from rainforests and beaches, moors and valleys, plains and mountains, highways and shantytowns: 'We are here!'

From then on, the mobilisations and the dynamics of the struggles led by native peoples and nationalities gained increasing visibility and had a growing impact on public events, from the commemoration of the 500 years of Indigenous, Black and popular resistance, to the Zapatista uprising of 1 January 1994 in Chiapas: from the water and gas wars in Bolivia to the boldness of the Nasa people in the Cauca region of Colombia, or the Mapuche insurgency south of the Bio Bio River.

Beyond their specific characteristics, this constellation of struggles had a series of shared features arising from their emancipatory impulse: direct action and territorial self-determination, community and pluri-nationality,[1] the recovery of shared symbols,

---

[1] The recognition of the different nationalities that live in the territory of Ecuador.

ancestral knowledge and collective identities and a common critique of the colonial heritage, a deep historical memory and a radical defence of life in all its forms, a plebeian upsurge, anti-capitalism and the questioning of liberal democracy. New categories of struggle and a new vocabulary were forged, which, over time, enriched alternative civilizational projects. The good life (*el buen vivir* and *Sumak Kawsay*) food sovereignty, to lead by obeying, (*mandar obedeciendo*), people's diplomacy, autonomy, communality, and interculturality, among others, became increasingly crucial concepts in the strategic debates in pursuit of the protagonism of those from below in the construction of their destiny.

As a result of this arduous, subterranean popular resistance, which included, as in the case of Ecuador, insurrections with the capacity to remove people from power and an enormous popular power of veto – in most of the region, centre-left forces, progressive coalitions and leaders from outside the traditional political structures came to power. They made an anti-neoliberal discourse the central pillar of their proposals. Nevertheless, it is essential to recognize that the cycle of challenge to neoliberalism in Latin America preceded those electoral triumphs, and had its own time scales and its own agendas which contradicted the trajectories of these governments, and even endured beyond their decline or fall, either as a result of the electoral defeats inflicted on them or of destabilization processes based on neoliberal policies.

We can even assert, and this book is an example of it, that, although we are living through the eclipse of progressivism as a continental phenomenon, the confrontation with neoliberalism – the contemporary expression of the capitalist/patriarchal/neo-fascist/imperial counter-offensive – based on antagonism, open confrontation and direct action in the streets, returned with new force and enormous radicalism through 2019 and up to the present. It also seems to have regained momentum in various parts of the Global South (also including the United States), echoing the multitudinous revolts, popular uprisings and mass strikes that broke out in the second half of 2020, especially during the tumultuous month of October.

II

But how did such a colossal rebellion occur? Was it a purely spontaneous explosion, or did organisational factors guide this healthy plebeian uprising? What caused this pressure to explode in those days and to continue for almost two weeks, opening unimaginable new horizons for the emancipatory struggle? We must recognize that the widespread colour-blindness of a large sector of Latin American progressive intellectuals had led them to ignore Indigenous nationalities and peoples as relevant actors, particularly in Ecuador. From always looking upwards, in the mistaken belief that the actions of governments were what constituted 'high politics', many of them ended with stiff necks as a result of their bad posture.

With the elevation to government of political figures who shared the neo-developmentalist discourse, the concept that political life was the monopoly of the state, and a shared commitment to extractivism, these struggles were branded as ultra-leftist or *pachamamistas*,[2] as corporate stubbornness or an infantile environmentalism only updated the 'sheepdog' syndrome, neither allowing Indigenous communities to gain access to the fruits of progress nor allowing others to enjoy them.

The fierce defence of ancestral territories in the face of the policies of dispossession and submission promoted by progressive governments (oil exploitation in the Amazon is perhaps the most tragic and illustrative example of this, together with the initiation of large-scale mining projects that have become mirages for the supposed development of the Ecuadorean economy), did not receive much media attention during the fragile hegemony of the progressives, and when they did it was mainly to criminalize or ridicule the resistance.

Until the October rebellion, an important sector of the Latin American and European progressive left harshly criticized and denigrated the Ecuadorean Indigenous movement, while at the same time staunchly defending the government of Rafael Correa and praising the man who was for many years his vice-president and main successor: Lenin Moreno. The pursuit of an electoral victory in 2017 came to be compared to the battle of Stalingrad, which sealed the capitulation of Nazi-fascism during World War II. According to this characterization, his assumption as president of Ecuador would inflict an inevitable and mortal defeat on the continental right wing. We know that the outcome was the diametrical opposite. To provide cover for such a blunder, the face-saving talisman word 'betrayal' was invoked, which served to veil and justify rather than shed light on what it claimed to explain.

2   People who extol the virtues of Pachamama –
Mother Earth – above all others. Used in a derogatory
manner here.

Although it may seem paradoxical, this type of government increasingly limited its actions to what Gramsci called 'petty politics', limited to the day-to-day and taking as read the dominant order, adapting to it rather than confronting it. Far from overturning the socio-economic structures and aspiring to create new relations, it preserved and defended these structures, focusing on inter-factional intrigue, opportunism and the electoral disputes which became a central pivot of their actions. Their aim was to consolidate their place within the existing balance of power. Indeed, during the height of the challenge to neoliberalism, what remained intact in these moderate or centre-left progressive projects was their infatuation with the management of the government apparatus. To survive within it at any cost became an end in itself. This resulted in a political model based on the individual figure of Rafael Correa (and on a broader level, in a major concentration of decision-making power in the executive), which had as its counterpart a repudiation of any type of organisational mediation, especially those with roots in strategic areas of accumulation by dispossession. The consequence was a re-ethnification of capitalist domination, combining class exploitation with re-colonization and the plundering of territory.

Within a short period, in parallel to an exacerbation of the primary-export neo-extractivist matrix, it became possible to implement certain redistributive and compensatory policies, and to set in motion infrastructural projects together with an expansion of consumption to include vast urban-popular sectors. At the same time, spurious alliances, the 'give and take' typical of the old politics, concessions to – and entanglements with – transnational corporations and local elites, were taking precedence within the state fabric. Corruption and perks as a bargaining chip, the underestimation and even repression of those who did not fully comply with the modernising project, and the disregard of those sectors that did not provide a significant number of votes or substantial investment income, undermined in an increasingly dramatic way the very bases that sustained the so-called 'Citizens' Revolution'.

Without underestimating the particularities of each case, we can say that something similar happened in other progressive processes in South America, such as those led by the PT in Brazil, Kirchnerism in Argentina and the Frente Amplio in Uruguay. Although we cannot study them here in depth, in the dialectic between 'power itself' and 'the appropriation of power', these experiences did not offer any integral critique of capitalism but tended to privilege subordination to the rules of the game of bourgeois liberal democracy. They made instrumental use of the institutions of the state inherited from neoliberalism with no intention of breaking with them; the result was the extreme fragility of the projects they claimed to build.

It is evident today that the timings and dynamics of elections in their traditional bourgeois configuration (to which practically all governments, as well as many supposedly left parties, submitted) were not compatible with the radical transformations pursued by the anti-capitalist forces. On the contrary, these involve long processes of maturation and hegemonic struggle, where the revolutionary perspective, class antagonism and the masses' activity must play a fundamental role in the complex construction of a socialist alternative.

III

'We must see the October rebellion as the climax of a series of previous struggles that developed across a wide historical spectrum, to relate to and connect with the accumulated experience of social struggle,' as the authors of this book suggest in one of its most interesting passages. This is a warning against immediatist readings or those that neglect the molecular processes and underlying resistances that, like moles, managed to erode bourgeois hegemony from below and create the conditions that contributed to such a powerful uprising.

In the notes written during his imprisonment as a political prisoner, Antonio Gramsci proposed a hypothesis that arose out of what happened during the long cycle that preceded the October revolution of 1917: 'In the study of a structure it is necessary to distinguish the 'organic' movements (relatively permanent) from the movements that can be called 'conjunctural' (which present themselves as occasional, immediate, almost accidental)'. We would venture to suggest that *Correismo*[3] was based above all on a power appropriated in a conjunctural and transitory way by electoral means. Its main support base was a diffuse individualized citizenry with strong roots in the urban middle classes, although at times it achieved a high percentage of votes and a certain legitimacy in some peripheral neighbourhoods of Quito and other cities of the coast. But these are the features of movement of an occasional type. The nationalities and peoples united in CONAIE, on the other hand, are founded on a power of their own, territorial and

3   The movement in support of Raphael Correa.

popular-communitarian that has endured over time, beyond occasional changes and the ups and downs of government. It can therefore be categorized as *organic*.

This should not lead us into a simple binary of white on black, nor into a metaphor of a division between a rotten and conservative layer above in absolute opposition to a layer below that is pure revolutionary potentiality. Each of these actors is far from being free from contradictions. On more than one occasion they have been forced to coexist in a heterogeneous field of forces characterized by disputes and ambiguities and torn by different interests and aspirations. However, we do highlight CONAIE as a multi-organizational and multi-societal movement, organic and permanent in character, and which, despite the constant attacks to which it was subjected throughout the Correa period, managed to stay on its feet, to become the key point of reference for the bulk of the popular sectors of the country. Today it is once again prominent in Ecuadorean and even continental political life as a joint project. CONAIE transcends its pure ethnic and identity condition to confront the four wheels that, according to Zapatismo, sustain the capitalist system: exploitation, dispossession, contempt and repression.

Without the support of this active rearguard, patiently sustaining for years and even longer periods a coordination of temporalities and organizational structures on the coast, in the Andes and Amazon regions, the process of mobilization and popular uprising in October 2019 would have been unthinkable. This book gives a first-hand detailed account of the leading role played by CONAIE, though not by CONAIE alone, in shaping the direction taken by the rebellion. This allowed it to achieve a mass and radical character, covering the entire country, and combining it with popular creativity, historical memory and social catharsis evidenced in countless spontaneous actions, both in rural areas and in major cities, particularly during the days when the 'Commune of Quito' remained in existence.

It would be a mistake to conceive CONAIE as an unchanging entity. 'We are the same, although different' is perhaps the most appropriate definition, to the extent that, although it was the sons and daughters of the first Indigenous uprising in 1990 who participated in the October rebellion and took up the reins of an ancestral resistance, this generational change, in addition to implying the updating of a dense historical accumulation of learning inscribed in persistent processes of struggle that brought together 'the wisdom of grandparents and the strength of youth', is marked by transformations in multiple dimensions of the Ecuadorean reality, as is well analysed in more than one section of this book.

In any case, these remarkable changes in the morphology of the protagonist of the rebellion (changes that respond to profound transformations in the productive matrix and the capitalist structure of the country, as well as a result of the reconfiguration of the socio-political actors and the territorial organizational networks in rural areas and cities), should not eclipse the continuity with that cycle inaugurated 30 years earlier, a continuity denied in the corporative or purely sectoral perspective on the Indigenous peoples and nationalities. 'Nothing for the Indigenous people alone' was a slogan that regained strength in the October uprising, articulating a range of experiences throughout Ecuador, in the same way as the Zapatistas called for 'Everything for everyone'. In this sense we can describe it as representing a *cathartic* moment in Gramscian terms, evidence of a qualitative leap forward resolving fragmentation and transcending immediate interests, allowing the struggle to become ethico-political, with the potential to build an alternative hegemony.

IV

This may be one of the most distinctive and original features of the uprising: the (re)composition of a unitary subject, with both ethnic and class contours, which embraces a diversity of subaltern identities and struggles for the commons, in which women and young people played a crucial role. This was a popular bloc unhampered by the specific bureaucratic logics typical of NGOs or the *realpolitik* which, in the not-so-distant past, blocked the bridges of communication and the radical encounters at the crossroads between the country and the city. It made possible the constitution of an anti-systemic project anchored not only in the Indigenous peoples and nationalities but also in the new forms of contemporary living labour, among them the increasingly widespread and heterogeneous precariat of the 21st century, which has become increasingly central to the capitalist machinery of our days.

If in the previous uprisings the Indigenous movement had been an almost exclusive and excluding actor – except for the revolt of the *Forajidos* in 2005 – on this occasion other subjects, agendas and organizational processes of an urban-popular character gained relevance. The street demonstrations and the embryonic territorial power generated during the outbreak involved students, feminists, neighbourhood grassroots movements, unions, leftist parties, poor peasants, the unemployed, environmentalists, state employees, precarious and migrant workers, day labourers, teachers, small merchants, squatters and, of course, Indigenous people belonging to CONAIE. But what also stood out was the number of groups and individuals not linked to any platform who participated, especially during the most critical days of the conflict, adding considerable dynamism and spontaneity to the most significant moments of confrontation, indiscipline and collective creativity. Invention.

It could be said that the course taken by this uprising was close to what Rosa Luxemburg called a mass strike, in which economic and political factors, objective and subjective conditions and conscious and spontaneous dynamics were dialectically combined to make possible a (pluri)national strike of immense proportions. The strike was not limited to the simple interruption of production by wage workers demanding partial demands, nor was it decided from above by union or party leaders. It was nourished by the accumulated anger of an enormous variety of grassroots activists, rebellious bodies, emerging social movements and networks of coexistence, many of them invisible until then, that converged and joined together on roads, streets and public places to confront the reforms with dignity, overflowing all institutional restrictions and directly challenging the State from a plebeian, anti-corporate and transversal perspective.

In the face of a neoliberal counter-offensive, which, in addition to the elimination of fuel subsidies, set out to impose labour flexibility and violate basic pension and contractual rights, the power of the popular-communitarian movement was reawakened, this time with high levels of articulation of the Indigenous movement with the working class, neighbourhood grassroots activism in the urban peripheries, feminist resistance and youth discontent, which together forged intergenerational links and a broad socio-political convergence in the praxis itself, between militants with long experience of struggle and a melting pot of unorganized sectors that defied the state of siege and joined the protest with added energy, focusing on the material realities of everyday life and opening new horizons of meaning in historical terms.

The outcome of the October conflict, however, did not go in the expected direction – which would have implied a complete breakdown of the dominant socio-economic and ideological-political order to build on its ruins a new historical bloc against the *imaginary* Ecuador. Even though the repeal of Decree No. 883 and the defeat of the IMF's neoliberal strategies were a resounding achievement, no progress was made towards an irreversible rupture in the existing correlation of forces. It is another major contribution of this book that, without disregarding the bloody repression and state terrorism exercised against activists in the streets, it also to analyses the limitations and weaknesses of the popular camp itself, which explain this outcome. That is the importance of this material, gathered in the heat of a sincere examination of the tasks yet to be fulfilled in the future confrontations and battles that will inescapably arise in the future.

Those who are looking for an objective, academic and objective study, blandly disengaged, will not find it in this book. What is offered here is an experience of struggle that will stimulate the political imagination which loses none of its rigour in the analysis of the conjuncture while taking a clear and committed position. The thought that threads through each of its pages combines knowledge with the project of the transformation of reality and a strategic projection of the struggle. And unlike most of the compilations and books that abound on the Latin American rebellions that took place in 2019, it is not the result of purely theoretical elucidations or research at a distance from the spheres of public discussion and the street mobilizations. It is a genuine product of that collective process that made the outbreak possible. It is an authentic systematization of the militant practices and purposes that constituted this rebellion, a passionate and meticulous text crafted by organic intellectuals emerging in the antipodes of cognitive extractivism at the very heart of the heterogeneous territories of resistance that always beats below and to the left. It arises out of the class struggle, and the accelerating insurgency of peoples and communities full of rage, the co-participants of the unprecedented mass insubordination of recent decades.

V

Its particularities apart, it would not be entirely fair to restrict the revolt analysed in this book to a series of events within Ecuador. The rebellion that began there in early October acted as a centrifugal force and radiated its potential to other latitudes of Our America and even of the Global South. Less than a week after the culmination of the popular insurrection in Quito,

Santiago de Chile was shaken by an unusual protest whose repertoires of action, contempt and forms of belligerence were reminiscent of those experienced in the Andean territory. This was followed by the days of disobedience in Colombia, with a similar political strike which filled the streets. In all these cases (to which we should add the always neglected precursor Haiti), those who shared the historical stage were not so much popular movements as *peoples in movement,* whose collective leadership became the rule with their combination of subterranean processes and uprisings in the public space. As the authors of this book demonstrate in the Ecuadorean case – a hypothesis that can also be extended to the other Latin American experiences – they cannot be defined as purely 'spontaneous' revolts. They have to be read as a conjunction of processes and events, that is to say of long-standing links forged over time, of products of an unselfish militancy and the day-to-day construction of movements from below that increasingly pierced the dominant neoliberal hegemony in these countries until they culminated in an explosion as massive as it was unexpected. At the end of 2019, these burst the bubble of the myth of a false democracy.

From then on, there was no doubt that the resumption of the cycle of challenges to neoliberalism was driven by a new antagonistic, self-managing and confrontational impulse, reacting against all forms of domination, exploitation or dispossession, anti-capitalist, anti-patriarchal and anti-racist, centred on the defence of life. October served as a watershed on a continental scale, inaugurating a period in which the subaltern classes and groups opposed to the dominant order at a regional level were emboldened. The people had reached their limits, and took their revenge by tearing down monuments and waving multicoloured flags, evading turnstiles and confronting the police, questioning all kinds of privileges and experiencing another temporality, stamping insubordinate slogans on walls and setting fire to emblematic buildings, at the same time as new instances of territorial self-government began to emerge, *Mingas* and community guards, welcome centres and *cacerolazos*, popular parliaments and front lines, under banners calling for daring and reciprocal care.

A few days before her assassination, submerged in an exceptional situation of barricades and combats in the streets of Berlin, Rosa Luxemburg affirmed that there are occasions in the history of humanity in which months are condensed into seconds and minutes and years into a few days. This book maps in great detail each of those days and nights of extreme intensity in which the extraordinary became an everyday occurrence in Ecuador. It tells a story that is not yet history, but rather a burning fuse and a fire that will smoulder in the memory of peoples and communities until the fire of rebellion is rekindled at the most unexpected moment.

But it not only invites us to create a detailed reconstruction of these 11 days, but, faithful to the spirit of Mariategui it assumes that 'images generate concepts, just as concepts inspire images', so that its pages are interspersed throughout with striking photographs of those days, which take us to those moments of danger where plebeian bodies configured an undisciplined visual narrative and exercised 'very different' ways of inhabiting the city and conquering it by assault. If, according to the Amauta (Mariátegui), 'the best way to explain and translate our times is, perhaps, partly journalistic and partly cinematographic', this book has created a montage of images (captured by activists and popular communicators who played a key role in breaking the media siege at that time) and the quick chronicles that, in the heat of events, fuse intelligence and imagination.

VI

The pandemic may have imposed a tragic and momentary pause in this arduous dispute, akin to the peace of the cemetery. Guayaquil, once a transitory refuge for the government and historical rearguard of the oligarchy, showed its most perverse face and turned necropolitics into a modality of disciplining and enforcing the extreme precariousness of the subaltern sectors. But even after a brutal criminalization of its leading spokespeople and referents of struggle in the days following the uprising, in a context like the current one, characterized by the most acute vulnerability, the rebellion is not something that can be left behind or consigned purely to the past. On the contrary, it is a dynamic objective to be aspired to in the midst of a planetary crisis, organic and structural, civilizational and integral, driven to the point of frenzy by a virus which appears to give no quarter.

This crisis can never be read as a prelude to certain victory, nor should it be read in a defeatist sense. Instead, it should be thought of as a *school of knowledge* and an anomaly in the life of a society, of which this book is a genuine product. All the expressions of resistance, both theoretical and practical, that are in the air these days point back to October, to those intense days that tore apart a world and simultaneously universalized it, that true 'festival of the plebs' in the words of Bolivian Marxist René Zavaleta. In those days a crack appeared that widened the horizon of visibility of the subaltern classes, making possible an exercise of collective (self-) knowledge of much of what, until then, had been forbidden: an understanding that, far from being a mere gathering of concepts, constitutes a vital experience of organisation that demands that the categories and notions of colonial-modern hegemonic thought should be 'sent into quarantine' together with the stagnant forms of liberal-bourgeois political praxis.

Today it is more evident than ever that for those of us who aspire to overcome the barbarism expressed by capitalism, patriarchy and colonialism in the cruel, repressive and apocalyptic phase through which we are currently passing, there is no guarantee of success. Our challenge is fragile, without certainty. At play is the possibility of building a society radically different from the present one that can ensure the survival of humanity and of Planet Earth as a whole. That is why it is urgent to relaunch, in the very heart of these processes of struggle and insubordination across the region, the urgent strategic debates based on fraternal dialogue and mutual listening.

In this framework, restoring socialism as a civilizational alternative is not only one option among many but a pressing historical necessity, articulated from the depths of a ravine or staring into the abyss. Faced with the decline and the evident limitations of the progressive projects in our continent, and in the face of a violent general counter-offensive of the right, the ruling classes and imperialism to overcome this crisis by whipping up fear and sharpening xenophobia, militarizing territories, discarding 'unproductive' bodies, increasing the plunder of the commons, degrading the environment, intensifying the precariousness of life and the super-exploitation of labour, we can only redouble our efforts to construct a socialist future. But it must be a socialism that can embrace many socialisms, as multicoloured and varied as the Wipala.

It will be necessary to look back to gather strength before we leap further. In the October cataclysm can be found the 'unprecedented and viable' situations and solutions that could provide clues as to how to resolve the organic crisis from which Ecuador has not yet been able to emerge. The answers, although they can be glimpsed in the pages of an essential book such as this one, will arise above all from the capacity for struggle, the self-awareness and organisation of the peoples, movements and communities, in both the rural and urban areas, who yearn to revolutionize everything. After all, as Rosa Luxemburg put it from her prison cell, 'Only experience can correct and open new paths. Only a life without coercion and overflowing into thousands of new forms and improvisations can take on a creative force and correct by itself all the errors of the past'. ★

Hernán Ouviña, Buenos Aires, July 2020

Hernan Ouviña is an Argentinean political scientist who teaches at the University of Buenos Aires (UBA). He is the author and editor of numerous books, including *Zapatism for Beginners* (2007) and *Rosa Luxemburg and the reinvention of politics: a Latin American reading* (2021).

Front line of the struggle of Indigenous peoples and popular sectors, Historic Centre of Quito (Photo: Daniel Andrade).

How do the peoples of Ecuador fight? By saying-doing, saying-doing, saying-doing. Damn it!

Introduction

Like a spear, eleven days of struggle crossed Ecuadorean history in October 2019. They were incorporated into the battles waged by the people in other parts of Latin America and the Caribbean during the turbulent period of civilizational crisis. Their multiple contradictions emerged in the struggles against capital as the working class, farmers and Indigenous peoples, youth and women sustained them in different parts of the world.

In October, different struggles converged – like streams that rise in the highlands, the jungles, the lowlands and the cities – to face the various forms of capitalist accumulation. Over the years, anger and indignation at precarious labour conditions, the dispossession of territories and the collateral effects of extractivism, added to the feminization and racialization of exploitation, came together. The insoluble contradiction of capital against labour, nature, women, etc., is the origin of the deterioration of human existence and Pachamama. That is why the rebellion mobilized, with such intensity, so many diverse sectors.

To paraphrase John Reed, the eleven days of the October rebellion[1] shook Ecuador to the core. Its combativity, authenticity and results are similar – or even greater – than the other milestones in the class struggle, like the First Indigenous Uprising (1990), the Seventh National Strike against Osvaldo Hurtado (1982), the April Days (1978) that brought down the military triumvirate, and the Glorious May Day of 1944.

The popular response exceeded the expectations of the organizers. It was not on the agenda that the mobilization would suddenly become a national insurrection. However, it should not be confused with spontaneous action. October brought together the organizational capacities of the Indigenous movement –the most powerful community network in Ecuador and the continent – with the traditions of street struggle of the popular urban sectors who had kept alive in silence the historical memory of combativity and solidarity to pass on to their Indigenous and peasant brothers and sisters. Added to that, multiple local and sectoral resistances strengthened in recent years through the struggle against the dispossession of territories and rights, permanently reinforced the need for a national

---

[1] This refers to John Reed's iconic description of the Russian Revolution in his *Ten Days that Shook the World*.

articulation of their demands. These were the factors that created the conditions for a popular mobilization that began for economic reasons to become a political insurrection that challenged the nature of domination in Ecuador.

In October, new forms of popular power appeared, and existing ones were strengthened. The State lost control for eleven days. A power parallel to that of the ruling classes emerged. It was made possible by the *crisis of legitimacy and hegemony* of the bourgeoisie, itself the result of the breakdown of the consent of the majority for its project. The crisis of hegemony degenerated into an organic crisis; however, it did not succeed in constituting itself as a revolutionary situation – as *dual power* – the highest level of struggle as Lenin defined it. Sensing the danger created by the people, the fractions of the ruling class compacted into an iron and monolithic bloc. It was different from other intense moments of conflict, for example the fall of several presidents of the Republic, which, despite their alliances, always produced rearrangements within the class bloc. In October, and despite their different forms of property ownership and their political differences, the different variants of capital, of electoral parties, the restricted state as a whole and the institutions of the expanded state[2] united in a single front. The actually existing powers[3] aligned together and closed ranks in direct opposition to the popular camp.

This dynamic, which may seem random, is in fact – as Rosa Luxemburg noted – the product of historical conditions, of years of agitation and political formation, of the emergence of popular leaderships, and of the unpredictable effervescence of a mass strike as it convulses the relations between social classes, without being able to decree from above the 'how' that will happen (Haug, 2019).

Luxemburg affirmed that neither the mass strike nor the revolution occurs or is determined only by a plan but rather by the confluence of movements that can develop, apparently, in opposite directions: 'It is not the mass strike that produces the

---

2   Banking, industrial, bureaucratic and commercial capital from the highlands and the coast joined forces, and a plethora of electoral parties – including some at odds with each other, the armed forces, the legislature, the official media, the Church, among others.

3   We use this combination of words to refer to modern bourgeois power in its extended form, and to differentiate this from the liberal formulation for which power is only expressed through government and elections. To put it schematically, power has an economic dimension (private property), an ideological-cultural one (hegemony) and a military one (the state). We do not reduce the state to a merely coercive problem, since it involves a set of complex and fraught social relations, implying social practices that reproduce domination with relative autonomy from the sovereignty of the state.

revolution, but it is the revolution that produces the mass strike'. Thus, the revolution is not a single act but a period of organization and events (Luxemburg, 2014, p.130). The October Rebellion – aside from its historical outcome – provides a laboratory for understanding the direction of Ecuador's social transformations. It also allows us to interpret the historical horizons of the struggle in the country, exposing the character of the state, elucidating the forms of struggle and the methodologies of organisation and agitation, the value of force as a determinant of political negotiation, the renewal of references and popular spokespersons, the politics of the broad fronts, the new forms of mass mobilization in the countryside and the city, the limits and perspectives of organisations and social movements, the itinerary for channelling the rising of the non-organic masses, the multi-sectoral participation, the new alignments of the bloc in power, among other aspects.

At the same time this book pays homage to the fighters of rebel October and conserves the historical memory of the Ecuadorean people whose roots lie in the singularity, diversity and convergence of interests of the exploited. This text is in line with the militant will of workers, farmers, Indigenous peoples, slum residents, market women, popular feminists, youth and the dispossessed.

Humanity is living through an unprecedented, ideologically tense, historical moment. While there is an awakening of the majorities in struggle, it is also evident that we are experiencing the rise of neo-fascist forces. The outcome is uncertain. Hence the future of our peoples depends on their ability to take advantage of this particular historical situation, bringing up to date the theses underpinning the uprising, building forms of political organization to confront the collapse of modernity, articulating the anti-capitalist forces, expanding the organizational fabric of the popular sector, and incorporating new forms of struggle.

This work is organized into three parts. Chapter One examines some features of the objective and material conditions for the crisis of capital accumulation in Ecuador, which led to the casualization of the labour force, the growth of the foreign debt, the deregulation of state intervention, the deepening of the extractivist primary export economy and the condition of dependence. The variations of political domination and the crisis of legitimacy of the representative system are then analysed. The contradictions of the statist regulatory project and its continuity with the deregulatory model are outlined. The subjective conditions and the accumulation of forces of the popular camp are described, starting from a breakdown of the struggles prior to October, the definitive rupture of the 'dialogues' with the government and the social outburst following the emission of Decree No. 883. In synthesis, the reasons and antecedents which explain why the October rebellion reached such a level of combativeness are shown, contradicting the visions that brand it as spontaneous or unforeseen. This chapter may be difficult to read, particularly the economic part. But we consider it indispensable to review the structural conditions that provoked the October emergency to then refer to the events that took place during the uprising.

The first part of Chapter Two describes the rebellion through empirical data and testimonies; it relates the events before the move of the Indigenous peoples to Quito, and the subsequent events that led to the outbreak of the insurrection. It goes on to explain the leading role of the Confederation of Indigenous Nationalities of Ecuador (CONAIE) in the mobilization. Thirdly, it analyses the participation of other actors such as the trade union movement and the working class, the emergence of the urban struggle, the leading role of women and youth, the solidarity of middle-income and academic sectors, the action of other Indigenous and farmer organizations, the positions of the institutional left and the polarization of right-wing narratives and the power bloc. The fourth point examines the pre-eminence of the coercive strategy over the consensual one on the part of the state and the reinforcement of the armed and repressive forces. Fifth, it reviews the management of official discourses and communication corporations in the service of power. The final section evaluates the performance of alternative and community communicators who confronted and broke the media blackout.

Chapter Three focuses on the lessons learned and the legacy that the October rebellion leaves for the struggle in Ecuador. With a view to a proposal, it establishes the conditions to capitalize on the levels of combativity demonstrated by the Ecuadorean people and translate them into a programme of anti-capitalist content. To this end it addresses the popularization of new tactics for the social struggle, and opens a debate that questions the daily use of violence by the ruling classes. It analyses the internal and external difficulties of the popular camp, as well as the dispute over the legitimacy and meaning of the use of force. Finally, it proposes basic premises for the anti-capitalist left to orient its work, emphasizing an essential element: the unity of struggle and action.

The epilogue considers the global emergency provoked by the COVID-19 pandemic, at a time of aggravation of the integral crisis of capitalist modernity, and explores the critical moments faced by the peoples of Ecuador in the aftermath of October.

Finally, October showed us that, as has always happened, the ruling classes, in the defence of their interests, have tried to misrepresent the consistent struggle of the Ecuadorean people, inheritors of the struggles against colonialism, latifundism and modern capitalism. They have used the media corporations to construct all kinds of conjectures about the existence of a great strategy of 'international sedition', 'external infiltration' or 'terrorist groups', to disfigure the revolutionary potential inherent in the spirit of October.

There was no international tutelage, only internationalist solidarity. Local and regional struggles multiplied; there were moving human gestures, and a confluence of multi-sectoral popular understanding emerged about how the powerful defend their interests in this country and in the world. Meanwhile, as Mama Dolores Cacuango believed, the working class, the farmers, the Ecuadorean Indigenous movement, the poor, the Cholos, the Blacks and the Montubios are working to build people's power for their liberation. This book is a humble contribution born, as Mariategui put it, of conviction and belief. ★

Mass for Inocencio Tucumbi in the main concourse of the House of Culture on 10 October 2019, the day after he was murdered (Photo: Fluxus Foto).

Dolores Cacuango
Mama warrior
On your path, comrade

Popular slogan of the October rebellion

For our heroes fallen in combat: not a minute of silence. A whole life of combat.

Popular Latin American slogan replicated in the October Rebellion

Imminence: Background, accumulated experience and rupture

1   A SLOW-COOKED INSURRECTION

In the face of an extraordinary phenomenon that disrupts the daily routine and disturbs the lines of historical development, simple questions arise: What happened in October in Ecuador? This answer is the spinal column of this book, moving inductively from less to more. What happened before the outbreak? What are the antecedents that explain the uprising of millions of people? It is unlikely that an event like a rebellion, which implies a broad mobilization of social resources, is produced by causes outside the structural framework. There is a background, beyond the circumstantial detonating factors, that allows us to understand why and how the explosion occurred. In the historical fabric of October, social relations were strained to the point of producing a rupture in the already weakened economic, political, social and institutional spheres.

Was the publication of Decree No. 883 the main reason for the rebellion? Does the incompetence of the government explain the rising of the majorities? Was the rebellion a spontaneous popular event? No. The circumstantial and spontaneous factors, the short-term events, were added to the long-term factors that had accumulated over time. It was not only the *paquetazo* – Decree No. 883 – that provoked the explosion of anger, but also the combination of innumerable micro *paquetazos*.

There was not an 'episodic' disorder in the administration of Ecuadorean capitalism that caused the crisis, because, as Bolívar Echeverría points out, crisis is the essence of capitalism. The growth of popular protest was not the result of government incompetence. The central mission of capitalism is not to stop revolutions, but to increase and centralize the profits that collaterally provoke them. It was not the *form* of the capitalist economy that was responsible but the nature of its economic relations. The causes of the October rebellion were not circumstantial: they were structural. It was not a particular problem: it was an integral, civilizational, systemic crisis.

It is the combination of short, medium and long-term factors that allows us to understand the October outbreak. The pro-business neoliberal programme that underpinned the spiral of crisis had begun years before.[1] Likewise, the cycle of economic boom had already ended previously, ending capital accumulation through a Keynesian form of economic policy. October produced a sudden and spontaneous response of the masses, which combined with the 'Progressive Days of Struggle' (Annex 1) and the struggles of the oppressed classes that developed in recent decades. In addition, there was a decline in the hegemony of the Moreno government, and a systematic loss of legitimacy in the institutional framework, expressed in permanent mobilizations, mostly local in character.

Decree No. 883, a symbolic milestone within an adjustment plan embodied in the Letter of Intent with the IMF, stipulated a disbursement of around 4 billion dollars, conditional on a set of measures. It set up the *paquetazo* and unleashed a social mobilisation that, in a few days, reached the level of an insurrection. The traditional Chinese proverb used by Mao Zedong was confirmed: 'A single spark can set the field on fire'. These structural conditions pointed ahead to a civilizational crisis, in a period marked by the difficulties of capital to raise the rate of profit, by recolonization and imperialist rivalry, an offensive against labour and the inability of capitalism to remedy the economic collapse. In this chapter we address the four elements that prepared the conditions for the October popular response:

1. The increasing precariousness of the conditions of existence of the majority of the population. This was due to the growing difficulty of the dominant groups to sustain the rates of accumulation and the need to unload the crisis onto the backs of the working class. Its most palpable expressions were the fall in the price of oil, the deepening of extractivism, the renegotiation and manipulation of foreign debt and the deregulation of state intervention through the application of the IMF rules.
2. Loss of confidence: the loss of confidence in state institutions translated into a crisis of legitimacy, a situation that

---

1 It began with the Law of Economic Reactivation and the Law of Productive Investment, and Employment Generation (known as the Trole Law No.3) that set in motion the deregulation of the economy and established tax cuts for the most powerful economic groups, condoning their fiscal debt by $2,355,000, according to the National Income Service, and the acceptance of up to $4,600,000 of total debt.

opens a cycle of instability similar to previous historical periods and which accounted for the erosion of the hegemony of the ruling class.

3. The permanent, silent and uneven escalation of conflict in various areas of the country. Although these sectors had not been involved in a structured list of demands, they maintained permanent focal points of mobilization at the local or regional level and managed, little by little, to unite into a larger network.

4. The resolution taken by CONAIE at the annual assembly of Ruku-llakta, on 23 August 2019. Here it was decided to withdraw from 'dialogues' with the national government and prepare the call for struggle. Such a stance created the conditions for responding to the imposition of Decree No. 883 which, among other aspects, eliminated the fuel subsidy, opened conditions for 'flexible' labour legislation, eliminated the rights of public sector workers and increased the profits of commercial and financial capital. This decree turned out to be a new, unforeseen element in the scenario of struggle, which inflamed the already heated tempers of the population.

1.1 CAPITALIST DEVELOPMENT IN ECUADOR: ACCUMULATION AND CRISIS

The most appropriate method for understanding the development of capitalism in Ecuador is the critique of political economy: to study the economy by looking at the social classes that benefit from the wealth created by labour and the conditions of its production.

In a capitalist society, an economic crisis is the result of the fall in the rate of profit for the dominant classes, when their gains fail to reach the level they aspire to. When that happens they decide to close their businesses and engage in more profitable activities, for example, by increasing their capital through financial speculation.

Therefore the crisis faced by the country was not only – nor mainly – a fiscal crisis. The imbalance of public finances originates in the difficulties faced by the production and circulation of goods and services in the domestic and international markets. Following Bolívar Echeverría's observations, economic policy is a device for administering the capital accumulation crisis and a tool to counteract it.

These are the premises on which we base our reading of the situation of capitalist production in Ecuador and its main limitations. We will consider the state's economic policy and its predicament at the time and then discuss the solutions proposed by Ecuadorean capitalists: casualization of labour, public indebtedness and primary export extractivism. Finally, we consider the stock market débacle of March 2020 – aggravated by the emergence of COVID-19 – and its consequences for the country's economy.

1.2 ECONOMIC DEPENDENCE ON THE WORLD MARKET

Since the beginning of the twentieth century, the development of capitalism in Ecuador has been characterized by a succession of economic cycles related to the international price of its main export commodities, in order: cocoa (1891–1920), bananas (1948–1960) and oil (1972–1979 and 2003–2014). This dependence on the world market inevitably made capital accumulation more difficult and unstable. Thus, for example, during the oil boom of the seventies of the last century Ecuador's Gross Domestic Product (GDP) showed a growth rate of 7.3%, while in the period 2003–2014, when a second boom was reported, it only increased at a rate of 4% (Central Bank of Ecuador, 2016).

After the deep crisis that culminated with the bank holiday and the dollarization of the Ecuadorean economy 1999–2001), the balance of trade – which represents the relationship between imports and exports – reached equilibrium in 2003 thanks to the increase in the international price of oil and other export products that reached their peak between 2011 and 2014, including the export of labour.[2] This moment was called by some authors the 'commodity super cycle'. However, the fall in the price of a barrel of Ecuadorean oil (Crude Oriente) from US$98.90 to US$38.85 between June 2014 and August 2015 led to the end of this period and the beginning of a steady decline of Ecuadorean products on the world market, together again with the deterioration of state finances.

The first factor to understand is the situation of Ecuador's foreign trade. On the one hand, the large private importers,[3] whose form of capital accumulation is based on the sale of

---

[2] From the capitalists' point of view there is no difference between exporting products and labour, since both are commodities that are paid for. The money sent home by emigrants outside the country is a central component of GDP. No government has acted to change this situation, despite the 'deep' ideological differences that divide them.

[3] Imports are divided almost equally into raw materials, capital goods, fuel and oils, and consumer goods, where the comprador bourgeoisie earns its highest profits.

manufactured products, produced a negative balance of non-oil foreign trade – which represents a quarter of the country's economy – and, consequently, a haemorrhage of dollars that only benefits a segment of the comprador bourgeoisie. That is to say, businessmen prefer to buy abroad to sell in the local market, rather than to produce in the country, an expression of their anti-patriotic attitudes. On the other hand, the commercial loss is counterbalanced by state oil extraction and agro-exports, which create a similar commercial surplus and allow the entry of dollars (Campaña, 2019a; SENPLADES, 2009, p. 66). Therefore, the entry of dollars into the country that allows capital accumulation depends mainly on oil and agro-industrial exports, sectors that have not substantially improved their level of production, reinforcing capitalism's dependence on world market demand.

The second factor is the deterioration of the terms of trade. The fall in the value of the main primary export products such as oil, bananas and flowers, among others – which reached 77.3% of total exports in 2012 (IMF, 2019, p. 23; SENPLADES, 2013, p. 256) – as well as the absence of substantial increases in oil production, stalled since the construction of the Heavy Crude Oil Pipeline (OCP) at the beginning of this century (Cantuña, 2015, p. 25), had a particular impact on the reduction of the profit share of companies engaged in agribusiness and produced, in general, a vicious circle in employment and production: production declines, unemployment rises, consumption is depressed, the economy goes into recession and a crisis ensues. Moreover, the phenomenon becomes even more acute if we consider that the lower oil revenues also thinned the fiscal accounts, which could not sustain the pace of public spending and investment, thus affecting the capitalists who profited from this spending in sectors such as construction.

The third element shaping the crisis of capital accumulation in Ecuador is the fall in world trade after 2014 – as a prelude to the trade war between the United States and China (WTO, 2017) which led to the appreciation of the dollar exchange rate (ECB, 2016) and, together with the almost general currency devaluation in Latin America, ended up making exports from Ecuador more expensive. The fact is more sensitive given that the economy is dollarised and, without its own currency, it does not have a monetary policy to patch up the crisis by reducing the purchasing power of the popular classes through printing money – that is, devaluation – and, at the same time, improving the competitiveness of export prices.

Domestically, the outlook has not been more encouraging for the capitalist class. The economic contraction in sectors such as construction or industry intensified from the beginning of 2014, due to three factors. First, the difference in production costs with respect to countries such as Colombia and Peru is caused by the intentional devaluation of their respective national currencies.[4] Second was the fall in sales of several industries such as textiles and floriculture, due to smuggling (Silva, 2019a), as well as the contraction of consumption and investments (IMF, 2019, p. 20). Third, there was disinvestment in local industry due to the fact that 'a large number of entrepreneurs in the footwear, furniture, textile, and vehicle assembly sectors, among others, turned to import activities, since it was more profitable to import goods than to produce locally' (Campaña, 2019b).

The cherry on the cake is added by the financial sector, the great historical beneficiary of dollarisation. As León (2020, p. 215) notes,[5] in the boom period 2010–2014 profits amounted to USD 1,572.7 million, which grew in the recession period, between 2015–2019, to USD 2,002.9 million. The point is that for the financial sector it is more profitable to deposit the money from its profits in a bank abroad than to invest it in the country.[6]

In this context the idea has circulated that the problem could be resolved by industrial metal mining – these are the siren songs of the 'experts' seeking ways of escaping the trap. But in fact its implementation would emphasize Ecuador's peripheral role in the world economy (as providers of cheap raw materials),

---

4 The dollar is a strong international currency. When used as a local currency in Ecuador domestically produced goods are consequently more costly than similar goods produced elsewhere, which limits their availability for external trade.

5 Leon synthesises the process thus. 'Local banks before 2000 linked currency exchange to the maximum issue of internal credits in dollars, driving what was called informal dollarisation. Miraculously, dollar credits exceeded dollar deposits. And the banks became creditors in dollars and debtors in the national currency. Liquidity was very limited and the banks had to inflate the amount of cash in circulation by seeking loans from the Central Bank whenever it faced a run on deposits. Thus, in the chaos of the currency market, caused by the inflation set in motion by the Central Bank in helping out the banking sector and by the flight of the population towards the dollar to defend the value of their savings, Itself a symptom of the death of the sucre when the violent increase in the exchange rate occurred, the banks liquidated their debts in the national currency and became, instantly, financially healthy and profitable.'

6 The flight of capital from the country into deposits abroad intensified despite the USD, $1,631.4 million between 2000 and 2009 and $22,130.0 millions from 2018-2019, a ratio of 137:1 compared to the first decade. A total of $23,726.4 million, close to the total quantity of money in circulation' (Leon, 2020, p. 211).

limiting national sovereignty in favour of the imperialist mining industry. Added to the flexibility of labour and the relaxation of environmental conditions it would lead to the degradation of extensive territorial areas. Mining is a manifestation of the search for profits in the context of crisis. In Rosa Luxemburg's terms it would open a new phase of primitive capitalist accumulation, and establish a line of continuity with the neo-developmentalist and neoliberal governments, between regulatory and deregulatory capitalism.

1.3 FOREIGN DEBT: THE FATAL RESULT OF THE UNTOUCHED ECONOMIC STRUCTURE

Dollarization is the state's renunciation of its monetary sovereignty. In this framework, the main instrument of economic policy is fiscal policy. This is the most important mechanism the state has to intervene in the economy and create conditions conducive to the enrichment of the capitalist class, directing public spending to the domestic market to expand it. During the period 2005–2018, public spending energised the market through infrastructure works, provision of services and supply of materials and products with large companies, as well as the incorporation of a significant contingent of male and female workers onto the state payroll who were then consumers of the same capitalist companies. The increase in oil tax revenues led to a growth in the General State Budget (PGE) and, together with this incentive to consumption and production, caused economic activity in general to revive. The high price of raw materials was transferred to the domestic market.

This dynamic improved the tax contribution which, in return, increased the state budget and set the tone for the cycle described above. It can be observed that the gradual growth in the value of tax collection is closely related to the boom cycle that began in 2003 and to the dramatic expansion of total public revenues in 2008 (from 13.4 to 22 billion dollars) and in 2011 (from 23.1 to 31.1 billion dollars), especially due to the growth of oil revenues; while, ironically, there was a relative contraction of non-oil state revenues (SENPLADES, 2009, p.139 Cantuña, 2015; Paz and Miño, 2015, p. 221). In this period, the pressure of foreign debt interest on current spending (annual) was not significant, salaries were the most relevant item in state spending, and until 2012 financing needs remained at a moderate level because the GEB (General State Budget) deficit increased slightly (it did not exceed 2%). However, after 2014

Graph 1: External public debt (in millions of dollars), 1976–2019

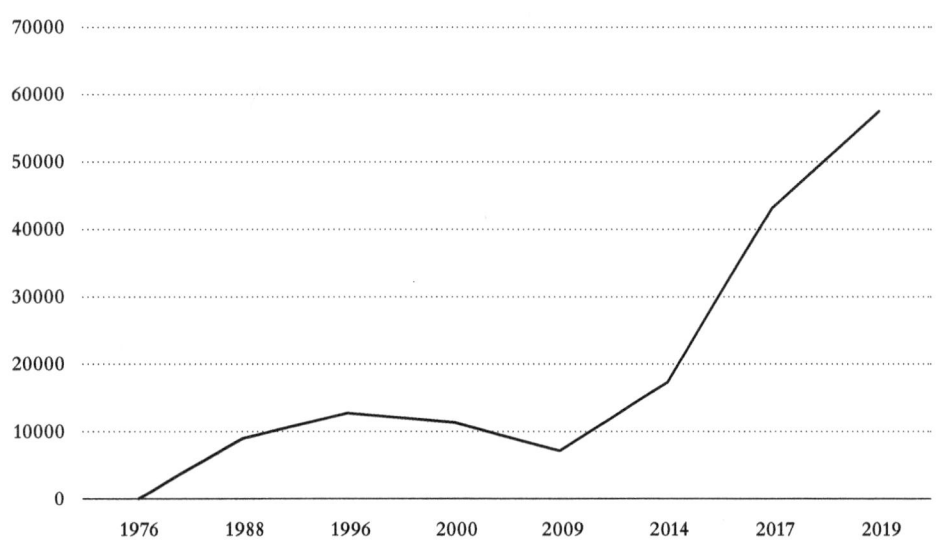

Source: Ministry of Economy and Finance. Own elaboration

the fiscal budget deficit grew and, with the fall in oil prices, led to heavy indebtedness to maintain state spending. Therefore the contraction of oil revenues is the most important variable to explain the fiscal crisis.[7]

The wild card to overcome this obstacle was public indebtedness, especially through foreign debt. Seen from this angle, it was the fatal result of the fact that the structure of Ecuadorean capitalism was not transformed at all during the 21st century and that, on the contrary, the pattern of capital accumulation left by neoliberalism maintained a line of continuity in the first two decades of the current century. In other words, there was no change in the so-called 'productive matrix'. As shown in Graph 1, the current public debt began its trajectory in 1976 with the credits contracted by the military dictatorship, in an upward spiral until 1996; then, it began a downward trend that ended in 2009 (SENPLADES, 2009, p. 251). From then on, debt growth was rampant until 2017, and in 2020 the contracting of credits to meet the same debt service – debt to pay debt – skyrocketed. In 2019 the spiral led to external debt representing 45% of GDP (BBC World News, 2019a); by January 2020 it was 53% of GDP and rising. Such levels of external debt are comparable to the value recorded five years before the great crisis of 1999.

From 2014 onwards, the increase in public indebtedness occurred under increasingly adverse and detrimental credit conditions for the country. This – together with the variations in the foreign market, especially in the oil market – caused international distrust to grow due to the country's risk of default. As shown in Graph 2, in September 2019 the country's risk stood at 630 points.[8] After the October rebellion it reached 783 points. However, when the price of oil declined (March 23, 2020) the indicator rose sharply to 6,063 points. Higher country risk means more expensive debt – higher interest rates. Therefore oil prices directly correlate with Ecuador's country risk (Weisbrot and Arauz, 2019, p. 8). The conditions of indebtedness are determined by the level of subordination of the national economy to the world primary-extractive capitalist market.

Gradually, the weight of interest and amortization – called 'debt service' – in the state budget increased (IMF, 2019, p. 22; Cantuña, 2015), touching 5% of GDP and almost one-seventh of the state budget in 2019 (Campaña, 2019b). The foreign debt, as well as a good part of the oil and mining, is controlled by foreign countries and companies, a symptom of how Ecuador is chained to the needs of imperialism; this condemns the country to the intensification of the condition of dependence on the needs of the central or emerging capitalist countries.

Consequently the Ecuadorean state has fewer and fewer economic policy tools to manage the crisis of capitalism. At this point, decisions related to the General State Budget (GEB) are of key significance for the bourgeoisie and are the source of disputes. From the perspective of the capital accumulation cycle, which is the key approach to understanding the capitalist economy, the conditions for insisting on a Keynesian state intervention – the model of state action sustained between 2007 and 2019 – no longer exist: the prices of oil and other raw materials are low, the disputes in foreign markets are growing, indebtedness is high and there are no other sources of state financing.

In this context, there are three fundamental economic tendencies that the capitalists adopt to face the crisis: a) increasing

---

[7] The dependence of the Ecuadorean state on oil income, however, is not 'congenital'. In 1970 tax income covered 86% of the total, falling in 1975 alone to 35% in the wake of the oil price boom. The logic of extractivism is the result of the incapacity of the bourgeoisie to develop a national capitalist project beyond the international division of labour and the interests of the imperialist powers.

[8] A country's default risk is an indicator of whether an investment is at risk due to specific factors like its political, economic or security situation and with an eye to the possibility that a sovereign state may find itself unable to fulfil its obligations.

Graph 2: Country risk 2010–2020

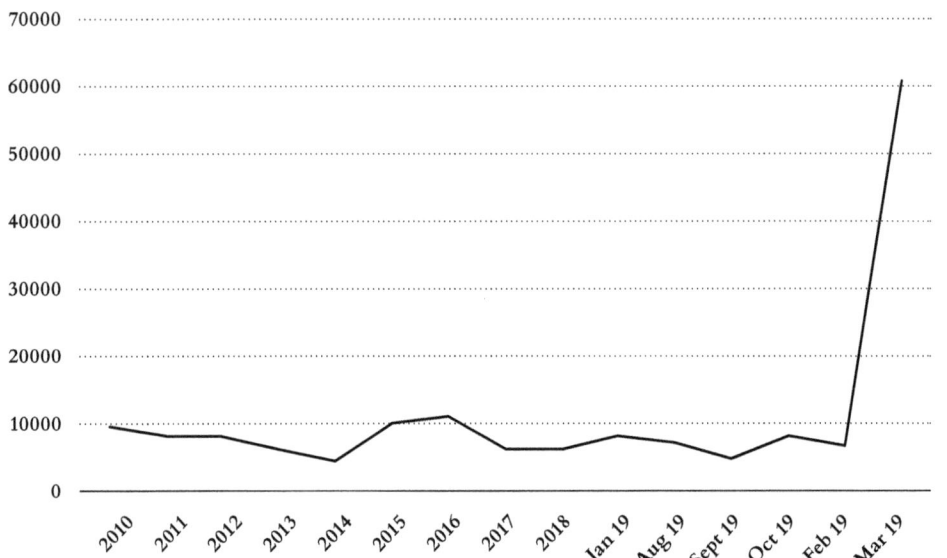

Source: Ambito.com Own elaboration

pressure on wages and working conditions to improve the rate of profit of large companies; b) an extractivist onslaught with the argument that resources will be injected into the economy to sustain the domestic market; and c) a shift in economic policy towards state intervention to deregulate the market.

1.4 THE PRESSURE OF THE CRISIS ON THE WORKING CLASS

In Ecuador, around 94% of the value of the country's production is in the hands of large capitalist enterprises, while medium and small 'enterprises',[9] despite being the overwhelming majority of production units, have control over only 4.7% and 1.4% of the wealth produced, respectively (Carrillo, 2009, p. 4). It is the large companies that set the fundamental guidelines in economic and productive matters.

The production of the capitalist sector is, for the most part, labour-intensive: large units of production, whose main cost

---

9 The Andean Community (CAN) classifies enterprises according to the number of workers employed – in small enterprises between 10 and 49, in medium enterprises from 50 to 199 and in large enterprises 200 and above (Carrillo, 2009, p. 49).

is labour. This means that the wealth produced in the country is basically generated by the exploitation of the labour force. Complementing this characteristic, it is fundamental to note that the extraction of surplus value has a patriarchal character: women receive between one and two-fifths less remuneration in waged jobs than men for doing the same work. In addition, they also contribute through unpaid work – that is, care tasks for the reproduction of the labour force – 'between 11% and 15% of GDP' (Madrid, 2017, pp. 54–55). Likewise, this pattern of accumulation makes the rural and Indigenous population precarious, since they serve as labour to ensure cheap raw materials for agribusiness and the production of abundant and low-cost food, which allows the working population to sustain their households on reduced wages (Madrid, 2018b, p. 107).[10]

The importance of the labour force in the cost structure of the large capitalist enterprises means that one of the main and most recurrent demands of the monopoly groups is the reduction of the wages of the working class. To achieve this, over three decades, they have used the most diverse, creative and extravagant methods: changes in the institutional regulation of productive activities (firing costs, flexible contracts and schedules, among others), modifications in the organization of the work process (productive and labour flexibility, increased work intensity), regardless of the consequences in terms of occupational accidents and occupational diseases (Madrid, 2017). All these measures resulted in increasing the precariousness of working conditions (Báez, 2020, p. 213; Chiriboga and Arias, 2020, p. 185). What is most striking is the decrease in stable jobs (measured by the rate of adequate employment) from 2014 onwards; in other words, given that between 2014 and 2019 two governments of different tendencies succeeded each other, we can conclude that the process of capital accumulation has a decisive impact on the precariousness of labour, over and above the ideological current of the government in power and that, therefore, the trend for the following years points to the deepening of this process.

The Gordian knot is the restrictions that dollarization places on the capitalist crusade against wages. The monetary system, once a price stability mechanism, is now a straitjacket. Big business

---

10 In general, the continuing tendency towards proletarianization of the country does not lead to an increase in the wage-earning population, but increases the informal labour force, impoverishing a segment of the working class that does not have nor will ever have stable employment. Unemployment from 1980 onwards remains around 5%, except during periods of recession; underemployment and autonomous precarious employment represent half of the country's labour force (Madrid, 2017, p. 50). The growth of precarity is one consequence of the deepening crisis.

tries to reduce its production costs, specifically labour costs, to compete with its peers in other countries producing the same or similar goods, but who have the advantage of devaluing the currency and, in this way, reducing the real wages of their workers. For this reason, since 2001, as an unintended effect of dollarization, real wages in Ecuador are among the highest in Latin America, a trend that has been accentuated since 2010. In parallel, the country's productivity has stagnated, resulting in slow economic growth (IMF, 2019, p. 41).

Not being able to devalue the currency, which is a measure that in practice allows states to reduce the purchasing power of wages, the Ecuadorean capitalist class took another option. When the Moreno government decided to eliminate the subsidy on transportation fuels, through Decree No. 883, it provoked a general rise in prices (inflation) that benefited the big companies with a measure equivalent to currency devaluation. Different calculations indicated that inflation could reach 2% annually, increase by 12% the price of transportation,[11] and add up to 5% to the basic family basket (Saltos, 2019; Acosta and Cajas, 2019a). Inflation causes a reduction in real wages; indirectly, it allows the cheapening of the labour force and the improvement of the profit margin.

The intention was the following: Decree No. 883 eliminated the subsidy for diesel for car use but not for industrial use (Villavicencio, 2020). It did not alter other areas of the cost structure of large capitalist enterprises, but, on the contrary, continued to subsidize the industrial and agro-industrial bourgeoisie by 0.70 dollars per gallon. Beyond the assumptions of wage growth (Baez, 2019a), we consider that the wage adjustment measures belong to the long period of economic contraction that began in 2014. In the long run, it perpetuated the process of 'wage implosion' that began in the 1980s. Consequently, the period 2003–2014 – which saw a real minimum wage increase – was a brief interregnum. Only in 2014 did wages recover their 1985 purchasing power, although they remained far from the real wage of the 1980s. From 2014 onwards, real wages stagnated with a subsequent decrease in the purchasing power of the wage, which is equivalent to a slow and steady wage reduction (Figueroa, 2017, p. 29); this impacted above all on working people.

---

11   The price of Extra petrol rose from 1.45 to 2.41 dollars a gallon, Exopais (Extra with ethanol) from 1.45 to 2.5 a gallon and Super from 2.3 to 3.07 a gallon (Machado, 2019b).

1.5 EXTRACTIVISM AS AN IMPERIALIST SYMPTOM

The Ecuadorean economy has been structured around the export of raw materials. It has been subjected to the rise and fall of successive booms in cocoa, bananas, flowers, prawns and oil on the world market. And in recent decades, with the Correa government's commitment to deepening this process, the ruling classes have developed all the instruments to promote the conversion of Ecuador into a mining country. In 2012, while opening the doors to large-scale mining with the signing of the first contract to extract copper with the Chinese firm Ecuacorriente (ECSA) in the Amazonian province of Zamora Chinchipe (south-east), former President Correa ratified the extractivist course initiated with the passage of the Mining Law in 2009 and the proliferation of concessions, stating that 'we cannot be beggars sitting on a sack of gold'.

Criticism of this form of accumulation is not based only on an environmentalist perspective, but also on the forms of dependency it generates and which deepen the vulnerability of the Ecuadorean economy in the face of cyclical crises of capitalism such as the one we are currently experiencing.

Dependency theorists have argued extensively about the link between the abundance of natural resources and underdevelopment, features that can be seen in the Ecuadorean case. Since colonial times, and especially since the beginning of the 20th century, the export of primary goods (agricultural or mineral) has underpinned the massive concentration of income in a few oligopolistic groups. These business sectors – due to their configuration and traditional links with commercial elites – historically act on the basis of a rentier mentality, encouraging the consumption of imported goods instead of investing in the domestic economy, and frequently taking their profits out of the country and managing their business with companies based in tax havens. The result is limited integration of the export sector with domestic production; no productive clusters are developed to diversify the domestic market, or even to expand the exportable supply or transform natural resources into higher value-added goods.

Although its discourse placed Ecuador in the new mining era in which the Ecuadorean state would play a regulatory role and capture a portion of the income for redistributive purposes, the political economy of these megaprojects shows that the major beneficiaries continued to be the business sectors contracted by the state. The liabilities, land dispossession and reduced employment generation translated into more poverty in the extraction zones. Nor is there any public investment policy for productive industrialization by import substitution: there is no strategy of 'deepening extractivism to get out of extractivism'.

In addition, the high demand for capital and technology in oil and mining production requires agreements with imperialist capitals (in the last decade mainly Chinese and Canadian) that demand environmental deregulation measures and state protection for their investments, and operate with an enclave logic that leaves the productive system subject to the uncertainties of the world market. That leaves the economy vulnerable to competition from other countries in similar conditions, who seek to sustain their income without worrying about price stability in the international market. Thus, in response to the cyclical falls in the price of these resources, the response in the primary exporting countries has always been to fall into the trap of expanding the extractive frontier, intensifying the cycle of dependence in times of crisis, which ends up benefiting the central countries: a greater supply in times of depressed prices leads to a greater reduction in their prices. This can be seen in the recent instances of significant acceleration of the extractivist policy, in 1995 and 2014, which coincided with periods of economic recession.

The urgent need for resources to maintain the economic dynamics set in motion on the basis of the injection of public investment and in response to the declining profits of the big capitalist companies meant that the country (community and peasant territories, the health of entire populations, water sources, the balance of ecosystems and the spiritual sites of peoples and nationalities) was handed over to imperialism in exchange for very little. Given the drop in oil prices, the position of the Correa government, and later the Moreno government, has been to give way to the demand of the imperialist companies to increase oil extraction in the Central Amazon, and to accelerate the extraction of minerals in the Southern Amazon and in the foothills of the mountain range that connects the sierra with the coast. As the Assembly of the Peoples of the South points out, this project put 8% of the national territory at risk, sparking conflicts with local populations throughout the country. Also – in view of the interest in expanding the map of mining rights transferred to transnationals – up to 15% of the territory is at risk, as announced by state officials: a new auction of mining concessions is expected at the beginning of 2021.

Large-scale extraction of metallic minerals and oil are the only branches of economic activity that have attracted foreign capital; the rest of Foreign Direct Investment (FDI) is just a discourse of the ruling class. The regulatory framework of the 1990s, which was drafted with the advice of the World Bank and whose spirit has not changed with the 2009 Mining Law – or its subsequent modifications – allows companies to gain, both through mining concession rights as assets in the country, and also by accumulating resources in the stock market, even when the extractive activity is in the exploration phase. This necessarily links foreign investment with speculative processes in times of high commodity prices, and the exacerbation of land dispossession in times of crisis.

The long-term social and environmental impacts of this economic policy undermine the endogenous conditions for developing productive clusters that underpin economic sovereignty, let alone proposals of a popular nature. By altering the ecological balance and appropriating the territories of the people, the state destroyed their capacity for economic reproduction, linked to productive, cultural and social practices. This leads to total dependence on imperialist companies in the areas of health, education, labour and recreation. The intervention of the transnationals turns them into an authentic state, which not only provides social services but also builds its own sovereignty through private guards that limit free transit over the territory, even outside the concession areas.

What was presented by the elites as a 'necessary sacrifice' to 'improve the living conditions of the poorest' is an illusion that cyclically vanishes. The logical consequences of the extractive rentier process, and the way in which capitalist groups operate with their profits, are that: the country's reserves are reduced, the territory is emptied of resources and destroyed nature is exported – a net loss in its patrimony – in exchange for a meagre and temporary flow of investments. This illusion has caused the development of capitalism in Ecuador to become dependent on raw materials and their fate: a viscous liquid or a few strange stones determine the fate or misfortune of entire populations, the structural weakness of the national economy and the outburst of state violence to intensify extraction in the face of the crisis.

1.6 DEREGULATORY STATE INTERVENTION

Since 2014 the economic policy that attempted to restore the profit rate of large economic groups based on an active use of state spending faced increasing difficulties. During the cycle of economic contraction, the governments in power avoided unleashing the strongest cutback measures. They resorted to palliative measures such as public indebtedness and a series of smaller measures (micro packages) that tried, drop by drop, to maintain the so-called 'multiplier effect of spending'.

Among these the following are worth mentioning: a) the growth of consumption through initiatives such as electronic money, the delivery of reserve funds to each affiliate or the growth of credit due to lower interest rates; b) the temporary restriction of imports, an area that has always been hindered by the commitments adopted between the governments and this sector of the comprador bourgeoisie; and c) the increase of taxes, in all imaginable ways,[12] but without violating tax inequality or the characteristic tax evasion.[13] [14]

These micro packages preceding Decree No. 883 were conceived to overcome the budget deficit and the liquidity crisis.

- According to ECLAC (2017), the average rate of evasion of Value Added Tax (VAT) [...] in 2015 [...] in Ecuador reached 31.8% in absolute terms and was equivalent to USD 2.8 billion (Campaña, 2017).
- 971 people who are major shareholders in the [most powerful] Economic Groups represented, together, in 2017, 0.006% of the total Ecuadorean population and control the equivalent in assets of 1.63 times the country's GDP with US$ 115.725 billion [...]. Of these, 236 (24 %) declared no income, and so paid zero income tax. On the other hand, 541 of them had, together [...] an income of USD 517 million per year. On average, their monthly income was US$ 79 773, which is equivalent to approximately 213 times the minimum wage (Baez, 2019a).

---

12 These include: a tariff on foreign post, a tax on fast food, a green tax on vehicles, increased costs for licences, tax on foreign currency exports, tax on banking, elimination of advance payments on income tax, the retention of taxes on micro, small and medium enterprises, return of taxes to exporters, simplification of taxes on the banana sector, extra taxes on plastic containers, e-cigarettes and digital services, on soft drinks, on use of mobile phones, 0.1% addition to tax on most profitable enterprises, limitations on personal expenses on tax returns, reduced taxes on craft beers and on technology.

13 From 1980, income tax fell significantly while the importance of indirect taxes increased

14 Tax evasion in 1968 touched 30% (Paz y Miño, 2015, p.150).

The ensuing measures were a condition for obtaining financing from the International Monetary Fund (IMF). The institution – after its expulsion in 2008 – returned in 2014 and, by 2016, 'delivered a credit of 364 million dollars' (Guanche, 2019).

This evidence refutes the 'theory' of 'state capture' or 'state decision capture', which would suppose that the ruling class vanished from the country for ten years and that, miraculously, it also recovered its capacity to intervene after 2016. Did they revive (Baez, 2020, pp. 196-197)? In fact the capitalists never ceased to obtain enormous economic benefits during the neo-developmentalist period, supported by an economic policy favourable to their interests. The demands of the economic groups were permanently picked up by state policy to the point that the structure of Ecuadorean capitalism did not suffer substantial variations; the unions, chambers and federations of the ruling class were never touched either judicially or politically; on the contrary, the bloc of agro-industrial, commercial and financial bourgeois groups benefited as never before.

This deserves to be underlined, since in Ecuador only one out of every ten jobs was created by these large capitalist companies, one more by the state, and the remaining eight were generated through self-employment, by small and medium-sized production units and other types of precarious labour activities. In other words, the greatest generator of employment is the working class itself, who subsist in an adverse context under the conditions of informal precarious work, or at the mercy of the state's clientelist programmes.

Consequently, poverty rates, especially extreme poverty, worsened after 2014 (Chiriboga and Arias, 2020, p. 188; Báez, 2020, p. 213). When the redistributive illusion faded and the crisis hit, the harsh reality of the poor returned to normal. If capital does well, they receive the smallest share; if it does badly, they bear the crisis on their backs. The propaganda of the Correa government regarding a supposed 'epochal change' was just that – propaganda.

The measures adopted since the beginning of the long cycle of contraction of capitalism are not even the worst facet of the crisis. From the perspective of capital, cosmetic solutions were not enough. However, measures of greater intensity were postponed due to the electoral calculations (March 2019 elections) of the different fractions of the ruling class.

Under the logic of managing the crisis of capitalism, the programme of anti-popular measures required by the capitalists

Graph 3: Incidence of extreme poverty by income, 2007–2019

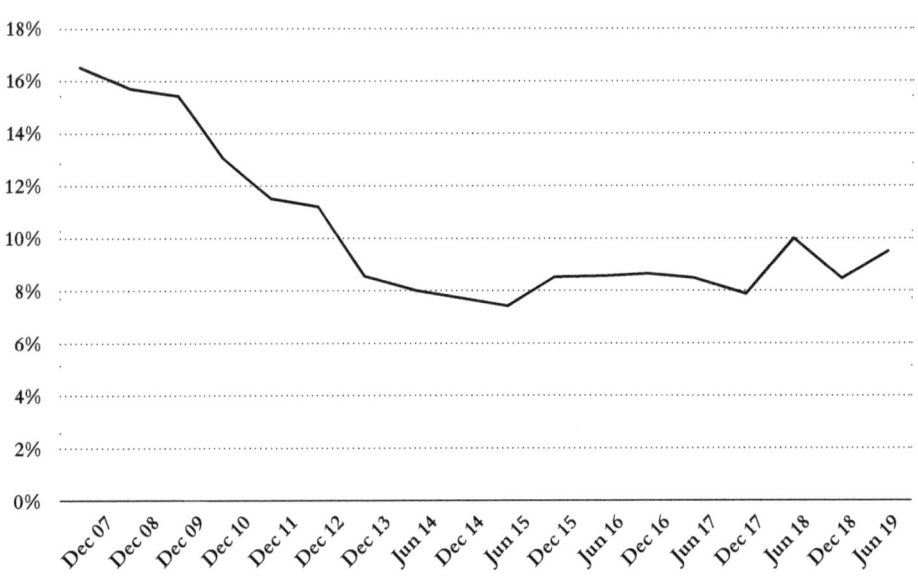

Source: Chiriboga and Arias, 2020, p. 187. Own elaboration

and implemented through a deregulatory (or neoliberal) state intervention includes:

1 External indebtedness, which would constitute the problem of the 2020s.
2 Elimination, in order of importance, of:
    a. fuel subsidies,[15]
    b. the subsidy on domestic gas,
    c. the human development bonus, which had already been reduced from 1.24 to 0.43 million beneficiaries, between 2009 and 2016 (OSE, 2019, p. 43),
    d. utility, housing and electricity rates – the electricity rate was increased in 2014 (Ruiz and Iturralde, 2013).
3 Privatization or long-term concession of public companies, more or less blatantly. It included the renegotiation of nine petroleum contracts of mature fields (El Comercio, 2016); the concession of the two most productive industries in the country: the Sacha and Auca oilfields, and the sale of the most economically profitable state-owned companies.[16]

---

15 The 85% subsidy on fuels was concentrated on diesel (35%), liquid gas (21%), Ecopais and Extra (28%) and on auto (68%) and domestic (21%) uses.

4 Labour reform. Returning to the policy of casualization included in the proposed reform of the Labour Code presented in 2014.
5 Massive layoffs in the state sector to reduce costs.
6 Promotion of the extractivist policy in the mining and oil sectors and, at the same time, reinforcement of the state policy of criminalization of social protest.

Neoliberal policies do not imply a withdrawal of the state but a proactive action to produce a public policy to reduce the state's regulatory practice in the economy, and to establish a deregulatory state intervention that supports the free market.[17]

1.7 TWINS AND RIVALS: KEYNESIAN AND NEOLIBERAL 'SOLUTIONS' TO THE CRISIS

As we have seen, the discourses of the capitalists to manage the crisis can be schematized in two variants: The first – social democratic or right-wing – focuses on a Keynesian or neo-Keynesian[18] type of policy that seeks to improve the efficiency of tax collection and stimulate consumption,[19] that is, to push so-called 'demand policies'. The second, sustained by the orthodox neoliberal right, seeks adjustment at all costs; the heterodox neoliberal[20] bets on 'social capitalism': '[...] the country grows, investment comes, tax collection increases, the state benefits [...] these are the only four things that need to be done' (Nebot, 2019a).

Both variants safeguard the interests of the capitalist class and to 'solve' the crisis they transfer the burden, ultimately, to

---

16 National Telecommunications Corporation (CNT), National Electricity Corporation (CNEL), National Electricity Corporation of Ecuador (CELEC), Petroecuador, Banco del Pacífico, Empresas de Agua, Flopec, Ecuadorean Railway, which are worth millions. 7 of the 21 public enterprises administered by the state produced a surplus of $1,757.4 million added to the general state budget (Campaña 2019a).

17 The central measures in the proposal are the reduction of public spending and in the size of the state, support and finances for multilateral entities, reduction of tax on corporations, special consumption and customs tariffs, simplification of the tax system to improve competitiveness and collection (on the Lafer formula), revising tax control measures, signing commercial agreements and legal reforms in favour of private productive investment.

18 Keynesianism also includes a variety of economic schools of thoughts, which may be called 'heterodox', i.e. the Forum of Heterodox Economists, Muños, Erazo, Pérez, Acosta Dávalos.

19 Among the measures proposed are reduction of VAT, elimination of income tax on micro and small enterprises, increased income tax or tax on currency exports by corporations, eliminating subsidies to big capital, increased customs duties on luxury goods, recovery of corruptly accumulated wealth, renegotiation of oil and media contracts, reducing the salaries and expenses of high officials, 0% electricity tariffs for small enterprises, lower interest rates and encouraging productive credit, large-scale public employment programmes, encouragement of small and medium business, popular markets, reduction of bureaucracy around productive activities, protectionism with free trade agreements and bilateral investment agreements.

20 Neoliberal is a problematic term because it embraces a number of schools of economic thought.

the majority of the population – through public debt, dispossession of territories and labour precariousness – to sustain the 'multiplier effect of spending', or the 'structural adjustment'. Nor do they question the paradigm of modern economics: that it is possible to order and humanize capitalism.

Hence the urgency of a critique that, based on political economy, responds to the needs of the majorities and prioritizes the most pressing problems of the working class, instead of seeking alternatives to manage the capitalist crisis as Keynesian or neoliberal, heterodox or orthodox, regulatory or deregulatory bourgeois economics have been doing. It is necessary to recover the concept of politics in public policy, since state measures crystallize a struggle between social forces where 'technical' arguments take second place, and economic interests prevail in a specific context of power relations.

A reading of these characteristics makes it possible to show that, at the economic level, the October outburst does not stem only from Decree No. 883, but from a chain of events that warn that capitalism is unviable, a historical framework of social and human organization and of the relationship with other forms of life. Responsibility for the October rebellion is shared between the working people (who fought to end exploitation and to stimulate a new future) and the exploiting classes who use political domination to save their decomposing civilization.

2 THE CRISIS OF LEGITIMACY OF THE POLITICAL SYSTEM

In Ecuador, periods of high prices for the main export commodities, such as bananas or oil, have created conditions that guaranteed relative political stability. These cycles have held to an approximate 12-year pattern (1912–1924; 1948–1960; 1972–1979; 2007–2019). All attempts to establish some political and institutional stability outside these cycles have failed. The crisis of legitimacy of the state is another dimension of the October uprising that demands explanation.

Since the so-called Transition Plan for the Return to Democracy in 1979 – or to give it its proper name 'the return to elections' – Ecuador has had a total of fourteen constitutional governments. Three of them were overthrown by huge mass mobilizations, which ended in coup d'états backed by the armed forces.[21] During the so-called 'lost decade and a half' (1981–1996), the systemic crisis of capitalism in Ecuador was so profound that intense disputes arose between the fractions of the ruling class. During this time, major political and structural decisions were shared among four large political organizations – Freidenberg and Alcántara (2001) called these groups 'the owners of power' though, strictly speaking, they should be called the 'owners of government' – Partido Roldosista Ecuatoriano (PRE), Partido Social Cristiano (PSC), Democracia Popular (DP) and Izquierda Democrática (ID).

Given the regional configuration of the dominant classes – due to differences in the form of economic accumulation, cultural patterns and ideological positions on the role of the state, we find that the first two parties enjoyed a broad influence on the Ecuadorean coast:

1. The Partido Roldosista Ecuatoriano, now Fuerza Ecuador, was characterised by a logic of capital accumulation specific to the bureaucratic bourgeoisie – using the state primarily to stimulate the growth of capital – in turn articulated to the needs of a sector of agro-exporters and the coastal commercial bourgeoisie. In addition, they took advantage of their bureaucratic position to shamelessly plunder the coffers and assets of the state to expand their private fortunes.[22] After the 'successful' decade of the PRE in 1980, and the short-lived presidential term of its leader in 1996, the party's image fell into a deep decline.

2. The Partido Social Cristiano represents the interests of the commercial bourgeoisie, which requires the free market to expand its zones of influence, and a segment of real estate, financial and agro-industrial bourgeoisie. Their businesses require favourable conditions for accumulation, which are achieved through regulation and public contracts. The centralized character of the fractions involved in the PSC provoked its regionalization; it became dominant in the zone of influence of the Guayaquil bourgeoisie. The death of the party's leader, León Febres Cordero, in 2008 led to a deepening of internal differences between party factions. A conservative wing appeared which adheres to the founding principles of Christian socialism and, on the other hand, a modernizing wing emerged, led by Jaime Nebot through the

---

21 We are referring here to the exit of presidents Abdalá Bucaram (02/1997), Jamil Mahuad (01/2001) and Lucio Gutiérrez (04/2005

22 The logic of capital accumulation is illustrated by the celebration of his first million dollars by Jacobito Bucaram, the wild child son of the leader of the party Abdalá Bucaram Ortiz supposedly 'earned' when he was in charge of customs.

Movimiento Madera de Guerrero, which supports the thesis of social and heterodox neoliberalism.

The predominant parties in the sierra region have two distinct origins:

1 Democracia Popular (DP) represented the most reactionary sectors of the ruling class, both ideologically and economically. A good part of this fraction originated from the landowning families that migrated their businesses towards finance and industry – mostly in the highlands, although also with participation in the coastal region. The prolonged crisis that began in the 1980s ruined their interests, which led the PD to turn to the state to sustain its forms of accumulation at two critical moments: the first through the nationalization of debt of large corporations (the 'sucretization of the debt'). The second stimulus developed through the liquidation of the most important banks in the so-called 'Feriado Bancario' and the dollarization of the economy, which allowed for an enormous concentration of capital in industry and finance. However, these operations led to the decline of party membership, especially after the collapse of the government of its representative, Jamil Mahuad, in 2001.
2 Izquierda Democrática (ID) tried to monopolise the political spectrum around social democracy, without fully succeeding. Unlike its North American and European counterparts, ID never established an organic link to any trade union.[23] ID's two main factions of support emerged in the 1970s: a middle-income sector that aspired to achieve social mobility through its link to the state, and a fraction of the industrial bourgeoisie that demanded permanent negotiation of capital-labour relations in order to improve its rate of profit. As a result of its deals with the other three main political parties, the electoral strength of ID was significantly reduced.

The factions of the ruling class represented by these political organizations maintained a frenzied dispute for decades. This often produced a pantomime resolution of their political differences.

23 Despite the efforts of some trade union leaders, who today enjoy considerable influence in the leadership of some national trade union organisations to win that backing.

The increasing precariousness of the population's living conditions increased the discredit of political representation, and explains the loss of confidence of the people in traditional state institutions, represented at this time by Congress, the judiciary and the party system as a whole.[24]

This did not mean the disappearance of the four hegemonic electoral forces, but rather their metamorphosis into other representations of the party system, and towards what is known as the 'camisetazo'.[25] The end of the century gave birth to 'new' party structures, as an outsider response to the crisis of political representation. The electoral space of the PRE was absorbed by the Partido Renovador Independiente (PRIAN) – later Adelante Ecuatoriano Adelante (AEA) – by Fuerza Ecuador (FE), and by the Partido Sociedad Patriótica (PSP). The remnants of the DP were reorganized under the acronym of the Movimiento Creando Oportunidades (CREO), a party led by banker Guillermo Lasso. Izquierda Democrática was absorbed by Alianza País (AP), which in turn incorporated Movimiento Ruptura de los 25 (R25), the remnants of the institutionalist left and the 'armed social democracy' of the 1980s – particularly Alfaro Vive Carajo (AVC) – together with some remnants of the right-wing parties. As an accessory, a multitude of minority organizations appeared, distributed in the margins of the electoral spectrum. These organizations revitalized the party system with the 'pluralist' illusion: Centro Democrático (CD), Democracia Sí, Avanza and Juntos Podemos (JP).

In parallel, some expressions of the 'left' have been institutionalized since the return of electoral democracy, such as the Marxist-Leninist Communist Party of Ecuador (PCMLE) and the Ecuadorean Socialist Party (PSE). These parties tried to institutionalize their social capital obtained during trade union disputes in the electoral process, with very poor results.[26] Their participation was always peripheral, leading to inter-party migration to other parties, including right-wing ones. The Movimiento de Unidad Plurinacional Pachakutik-Nuevo País (PK), founded in 1996, is also part of this although its trajectory included nuances of a different origin. PK was founded as one of the products of the cycle of mobilizations of the early 1990s. Establishing itself as a 'political arm' of CONAIE, PK gradually became an institutionalized party in permanent conflict

---

24 By 2005, a majority of the population rejected all the institutions of state. The slogan, 'out with them all', which became popular in the Quito rebellion of that year, summed up the social, economic and political discontent of the people.

25 We are referring here to leaving one party for another.

26 In the case of PCMLE into the popular Democratic Movement (MPD), and of the PSE into the Frente Amplio (PSE-FA).

with the organizational structure of the Indigenous movement. Several of its cadres would end up in other political parties.

The restructuring of political forces is closely related to the conditions caused by the dynamics resulting from the peak of the period of deepened political crisis and the subsequent stability derived from the economic boom that began in 2007. The conditions which led to a recovery in public finances and the trade balance allowed for relative trust in the state and political parties, relative because even under those conditions almost one out of two Ecuadoreans still distrusted the state and the public administration (Latinobarómetro, 2019).

Government approval cycles correlate with the prices of the main export products and with the degree of social conflict. Social approval of the government improves when there is an economic boom, and decreases in times of crisis. Processes of social struggle, in the same way, increase in a period of economic crisis. The cycles of political legitimacy must be read through the filter of the expansions or contractions of capitalist markets, and the variations in the class struggle. Thus, for example, the growth in disapproval of the Correa government coincided with the fall in WTI oil prices and with the cycle of mobilizations of 2014–2015.

In 2014 a new period of crisis emerged, when: a) the government's approval rating and the rate of profitability of exports began to drop; b) tensions around extractivism deepened; and c) demonstrations began to happen. Progressively, cracks emerged in the dominant bloc, and the organized working class confronted Correa's government.

So, it is not true, as some opinion researchers claim, that mistrust in state institutions began after the first year of Lenin Moreno's government (*Perfiles de Opinión en Kolectivoz*, 2019). The interval of relative 'calm' between 2017 and 2018 was the result of the conjunction between the closing of a decade of Correa's governments (marked in parallel by high levels of criminalization of social protest and conflicts with a faction of the commercial bourgeoisie and certain media) and the national 'dialogue' promoted by Moreno, in an effort to restore the deteriorated structures of domination, appease social mobilization with superficial and accessory measures, and provide the bourgeoisie with guarantees concerning the nature of the policies that would emerge in 2018 in order to manage the crisis. This precarious political stability lasted until CONAIE broke off 'dialogue', although before that a scenario of weakened political power could already be perceived.[27]

Graph 4: Approval rating of the government, 2002–2018

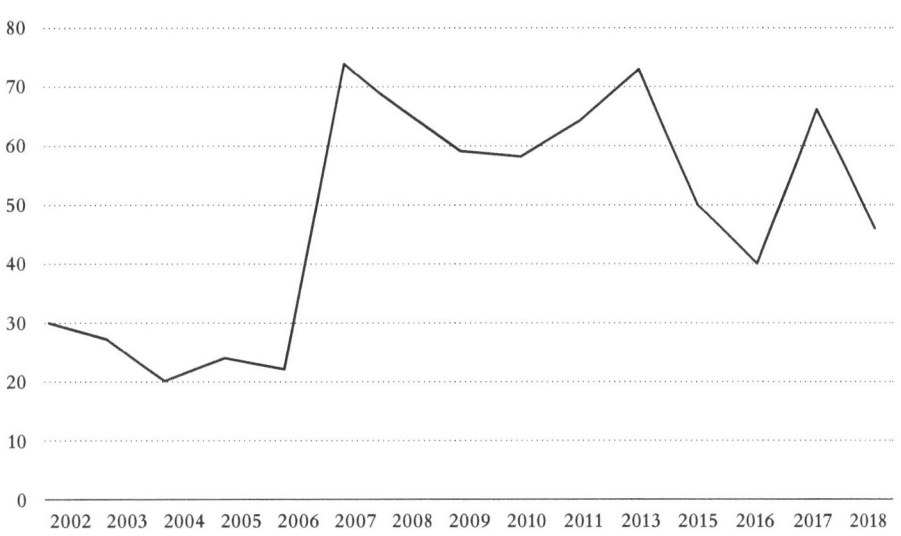

Source: Latinobarómetro, 2019. Elaboration; authors

The October rebellion devastated the deterioration of governmental legitimacy and bourgeois hegemony. Disapproval of the executive and the legislature exceeded 80%, and half the country failed to even recognize Vice-President Otto Sonnenholzner (Opinion Profiles in *Kolectivoz*, 2019). This was the result of the inherent capitalist crisis, and not of the President's incapacity and lack of leadership, as some factions argued. The October rebellion only worsened the outlook for political domination, as recognized by the Social-Christian assemblyman, Henry Cucalón: 'The political class as a whole has lost'. The overtone has provided the popular perception that in the country only 'power groups' benefit. We will now go on to address these issues.

Ecuador is in a period of deep crisis of legitimacy of the state, related to the end of the cycle of governmental stability and

---

27 Some of the factors that confirm these internal divisions in the official bloc are: the dismissal of assembly members for different reasons, including demanding payment from their staff or absence from work; the dismissal of two vice-presidents (one jailed and one put on trial); questions raised in parliament with the judiciary about costs added to contracts; political trials of the Comptroller General and members of the national cabinet; dismissal of officials overseeing control and transparency; suspicions of electoral fraud and switching of parties by assembly members. Yesterday's orthodox Correístas became today's pure Morenistas, as the Correísta Franklin Ramirez confirmed.

Graph 5: Social perception of who benefits from state policy
Dark line: What benefits the powerful alone. Light line: what benefits everyone.

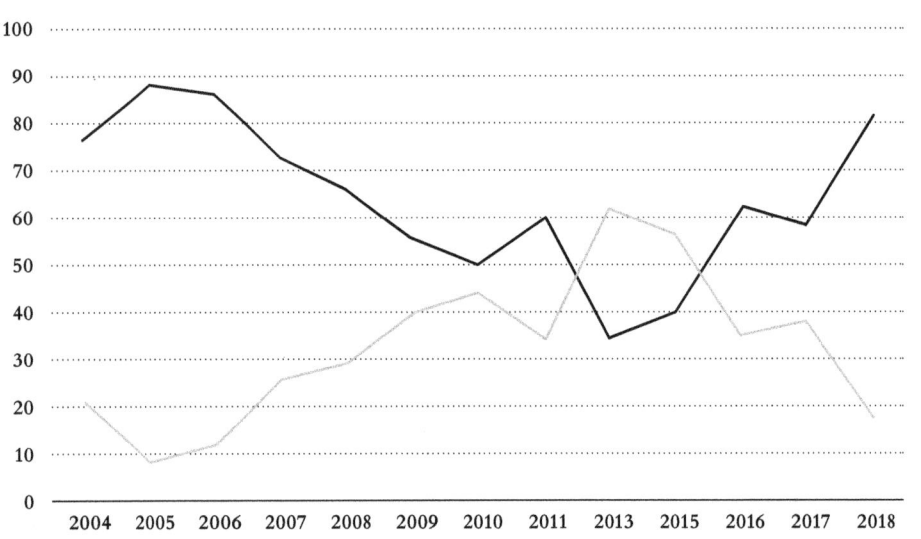

Source: Latinobarómetro. Elaboration: The authors

to the growing questioning of actually existing power. In the terms of the analysis put forward by Italian Marxist Antonio Gramsci, we are on the verge of an organic capitalist crisis, which manifests itself in difficulties for the accumulation of capital, in the loss of hegemony of the elites, in the deterioration of the living conditions of the subaltern masses, in the increase of social mobilization processes, and in the growing optimism of a revolutionary spirit. These last factors will be discussed below.

3 THE SPECTRE OF CLASS STRUGGLE IS HAUNTING ECUADOR

If cycles of stability or crisis of the capitalist system do not fit into the pattern of electoral or governmental terms, neither do the mobilizations they provoke. It is necessary to understand the October rebellion as the climax of a series of previous struggles, immersed in a broad historical cycle that links the class struggle as a whole.

Prior to October 2019, the most conflictual period occurred during the presidential oustings, between 1997 and 2005. The first to be overthrown, by a general mobilization, was Abdalá Bucaram, while attempting to achieve convertibility in the midst of high levels of corruption linked to the lumpen logic of the elites, and the general degradation of bureaucratic institutions. After that the period of crisis from 1999–2000 led to the 'Feriado Bancario', dollarization and the deterioration of living conditions (maximum historical unemployment and migration). Mobilizations led by the Indigenous movement also followed, ousting Jamil Mahuad.

From 2001–2005, social upheaval continued, but combined with a revival of the economy after the disastrous social and economic indicators of the 1990s. In 2001 there was a strong mobilization against the oligarchic government of Gustavo Noboa, which included the occupation of Quito, road closures, occupations of public institutions and hunger strikes. In 2005, then President Lucio Gutiérrez was ousted after attempting to implement neoliberalism in 2005 through a populist government, by a popular uprising in the city of Quito known as the 'rebellion of the Forajidos'.

The purpose of this subchapter is to develop an understanding of the cycle of social struggles that took place between the fall of the presidents of the republic and the October rebellion. In this interval, the class struggle, social conflicts and political tension did not disappear – despite the fact that the president was not ousted.

History, far from being linear and progressive as Hegel believed, has its ups and downs. It is naturally discontinuous, more like a doodle than a straight line. Between 2008 and 2019, silent and persistent struggles emerged, which gradually increased the weariness, the discontent and the resistance. They did not emerge to confront neoliberalism, but its bastard brother: State centrism. In this period the uprising of 2010 stood out, the March for Water (which went from Pangui to Quito in 2012), and especially the People's Strike of August 2015. The authors organize this section in the following way: economic recovery and return to a critical period, from 2007 to 2016, followed by a period of relative 'calm' between 2017 and 2018, and the massive return to the streets in 2019.

Graph 6: Evolution of conflict, 2008–2019

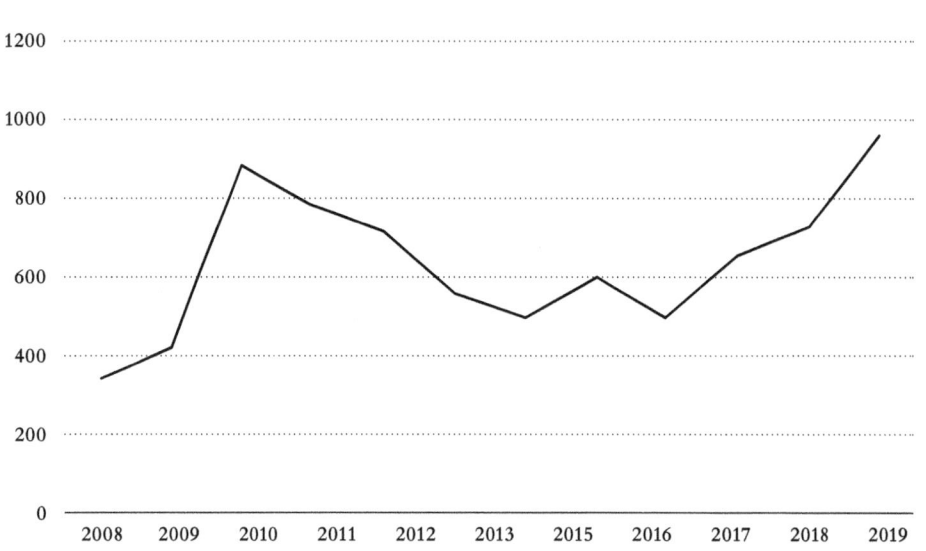

Source: caap, 2019, p. 30. Elaboration: The authors

3.1 RECOVERY AND THE RETURN TO A CRITICAL PERIOD, 2007–2016

After multiple and unsuccessful trials of models of domination that provoked political revolts and civil disobedience, Ecuadorean capitalism finally discovered an appropriate strategy to overcome the organic crisis – the Alianza País project. This movement capitalised on the erosion of the political system with a centre-left rhetoric, projecting a model of social capitalism, modernisation of the state and reinstitutionalization of political relations. Alianza País designed a bourgeois reform, with the intention of achieving the stability of the capitalist process of domination and stimulating the increase of capital accumulation, according to the Keynesian logic of regulation.

The emergence of AP in 2006 ushered in a period of declining protest action, in which the efforts of popular organizations and, in particular, the Indigenous movement, were the exception not the rule. The project of a 'Citizens' Revolution' (AP) quickly clashed with the sectors that contested extractivism and the deregulation of labour relations. Although the economic bonanza resulted in the restructuring of the state and created political stability, processes of class struggle remained in place.[28]

After the new constitution was approved in 2008, social conflicts started to multiply. First at the level of super-structure, the configuration of the secondary legislation that formulated the new state model and the economic regime (Vogliano and Castro, 2020). Specifically, five elements led to the definitive rupture of the Indigenous movement and other working-class organizations with the government: 1) the attempts to reform labour legislation to guarantee an increase in the rate of profit for companies, undermining the organization of the working class; 2) a series of reforms (Organic Code of Production, among others), which strengthened a transnationalized national bourgeoisie possessing great influence at the centre of Correa's political project; 3) the dilution of constitutional principles such as the deprivatization and redistribution of water, the deconcentration of land, the prohibition of transgenic crops, among other norms that contradicted their rhetoric; 4) the approval of a new Penal Code (COIP), which outlined the framework that criminalizes social struggle; and 5) the false affirmation that change in the social model is the direct result of a new productive paradigm, whose constitution would demand an expansion of extractivism. A legal framework was established to allow the influx of transnational mining capital, new bidding rounds for oilfields in the Amazon were initiated, and state oil and mineral pre-sale contracts were signed with transnational companies (Vogliano and Castro, 2020).

Between 2009 and 2014 – despite the stability generated by economic recovery and public investment sustained by high commodity prices – multiple points of resistance appeared in Ecuador, which fought to expose the true interests of the capitalist class: extractivism, debt with China, constitutional amendments to undermine acquired rights, and setbacks in labour rights, among others. The most significant reactivation of social protest occurred in 2010, through the mobilization around a reform on water and mining laws; the outburst became massive during the March for Water and the Dignity of the Peoples (2012), and reached its peak with the *Paro del Pueblo* (People's Strike) in August 2015.

A key moment for the resurgence of class struggle was May Day 2014,[29] a date that corresponded to the first signs of deterioration of commodity prices on the international market. That year a series of mobilizations took form, triggered by the

---

28   One popular slogan in this context was, 'What is the Alianza Pais government? A caricature of revolution'.

29   On that day the call for participation by the trade unions doubled the size of the anti-government demonstration which was pushing through the reform of articles 229 and 326 of the Constitution, limiting the rights of trade unions in the public sector.

trade union movement;[30] the Indigenous movement and other sectors soon joined in. Finally, on 2 August 2015 the March for Life and Dignity of the Peoples started in the south of the country; its objective was to take Quito on 12 August in the 'People's Strike', a mobilization that brought together on one day alone around 300,000 people.

Ideologues of the Correa administration argued that this cycle of protest began with objections generated by the right wing to the draft 'Ley de Herencias',[31] which taxed patrimonial inheritance. However, a part of the right wing that was not in government tried to take advantage of the opening of social conflict that had begun a year earlier by the working class, but never managed to lead it, since its central concern was the violation of labour rights and the siege of extractive industries in peasant and Indigenous territories.

The 2015 strike was followed by a series of smaller protests. They included road closures and clashes with the police. 2016 was marked by conflicts in mining areas; the most significant was the recovery of Shuar territory in Nankints, which had been grabbed by the Chinese company ECSA. The social tension led to the establishment of a state of emergency, the militarization of the Amazon region and the persecution of several leaders, among them the prominent fighters Luis Tiwiram and Domingo Ankuash. Towards the end of that year, protests to reject the imposition of a package of constitutional amendments occurred, eliminating union organization in the public sector. The state's response was criminalization of social struggle.

CONAIE denounced the fact that, in the course of two years, 200 leaders and grassroots members of its organizations were subject to preliminary inquiries and trials, accused of resistance to authority, terrorism, sabotage or incitement to civil unrest. Some of the most emblematic cases took place in the provinces

---

30 In the same year there were further mobilizations on 17 September, 19 November and 2 December, mobilized by the unity platform of rural and urban organizations all agreed at the National Convention of Guayacil on 18 October. This in turn ratified the agreements reached at Cuenca on 16 august, the main demands turned on the rejection of the Free Trade Agreement with the EU, which was driven by agribusiness and export agriculture based on single crop cultivation and so undermining the peasant and Indigenous economy; the meeting also repudiated the increase in the cost of public transport, defended the right of the young to study and rejected the constitutional amendments which included indefinite re-election.

31 One example of this argument, which we reject as superficial and external, was offered in a speech by Franklin Ramirez: 'Through 2015 the political lines were drawn. In June that year Correa sent various proposals to the legislature that taxed inheritances and some property speculation. The resistance from the powerful came immediately – street demonstrations and capital flight put the government up against the wall. Trade unions and indigenous groups confronted the policy of regulating imports and in the midst of a conflict over 'Marxist taxes' several marches were organised to oppose government reforms relating to labour rights, environment and social security among others'.

Graph 7: Cycle of popular mobilisations, September 2014–December 2015
Light blocks: Number in cities. Dark line: Number of people in thousands.

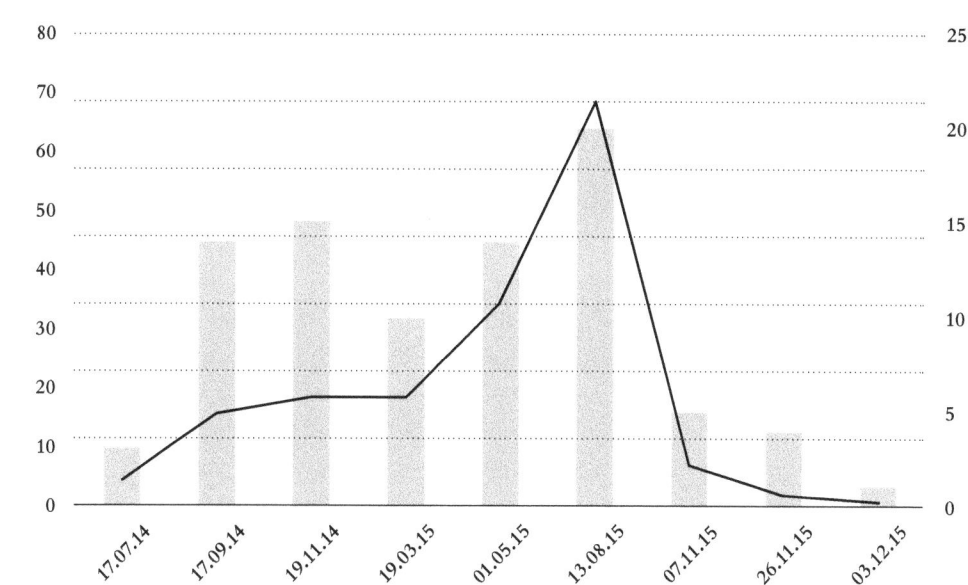

of Loja (Saraguro) and Cotopaxi. Also important are the cases of those criminalized in the 'El Arbolito' park, and the prosecution of more than 50 people in the provinces of Morona Santiago and Zamora Chinchipe, in addition to the criminalization of students, teachers, trade unionists, women, youth and militants of the anti-capitalist left. During those years, however, there was no pause in the class struggle.

3.2 THE PERIOD OF 'CALM': 2017–2018

The characterization of this period as an interval of 'calm' between the People's Strike (2015) and the anti-mining struggle (2016) up to the October rebellion, did not imply an ending of class conflict, but the struggles provoked by the new government strategy of 'dialogue' for the reconstruction of hegemony[32] did decrease as the working-class organizations of

---

32 The Indigenous movement took part in the talks with the slogan of achieving the release of hundreds of leaders, but publicly denounced the lack of conditions or political will on the part of the government to make progress on fundamental issues such as restoring rights or debating the model of development. On the contrary, the 'business dialogue' quickly handed over control of the country's economy to the chambers of commerce and representatives of big business, placing prominent members of the bourgeoisie in the top positions of state; moreover, the economic measures placed the burden of the crisis on the working class, facts that show the reconfiguration of neo-liberal business power – over the pro-state sector – in the heart of the government.

the previous period were weakened by criminal charges, extrajudicial executions, persecution, division – and the beginning of a period of elections.

The imminent presidential elections of 2017 shaped the political-institutional scenario, with the precondition of reducing social conflicts and establishing alliances for running for government. The right and institutional left[33] parties participated in the project. The elections faced a polarized political terrain and the electoral 'alternative' was posed between Guillermo Lasso (an orthodox neoliberal banker and owner of Banco de Guayaquil) and Lenin Moreno (former Vice-President and leading candidate of Correa's political project). The institutional left forged an alliance with the right in order to dislodge Alianza País from government. Thus, Unidad Popular (UP-PCMLE), Partido Socialista Ecuatoriano and a group of the Pachakutik leadership supported Guillermo Lasso in the second round of the electoral process. Yaku Pérez, Prefect of Azuay and member of PK, expressed his support for him (Pérez in *Plan V*, 2017). Geovanni Atarihuana, director of UP, justified his personal and party support as 'the only way to defeat ten years of Correísmo' (*El Universo*, 2017).

Outside that framework, in a minority, several fractions of the Indigenous movement, certain labour unions and autonomous leftist organizations maintained that the advance of structural adjustment and the neoliberal right-wing turn of the state would occur in any of the given scenarios. They opted – in the face of the misunderstanding of the Latin American progressive left – in favour of blank votes, in opposition to both candidates. However, electoral demobilization continued during the 2018 referendum; it continued, with less intensity, until the 2019 sectional elections, when coalitions between the institutional right and left were reformed, due to the disputes over local governments.

The party system is one of the most precious and functional tools of processes of political domination when it comes to composing social discipline, the antithesis to the October rebellion. This interval ended with the return to the agenda of mass struggle in 2019.

---

33 By the institutional left we understand the parties that describe themselves as of the left but whether they realise it or not are part of one of the most important guarantors of the contemporary order – the system of political parties.

3.3   MOBILIZATION GROWTH IN 2019

It is incorrect to assume that the October rebellion emerged from the political and economic situation of the moment. It would have been impossible without the build-up of struggles. Once the interval of 'calm' was over, social protests were continuous. In 2019 a new social subjectivity was forged in the heat of actions on a local or sub-regional scale, which gave legitimacy to the use of direct action (the only way to achieve social victories) in the face of a dysfunctional institutional framework. October increased the level of combativity, overcame dispersion and made visible the persistent local struggles that had been relatively silenced by the mainstream media. Class struggle is never fruitless, even if it develops in a discontinuous manner. When projected in unity, it paves the way for the escalation of the struggle to a higher level.

During the first nine months of 2019 there were nearly thirty mass protest actions. In some cases they were sustained for more than a week (the Carchi strike, Chonta Punta, a hunger strike led by organised pensioners) and some took place simultaneously in various parts of the country. Others were a continuation of struggles that had started years earlier (the Huaorani, Piatúa, informal workers, missing persons, protests in favour of abortion and equal marriage laws). Although most of them did not go beyond specific demands, there were glimpses of more comprehensive political platforms.

The array of local and sectoral struggles in the months preceding the uprising include:

- Road blocks in Cotopaxi, Cayambe and Pichincha in the Highands and Guayas, Santa Elena and Esmeraldas on the Coast, to demand better prices for agricultural products and oppose illegal logging, among other things;
- Regional stoppages or strikes in several parts of the Amazon and in Carchi in the northwest, to demand social and environmental safeguards from the state oil company, more regional aid and suspension of the government's agreement with the IMF;
- Occupations in the Amazon, the central Highlands and the Coast, against land grabs and evictions by mining projects, a hydroelectric plant and a giant prawn farm.
- Numerous marches and rallies in different parts of the country, against layoffs, labour reforms and privatisations, in defence of informal workers and Venezuelan migrants, and to demand abortion rights and gay marriage.

During the first nine months of 2019 there were nearly thirty protest actions. In some cases they were sustained for more than a week (Carchi strike, Chonta Punta, a hunger strike led by organized pensioners) and some took place in various parts of the country. Other protests continued struggles that started several years previously (Huaorani, Piatúa, informal workers, missing persons, protests in favour of abortion and equal marriage laws). Although most of them did not go beyond specific demands, there were glimpses of more comprehensive political platforms.

By 2019 there was almost a demonstration every week. The circumstances produced the conditions for the rise and articulation of the October rebellion. Despite the limits, the dispersion and low visibility of the previous actions, they gave credence to the slogan: 'The struggle is the way'. They also strengthened social movements, raised working-class morale and, at the same time, confronted the growing pessimism of the institutional left, who justified their inaction with excuses such as 'the necessary conditions do not exist'. October struck a significant blow to the power of the bourgeoisie and its lawyers dressed in sheep's clothing.

4   VIRTUE AND CHANCE: THE COLLAPSE OF 'DIALOGUE' WITH THE GOVERNMENT AND THE X FACTOR

Moreno assumed his presidential mandate with the promise of opening a national 'dialogue' with working-class sectors hit by the criminalization of the social struggle, as well as big media outlets and business sectors with which the Correa regime had come into conflict. From the inner circles of government, the strategy focused on ridding the country of the continuing influence of Correa.

The President used a script of supposed 'criticism' of the previous administration, drafted by certain sectors of the bourgeoisie in collaboration with the institutional 'left'. Its provisions included: (a) 're-institutionalization of the state', that is, a clean slate in governmental administration; (b) denying that in economic matters 'the stage was already set' and that the country was experiencing a 'fiscal crisis', hiding a much deeper crisis of capitalist accumulation; (c) adoption of the slogan of the 'struggle against corruption', focusing exclusively on the state structure, and exonerating the private business lobby group of any fiscal or legal responsibility; and (d) adoption of the tactic of 'dialogue' with social organizations to overcome a period described as 'despotic'.

This implied the reproduction of a neoliberal government agenda, different from that of his predecessor and its state-centrism in light of renewed circumstances: the impossibility of containing the crisis of capitalist accumulation; the difficulty of continuing the welfare state strategy due to the collapse of oil prices, and the intention of transferring the burden of the economic crisis to the working class.

The project of 'de-Correization' was a set of terms that gave all interested parties the opportunity to take a slice of the state's cake, while avoiding any critique of the central causes of the crisis. The institutionalist left paralysed any possible project that could come from the working class by limiting everything to a Correista/anti-Correista dichotomy, swept aside the disputes within the ruling class and undermined the political autonomy of the programme of the working class.

Two years of complaints against Correa, as well as ten years of apology, did not help to define or cement the social struggle. The anti-Correa 'criticism' was blatantly bourgeois, thanks to their front-men embedded in the social movements. Since this 'critique' did not overcome the inter-bourgeois class disputes, it never arrived at an integral critique of capitalism as a whole. Whether it was Keynesian or neoliberal, statist or monetarist, regulatory or deregulatory, it was content to cover conjunctural problem with a band aid.

Confrontation with any government of the ruling classes, whoever its temporary representatives are, is an imperative of the working-class movement. The class nature of bourgeois democracy tends to satisfy the needs of capital reproduction, as this statement from one of the previous government's administrators confirms:

> In our Government, the business sector itself, the oligarchy, the bourgeoisie, did very well [...] in my ten years of Government they tripled their profits; they increased profits more than the basic salary, which is shameful for a leftist government (Rafael Correa on RT live, 2019 [Our emphasis]).

The search for the common good? The homeland belongs to all? Sovereignty lies with the people? A representative or participatory democratic system? The government of all? Leaving aside the decorations, we live in a corporate dictatorship.

One of the lessons ratified by the October rebellion is telling: in capitalism there is no 'dialogue' with the government unless it is accompanied by social protest. The government and the actually existing power are not willing to yield privileges if there are no changes in the correlation of forces; otherwise, instead of dialogue there is imposition camouflaged by inclusive, pluralist and superficial rhetoric. The breakdown of the so-called 'dialogues' with the Moreno administration demonstrated that the mechanism for tipping the balance in favour of the working class depends on the organization of the masses in trade unions, federations, confederations, communes, centres, communities, associations, blocs, movements, fronts, as well as the spontaneous uprisings of the people.

CONAIE's announcement of a national protest at the annual assembly in Rukullakta, after the formal break with the Moreno government on 23 August 2019, constituted one of the substantial elements that would shape the October rebellion a month and a half later. The communiqué issued by CONAIE set out a strategic perspective.

> We left the talks with the government because of the enormous benefits that the bourgeoisie continues to receive via economic recovery policies or, to put it bluntly, the millionaire profits that the rich in this country get thanks to the policies of their servants in the state of raising the rate of profit, whether or not they are sued for corruption.
>
> The government serves the ruling elites (as does any government under capitalism), but it does so in a more direct manner, without the insignificant 'leftist' disguise of its predecessor, although sustaining the policies of social welfare. This is, in short, a transition stage from Correa's regulatory state interventionism to a deregulatory state interventionism. Both strategies are typical of a government of the rich, but in different contexts: the first at a time of economic boom and the second at a time of recession of capitalism (Annex 1).

Unlike the call for struggle in other national strikes – such as the one carried out by the National Citizens' Assembly (ANC) during the third week of July 2019 – CONAIE's call generated greater expectations. This happened in the first instance because

CONAIE is an organization that, despite the demobilizing onslaught of the previous governments, has maintained an organizational structure on a national scale with a combative capacity. The Rukullakta resolution called on the movement 'to confront extractivism, labour flexibilization and neoliberalism'. It demonstrated the will to struggle, the need to articulate actions and stimulate a more vigorous uprising. This declaration turned out to be another of the cornerstones of the October rebellion.[34]

'The Programme of Escalating Struggle', together with the Frente Unitario de Trabajadores (FUT), were scheduled for 14 October. However, the October austerity package changed the scenario. The approval of Decree No. 883, in full compliance with the provisions of the International Monetary Fund, inflamed the outraged working class. In particular, the proposal to raise fuel prices compelled one faction that had not been originally in support of the declaration to take a stand: the transportation sector. We should not forget that Osvaldo Hurtado (1982) was on the verge of impeachment, and Abdalá Bucaram (1996) was ousted for attempting to raise the price of gas for domestic use.

The 'paquetazo' contributed to detonating the previous discontent, raising it to unsuspected levels and, as Jorge Luis Borges would say, reality surpassed fiction. In spite of the conditions we have examined – economic crisis, loss of legitimacy of the state, previous struggles – which contributed to the events of October 2019, class struggle is unpredictable, susceptible to chance and indeterminism, factors that can propel the conflict in unexpected directions. In this particular case, the unpredictable X factor took on a number: Decree No. 883. ★

---

34 For the full declaration see Appendix.

March in Quito of Indigenous peoples and nationalities and popular urban sectors (Photo: Luis Herrera/Audiovisual Cooperative).

Youth confronts the National Police in the Historic Centre of Quito, 3 October 2019 (Photo: Fernanda Gallardo).

Cartridges fired by National Police and Armed Forces against the people
(Photo: Andrés León/Kapucha Communications).

A student shouts at a policeman outside the Social Security Offices, 4 October 2019 (Photo: Santiago Fernandez).

If this is not settled
War, war, war
And if there is no solution
There will be revolution

What does it take to
be president?
To be a miserable scumbag
who lies to the people!
What does it take to be
a congressman?

To be an opportunistic pig!
The fire of the heart
is stirred by our action!

Popular slogans in the October Rebellion

Awakening, determination, struggle and resistance

This chapter will address the events of October in detail. We will move away from a linear reading or a descriptive chronology of the facts, and contrast the events, developments, protagonists, etc., problematizing the endogenous and exogenous issues that occurred during the rebellion. First we present, statistically, the places where roads were blocked, the provinces that were the scene of the struggle, the signs of support from some sectors of society (such as transport cooperatives) and the movement of protesters to Quito, among other things. A timeframe is set out, subdivided into four stages: a) the start of the rebellion (3–6 October), b) the rising of the Indigenous movement (7–10 October), c) the development of the rebellion (11–13 October), and d) negotiation with burning barricades (13–14 October).

Secondly, it looks at the role of the Indigenous movement in leadership and development, as well as controlling the turning points of the mobilization. CONAIE's significant role, as a presence at the national level, as well as the affirmation of an anti-capitalist position in its midst, warns, to a large extent, of its withdrawal from the mediation of non-governmental organizations (NGOs) and international collaboration during the rebellion.

The third approach analyses the participation of other forces in *Octubre,* and reviews the limitations of the trade union movement. It explores the historical participation, in Quito, of the *barrios,* the middle class, women and youth, as well as the actions of other peasant and Indigenous organizations such as the Ecuadorean Federation of Evangelical Indigenous People (FEINE) and the Ecuadorean Federation of Indigenous and Black Peasant Organizations (FENOCINE). At the end of the chapter there is a critique of the political parties. The institutionalist left, through outrageous examples, created grotesque parallel universes, functional to the system, to justify its latent incapacity in historical events of great magnitude. The partisan right on the other hand evidenced the racist, imperialist and anti-popular character of the dominant classes; although they are armed, they are visible, especially in the urban centres of Quito, Cuenca and, particularly, Guayaquil.

In the fourth place, we review the strengthening of the state, carried out through the modernisation of the armed forces and the shift from consensual to coercive domination. In the fifth, the role of the media corporations in the service of power and support of the government, in frank adherence to right-wing discourse, and on the other hand the counter-hegemonic rupture generated by the community and alternative media, are evidenced.

The contributions of the October rebellion confirm the need for rationalisation and planning political struggle, as well as the richness of spontaneous action by the masses; at certain moments they combine popular creativity, historical memory and social catharsis. Spontaneous and planned actions pose urgent challenges, such as generating effective and high levels of struggle, aimed at allowing the accumulation of forces, insisting on popular unity to confront a modernised repressive and authoritarian apparatus and, ultimately, strengthening a project of anti-capitalist character.

1 POPULAR UPRISING AND ESCALATING REPRESSION

The trigger was the increase in fuel prices, following the elimination of subsidies; but its deeper roots were the inability of the administrations to solve the capitalist crisis in the last five years, the fall of institutional legitimacy and the accumulated expressions of discontent and struggle during recent years, particularly 2019. In this context, the government took a series of decisions to counter popular anger, based on repression, arrests, extrajudicial executions and misrepresentation of facts. These actions were not only inefficient, they stirred up already heated tempers.

The government's intention to contain the mobilization backfired. Not only was it impossible to mitigate it, but it was exacerbated to the point that the actions of struggle and resistance, objectively read, turned into the largest rebellion in the recent history of Ecuador. During the takeover of Quito, in the Indigenous uprisings between 1990 and 2015, the number of protesters arriving from the provinces ranged from five to eight thousand people, grouped in a single location. In October the mobilization was far larger. 'According to official data, 25,000 people arrived, but up to 50,000 Indigenous people are estimated to be involved' (Herrera, 2019). Several shelters were needed for rest, medical attention and supplies, which were provided by the people of Quito and other localities.[1]

Chart 1: Chronology of state actions, 3–13 October 2019

03	• Decree No. 884 and state of emergency. • Suspension of classes in the entire school and university system.
04	• Arrest of leaders of the National Federation of Taxi Transport Operators (FENACOTIP) and other unions. • Mass arrest of protesters in Quito and Sucumbíos. • Military patrolling the streets in the south and north of Guayaquil.
05	• Increase in the price of urban transportation fares (5 and 10 cents).
06	• Media and government conceal the Indigenous uprising and popular strike. They claim that there is only a transportation strike. • The centre of Quito is fenced with barbed wire, electrified barricades and armoured vehicles.
07	• Relocation of government headquarters to Guayaquil. • Closure of the National Unity Bridge and paralysis of public services by the municipality of Guayaquil. • Increase in fares and prices of basic necessities continue.
08	• Curfew in the centre of Quito. • State of emergency declared in Quito and Cuenca. • Call for a 'peaceful solution' by the Autonomous Decentralised Governments (AME, CONAGOPARE, CONGOPE, COMAGA). • Decentralised governments' (AME, CONAGOPARE, CONGOPE, COMAGA) proposal for the creation of a group formed by the UN and the Archbishop of Guayaquil to begin dialogue.
09	• Heavy cargo transportation rates increase up to 30%.
10	• Public call for dialogue by Lenin Moreno Garcés.
11	• Meeting of the Association of Municipalities of Ecuador (AME) to seek a solution. • The Federation of Industrialists of Ecuador, through an appeal, requests the immediate intervention of the armed forces.
12	• Curfew and militarization of Quito announced at 14.20; the measure begins at 15.00.
13	• Confirmation of the negotiation table. • Restriction of curfew, with the exception of downtown Quito. • Repeal of Decree No. 883.

At the same time, all over the country people took to the streets in struggle and held mass marches, set up barricades, confronted police and military repression, flouted the state of emergency and the curfew, channelled food, medicines and supplies to the frontline, and defended the interests of the majority of impoverished households.

The following is a timeline to understand the chain of events that convulsed the country, due to the esprit de corps of the subaltern sectors. The events unleashed a repressive strategy by the state and plunged the really existing power into despair.

---

1 In addition to other institutions with smaller capacity in neighbourhood houses and schools, the following were opened as reception centres: the Agora de la Casa de la Cultura Ecuatoriana, the Universidad Central del Ecuador, the Universidad Católica del Ecuador, the Universidad Politécnica Salesiana, the Universidad Andina Simón Bolívar and the Facultad Latinoamericana de Ciencias Sociales, among others.

1.1 START OF THE NATIONAL OUTBREAK, 3–6 OCTOBER

The unexpected announcement of the elimination of fuel subsidies caused a domino effect. Transport unions called for a national strike, CONAIE brought forward the date of the planned uprising to mid-October, there was a generalized popular emergency, and the youth surged to the front line. The blockade of roads and highways was fundamental in order to affect the movement of capital and the interests of the ruling classes. The transport strike disrupted the cities and the regular interprovincial flow. CONAIE's declaration of an indefinite strike led grassroots organizations to block traffic on the Pan-American Highway, the Amazonian Trunk Road and the inter-Andean communication routes to the coast.

> On 3 October 2019 protests began in Ecuador after President Lenin Moreno signed a series of austerity measures that eliminated a USD 1.3 billion gasoline subsidy. Cab and bus drivers, student organizations and thousands of members of Indigenous peoples led by the Confederation of Indigenous Nationalities of Ecuador (CONAIE) participated in protests that lasted several days. On 3 October the government declared a state of emergency (HRW, 2020).

The stoppage of urban, city to city, province-to-province taxis and freight transport cooperatives was sustained through road blockades, especially with burning tyres. The spread of the protests forced the interruption of the circulation of labour and merchandise in various parts of the country. Thus, at the beginning of the mobilization only 60 out of 416 transport cooperatives at national level provided service, and 13 out of 24 provinces were paralysed. Roads near airstrips were also blocked to interfere with airport activity.

On the first day of the outbreak, demonstrations and tyre burning took place in several cities. Road closures were reported in Ambato, Latacunga, Ibarra, Babahoyo, Quevedo, Manta, Montecristi, Portoviejo, Machala, Santo Domingo, Esmeraldas, Cuenca and Loja, and also in smaller towns such as Jujan, Milagro, Durán, Samborondón, Santa Elena, Bucay, Jipijapa, Palenque, Pasaje, Quinindé, Gualaceo, Santa Isabel, Girón, Molleturo, Pujilí, Cayambe, Tabacundo, Guamote, Colta,

Penipe, Pelileo, Macas, Puyo and Tena. Likewise, markets in the highlands were partially closed. Artisanal fishermen in the provinces of Santa Elena and Manabí also complied (Jairala, 2019). On 3 October 'at 21:00 at night, Guayaquil was a ghost town' (Sucre TV Online 2, 2019).

In Quito, during the morning, several main roads in the north, centre, south, surrounding valleys and main approaches were closed. The demonstrations reached the vicinity of the Carondelet Palace, generating pressure on the police barricades guarding the seat of government. During the afternoon, a massive march was held in San Blas, in the centre of the city, which constituted the first sign of the onset of the rebellion. The resistance at that point was fierce. The police used horses, motorized and armoured vehicles to pursue, attack and arrest demonstrators, even those who were not actively participating. This was the first sign of the state's death drive.

Meanwhile, in Guayaquil, many streets and shopping centres were closed, and looting took place, especially in Isla Trinitaria and Guasmo, in the south of the city. 'The result of that day was 3,159 calls to the state emergency service coordinated by different agencies (Police, Fire Department, Ecuadorean Red Cross, etc.) – known as ECU 911 – 230 concentrations in cities and 20 provinces on strike' (Le Quang, Chávez and Vizuete, 2020, p. 59).

The struggle escalated on the second day of national mobilization. There were 281 points of protest, 215 roads affected and 13 partially closed (Jairala, 2019). The sustaining of the blockades and marches were met with increasing repression. For example, in Quito, police forces deployed armoured vehicles and tanks in the streets, from which huge amounts of tear gas were fired, especially in the sector of El Ejido Park, the Caja del Seguro, the provincial government of Pichincha and the Central Bank. The gas even asphyxiated the relatives of those arrested the day before, who were waiting for news at the police station. The first confrontations and excessive police and military repression took place in rural areas; in La Esperanza, Imbabura Province, the houses of community members were invaded. Simultaneously, other localities in the central and northern highlands joined the stoppage.

During the weekend (5–6 October) protests continued in Quito and the intensity of the national strike increased, especially in rural areas. The highlands and the Amazon were blocked, and confrontations with the army persisted in some areas such as the province of Cotopaxi.² There were several confrontations and cases of repression in the Amazon, such as at Kilometre 51 on the road between Puyo and Macas in the Province of Pastaza, where communities of the Shuar nationality faced 200 soldiers. In the 'sector of Lasso (Cotopaxi Province), demonstrators of the Union of Indigenous and Peasant Communities of Cotopaxi of the Pujilí and Pastocalle district detained military and police officers. Heavy military repression was also reported in Santa Isabel (Azuay Province)' (Le Quang, Chávez and Vizuete, 2020, p. 59).

At the same time, rallies and gatherings were set up in hundreds of communities and rural organizations to organize the occupation of Quito while in other cities preparations were being made for the arrival of the Indigenous movement in the capital. This situation differed from the attitude of transport leaders who compromised with the government, formally ending their stoppage. 'Around that time, the National Federation of Heavy Transport, in a meeting with the Ecuadorean Business Committee, announced that it was withdrawing from the strike, but called for freight rates to be raised' (Le Quang, Chávez and Vizuete, 2020, p. 59).

Despite this, some companies disregarded the ruling; interprovincial service remained scarce and, in some cities, was reduced to a minimum.

1.2 THE TAKING OF QUITO: THE COUNTRY BURNS FROM NORTH TO SOUTH, 7–10 OCTOBER

In the second stage, the intensification of repression was notorious, in the midst of which the arrival of the Indigenous movement in Quito, the defence of strategic positions in the city, and the increase of the paralysis across the national territory took place. The first of the factors that led to these circumstances and to the massive incorporation to the struggle, especially of the urban youth, was the increase in prices of some goods such as gas for domestic use and basic foodstuffs. The price of a bag of potatoes in Guayaquil doubled, and 'green bananas were sold more expensively in Ecuador than in the United States' (Jairala, 2019).³ Fuel shortages were evident in 11 provinces:

---

2   Clashes with the army and police took place in the area of Chasqui, Lasso, the entrance to Saquisili and Guaytacama, Cinco de Junio bridge and in various parts of downtown Latacunga, as well as at the entrance to La Victoria, in Pujili, in Panzaleo and in La Maná. Other areas were totally closed.

3   Green banana is a variety of plantain that is heavily consumed in Ecuador. It has the same role as bread or potatoes; it is an important source of carbohydrates in the regular diet on the coast and in the warm areas of the subtropics and the Amazon.

Imbabura, Carchi, Azuay, Bolivar, Cañar, Cotopaxi, Chimborazo, Tungurahua, Orellana, Pastaza and Zamora Chinchipe (Jairala, 2019; Borja, Basantes and Castro, 2019). To this must be added the arrival of the first 20,000 members of the Indigenous movement in Quito. Both in the south (Aloag, Machachi, Tambillo and Santa Rosa) and in the north (Calderón and Carapungo), the population clashed with the police to allow this influx of people to enter the capital (TVC *El Comercio TV*, 2019).

The night of their arrival, delegations organized themselves to determine where to stay. Some of them stayed at the *Casa de la Cultura Ecuatoriana* and others went to different places, arranged in solidarity. People spent the night almost without blankets, mats or mattresses that could help them rest; however, the fighting morale of the community overcame fatigue. In the morning, after assembling in El Arbolito Park, the march headed towards 10 de Agosto Avenue, but was surrounded by the police and took cover in 6 de Diciembre and Tarqui avenues. From there, the crowd planned to advance towards the National Assembly, which produced confrontations with the police and a military cordon that prevented their advance. At the same time, there was an evident failure of certain transport leaders who declined to strike, since in several provinces no buses or heavy transport were circulating (Jairala, 2019; Morán, 2019). Finally, seven governorships were taken over by Indigenous organizations in the Amazon and in the Central Highlands, and others saw their facilities destroyed, as is the case in the city of Ibarra, Imbabura Province. In addition, large flower and dairy companies were looted.

On 7 October large mobilizations were called to receive the Indigenous movement in Quito. Massive acts of protest were registered in Guayaquil, Ambato, Manta, Quevedo and Santa Lucia (Jairala, 2019; TVC *El Comercio TV*, 2019), including the closure of the Riobamba market and the Ambato wholesale market. Taking advantage of the fact that media attention was concentrated in Quito, police action intensified in other places. So there were serious confrontations in Lumbaqui (Sucumbíos), Durán (Guayas), Puyo (Pastaza) and Cayambe (northern Pichincha) (TVC *El Comercio TV*, 2019; Morán, 2019).

In the Shuar community Tsurakú (Pastaza), a platoon of 200 military personnel indiscriminately attacked the population, 'regardless of the presence of women, children, youth and the elderly'. Similarly, in the Shuar Kunkuk community (Pastaza) '10 military trucks arrived', and in Cayambe the police used rubber bullets (Morán, 2019). Also in the Province of Santa Elena 'the FEDECOMSE [Federation of Communes of Santa Elena], member of CONAICE [Confederation of Indigenous Nationalities of the Ecuadorean Coast], called a meeting and initiated the strike. These leaders led protests with four communes: Libertador Bolivar, San Pedro, San Pablo and San Vicente. The following day Valdivia, La Enrada, Montañita, Olón, Manglaralto, Sitio Nuevo, Cadeate and Barcelona joined' (Álvarez, 2019).

On 8 October, with the bulk of the Indigenous movement already installed in Quito, the ECU 911 emergency system reported that all entrances to the capital were closed, as well as 7 roads in Imbabura, 4 in Cotopaxi, 12 in Chimborazo, 15 in Tungurahua, 12 in Bolivar, 4 in Azuay, 3 in El Oro, 10 in Loja, 11 in Los Rios, 16 in Guayas and Santa Elena, 6 in Esmeraldas, 3 in Santo Domingo, 3 in Manabi and 12 in the Amazon. In total, more than 120 main accesses were blocked throughout the country (Jairala, 2019). This, despite the fact that Military Intelligence and Political Security had warned that it was strategic to move the seat of government to Guayaquil to lower tensions and bring about calm (Jarrín in El Comercio, 2020). This did not happen. The country continued to burn and the coast mobilized.

The agitation of the coast was a pleasant surprise, since it has been the region of the country most affected in the capacity of autonomous popular mobilization in the last decades. The high point of the day on 8 October was the storming into the National Assembly by demonstrators, which was the first bellwether of the force of the rebellion, in a place emblematic of the political power of the Ecuadorean state.

9 October dawned with enormous expectations. The Indigenous uprising, the industrial strike and the general strike were scheduled for that day simultaneously. The anticipation was palpable. The country remained completely mobilized and transport was almost non-existent. In Guayaquil only 12 of the 92 cooperatives operated and, nationwide, 177 main roads were closed (Jairala, 2019). In this city, a march was held as part of the national strike, which was harshly repressed by the police while the military prevented Indigenous people coming into the city. For his part, Jaime Nebot, with the support of business chambers and rightwing groups, organized a weak counter-march. 'In Cuenca there was a robust mobilization that began as a peaceful march. During the course of the day, however, the citizens moved towards the centre of the city,

Chart 2: Protests during the national strike

Province	Protest	Province	Protest
Carchi	3 of 6 districts: Tulcán, San Gabriel and Mira	Esmeraldas	Esmeraldas district, several protests in city centre 5 protests in other districts
Imbabura	Marches in Ibarra 8 roads closed	Santo Domingo de los Tsáchilas	Marches in Santo Domingo 3 roads closed
Pichincha	4 roads closed (all entrances to Quito) Total closure, marches and demonstrations in Quito	Guayas	Total closure (15 cut-off points) 4 rallies in Guayaquil Protests in Durán
Cotopaxi	9 roads closed	Los Ríos	10 cut-off points Quevedo closed
Tunguragua	9 roads closed March in Ambato	Santa Elena	7 cut-off points
Chimborazo	12 roads closed	El Oro	Road closures March in Machala
Bolivar	12 roads closed (highlands and subtropical zone)	Manabí	2 roads closed
Cañar	Takeover of the governor's office Total closure of roads (two roads)	Morona Santiago	March in Macas Total road closures (6 roads) Takeover of the governor's office
Azuay	3 roads closed Total closure and marches in Cuenca	Pastaza	Attack on UPC Takeover of the governor's office Total road closures (6 highways)
Loja	9 roads closed	Sucumbíos	5 roads closed
Zamora Chinchipe	Total road closures (5 roads)	Orellana	1 road closed
Galápagos	1 sit-in	Napo	1 road closed

Source: Security Service ECU 911. Elaboration: own

while more demonstrators arrived from neighbouring districts who took part in the seizure of the Azuay governor's office. It is estimated that there were more than 10,000 people in the streets' (Le Quang, Chávez and Vizuete, 2020, p. 69).

The march held in Quito was one of the largest in Ecuador's history. In spite of the fact that the official media and those linked to business disseminated conservative estimates, the truth is that CONAIE exceeded what they expected. Around 50,000 Indigenous people came to Quito, while the FUT had a more limited organic call, no more than 5,000 workers.[4] There were other social groups participating and, above all, the overwhelming self-organization of popular sectors lacking a determined organic relationship. The rallies, throughout the city, took place in around fifty places, where there were road blockades and confrontations with repressive forces.

At the end of this phase (10 October) there was a retreat in the mobilization in Quito, due to the murder of demonstrators by the police the previous night. The Indigenous movement concentrated in the vicinity of the *Agora de la Casa de la Cultura Ecuatoriana* and held a ceremony in homage to the fallen. At the same time, there were marches in Ambato, La Maná, La Troncal, Guamote, Nueva Loja, Paute and Machala, which blocked 104 roads across the country.[5] The army and the police, driven by this repressive logic, went on a rampage against the Yanucocha community in the province of Sucumbíos, despite the presence of children there. (Alianza de Organizaciones por los Derechos Humanos, 2019).

1.3 'CURFEW AND RESISTANCE', 11–13 OCTOBER

The arrival of reinforcements of the Indigenous movement from the Amazon, Tungurahua, Chimborazo and Bolivar was of vital importance for the rebellion. (*TVC El Comercio TV*, 2019). Despite the fact that the government decreed a holiday, the number of roads closed increased to 117. In Guayaquil only one third of transport cooperatives operated normally.

In Quito, there were close to one hundred barricades on the main roads, but the greatest resistance took place in the

---

4 This contrasts with the capacity demonstrated by the FUT in previous years. For example, in August 2015 it managed to convene at least 50,000 grassroots members in Quito alone.

5 According to ECU 911, the closures include: 6 in Imbabura, 9 in Loja, 1 in Carchi, 2 in Cañar, total blockage in the Central Highlands (5 in Cotopaxi, 12 in Chimborazo, 12 in Bolivar, 7 in Tungurahua) and in the Amazon (25 closures in total), 4 in Pichincha, 5 in Azuay, 7 in Los Rios, 1 in Manabi, 3 in Guayas, 3 in Esmeraldas and 3 in Santa Elena.

Table 1: Protests on 11–12 October

Province	Protest	Province	Protest
Carchi	1 road closed	Esmeraldas	4 roads closed
Imbabura	7 roads closed	Santo Domingo de los Tsáchilas	No data
Pichincha	4 roads closed. Closures in Quito in 13–90 places	Guayas	2 roads closed. Marches in Guayaquil
Cotopaxi	6 roads closed	Los Ríos	9 roads closed
Tunguragua	8 roads closed	Santa Elena	2 roads closed
Cotopaxi	14 roads closed	El Oro	No data available
Bolivar	19 roads closed	Manabí	1 road closed. March in Manta
Cañar	1 road closed	Morona Santiago	9 roads closed
Azuay	5 roads closed	Pastaza	5 roads closed
Loja	March in Cuenca	Sucumbíos	5 roads closed
Zamora Chinchipe	9 roads closed	Orellana	No data
Galápagos	5 roads closed	Napo	1 road closed

Source: Security Service ecu 911. Elaboration: own

area of El Arbolito Park. At midday, members of the National Police guarding the National Assembly waved a white flag. The demonstrators welcomed this truce. Thousands of men, women, elderly and children gathered around the building and shared their food with the security forces.

However, after police and military helicopters landed several times on the roof of the Assembly to provide supplies to the officers, they began an intense barrage with vehicles and tear gas. The event provoked a stampede in which dozens of people were crushed and suffocated by the tear gas and the crushing of the crowd. Activists and community media considered that the event was an ambush. Early that morning, the explosion of a gas tank caused a 'roar [that] was heard 4 kilometres away' (El Comercio, 2019). With outrage in the air, the battle intensified from Saturday morning through the night, and ended only on Sunday afternoon. The area of greatest repression was the central part of Quito, subjected to a tense military and police siege.

On 12 October mobilization and blockades were intensified at the national level. 392 roads remained closed and 1228 points of conflict were registered in rural areas (*DemocraciaTV*, 2019).

During the morning, in Quito, a feminist demonstration marched through the streets to oppose the colonial tradition of 12 October – known as 'The Day of the Race' – which covers up the invasion of Abya-Yala. The protest included dyeing the statue of Isabel II in red. In the afternoon, Decree No. 888 was extended, establishing a curfew, which came into force at 3:00 p.m. and was publicly announced a few minutes after that. It should be noted that, for the first time since the return to democracy, a 'curfew' was decreed (Luque, Poveda and Hernández, 2020, p. 19).

In contempt and defiance of the government's ruling, the population in rebellion declared that they would resist the curfew. Massively, the population called for a *cacerolazo*, the mass banging of pots and pans, which shook the atmosphere of the country's cities. In several cases it led to rallies, marches and burning tyres. In the evening, a dialogue took place between the government and the Indigenous movement, which acted as representatives of all parties in the conflict. The tense meeting led to a review of the elimination of subsidies and, in the end, to the gradual return of fuel prices, passenger and cargo transportation and basic necessities to their previous rates.

1.4 NEGOTIATION WITH BURNING BARRICADES, 13–14 OCTOBER

On 13 October the Ecuadorean people, led by the Indigenous movement, achieved a historic victory: they confronted the President of the Republic and the bulk of his cabinet (representing the IMF and the capitalists) at a round table. The will of the architects of October prevailed.

Power was slapped in the face, which was broadcast openly in all the national and international media. This blow was painful for the government and its representatives, since the results of the negotiations slipped from their hands. Not even the government's 'demand' to stop the mobilization in order to negotiate and, even less, its 'refusal' to repeal the decree eliminating subsidies had the slightest weight.

The negotiations took place under the following conditions: 1) those who struggle will be represented; the social-democratic and institutionalist left tendencies, groups previously assiduous at the negotiating tables, were displaced; 2) negotiations are carried out while barricades continue burning; the bourgeoisie had to accept its defeat with the whole country paralysed; 3) negotiations are carried out publicly; the mass media transmitted, without editorial interference, the position of millions of people who rejected the *paquetazo*, the deal with the IMF, as well as the clumsy discourse of its defenders; 4) the IMF's demands were watered down; a blow was dealt to imperialism and the bourgeoisie through the elimination of Decree No. 883.

> The protest was unstoppable. It overflowed the streets and, in its composition, extension and logic of collective bargaining, it also overwhelmed the haggling schemes of corporate politics. The round table that was set up after 11 days of protest was called by the popular movement as a 'delivery of their mandate' (Coronel, 2020, p. 313).

The attempts by representatives of the Moreno regime to divide the interests of each group proved fragile, and were denounced as fallacious by the popular leadership at the negotiating table. Attempts to refer the process to 'commissions' in order to reach particular solutions were not accepted either. At the end of the meeting, CONAIE expressed its gratitude for the struggle of the popular sectors of the country. That night, Quito celebrated the victory with pyrotechnics, village bands, dances and hugs.[6] In Riobamba the celebration extended to the whole city (*TVC El Comercio TV*, 2019). The same happened in Guayaquil and Salinas (*Ecuavisa*, 2019).

> We had a loudspeaker to broadcast the event. At 9:40 p.m. the shouts of triumph burst throughout the area, we won, the decree that eliminated the gasoline subsidy had been repealed. We celebrated, we danced, we sang, we hugged, we cried, we thanked each other (Noriega and Criollo, 2020, p. 143).

The following morning, the demonstrators and volunteers carried out a *minga*, a small march in Quito, to clean up the remains left by the battles and organize the place where the members of the Indigenous movement and the people who organized for the rebellion were laid to rest.

A digression is in order. The result of 13 October was a victory for the popular sector; the general jubilation at the outcome of the table is faithful testimony. However, subsequently, a scenario of defeat was concocted from Correa's institutional left. It is not

---

6   'As the news of the agreement spread, *mestizo* families living near the area of the *Casa de la Cultura* began to join the celebration. The festive atmosphere extended from Patria Avenue northward, following the route of 12 de Octubre Avenue, reached the Catholic universities, where volunteer brigadistas, wearing aprons, approached the gate to greet the demonstrators' (Vaca, 2019).

accurate to claim that some popular organizations fell into a trap at the negotiating table, while others did not. The outcome was the result of an imposition by the popular sector. Perhaps more achievements were possible, for example the amnesty of all those charged in October; however, the excitement at one of the most decisive social events in the history of Ecuador, at certain moments, caused short-sightedness.

The identification of errors after the fact seeks to weaken the heart of self-criticism: to move forward. Don't forget, however, that those who promote the liberal 'betrayal theory' – which impairs the explanation of political phenomena – endorse it from a transatlantic distance and for electoral calculation. Don't forget that they were the ones who mounted and ran the campaign of their favoured candidate – Moreno – governed with him for a year together, and an enormous number of his colleagues were and are, covertly, in the bureaucratic leadership bodies. Another of the characteristics of the institutionalist left is hypocrisy. However, the important thing is to learn the lessons received and to be sufficiently self-critical to push the projects of the people towards the achievement of better preconditions for living.

2 THE LEADING ROLE OF THE ECUADOREAN INDIGENOUS MOVEMENT

The social movement involved in October was heterogeneous. There were hauliers, workers, young people, peasants, Indigenous people, residents of suburban neighbourhoods, students, professionals, children, intellectuals, women and whole families. A significant percentage of those who sustained the confrontation in the streets, highways and squares had no organic link to any organised body. Of these, those who contributed the largest groups were residents of the *barrios,* the Indigenous movement, women and youth. On the organised side, CONAIE stands out as the main political actor due to its capacity for mobilization and leadership, despite the difficulties. When CONAIE burst onto the scene as an actor that joined the mobilizations, the government hoped to use the same negotiating tactics that worked with the transport unions: 'indigenize' the conflict in order to deactivate it. That did not work' (García and Soria, 2020, p. 399).

The Indigenous movement, like any organisation, has moments of ebb and flow. The same, in its time, had happened to the union movement. After an ascending struggle during the seventies and eighties, trade unionism suffered a significant weakening due to uncontrollable external factors, such as the collapse of class ideology at an international level, and the development of a system of electoral parties. It was also affected by internal factors such as the bureaucratization and loss of membership by the unions, and a lack of understanding of the ways, means and instruments of modern exploitation. The vacuum left by trade unionism was filled by the Indigenous movement (CONAIE, FENOCIN, FEINE), which assumed the leadership of the left-wing political struggle in Ecuador during the 1990s.

The main contribution of the Indigenous movement was to integrate the critique of ethno-cultural oppression stemming from colonialism with a critique of the relations of capitalist economic exploitation, which has been linked to mass actions across the country, including, on several occasions, the takeover of Quito. The Indigenous movement has incorporated concepts such as spirituality, territoriality, anti-extractivism, administration of Indigenous justice, grassroots community democracy and defence of Mother Nature into its agenda of struggle. Its organisational and political core questions capitalist modernity and the crisis of civilization. It challenges the monocultural model of the nation state, which has been maintained and reproduced despite its plurinational rhetoric. The struggle of the Indigenous movement has challenged the process of accumulation and dispossession, based on formulations that propose the defence of life in a wider sense, not only of the human species.

At the beginning of the 1990s, in the context of resistance to neoliberalism and the removal of presidents, CONAIE achieved its greatest prominence and broad representativeness. It brought together thousands of communities, organically articulated through a complex structure relating to the three regions of the country: Ecuador *Runakunapak Rikcharimuy* (ECUARUNARI) in the Sierra, the Confederation of Indigenous Nationalities of the Ecuadorean Amazon (CONFENIAE), and the Confederation of Indigenous Nationalities and Peoples of the Ecuadorean Coast (CONAICE). The immanent power of the Indigenous movement has been rooted in grassroots community democracy – one of the characteristics behind its great mobilizing capacity – as well as in a broad set of strategies for struggle, inherited from its articulation with the Marxist left. In this way, the combative character of the indigenous movement stems from its historical emancipatory deeds, expressed in the struggle for territoriality and self-determination, both dysfunctional elements of capitalism insofar as they acquire an integral counterpoint to its structure and dissociate themselves from the autonomist logic.

At the beginning of the millennium, as certain leaders began to adapt to the logic of the state, the party system and NGOs, the organization began to lose ground. Despite this, it continued to be the strongest social organization in Ecuador, and promoted – with other actors – important mobilizations during the last few years: the March for Water in 2012 and the People's Strike in 2015; in the latter, the alliance with the trade union movement should be highlighted.

The October rebellion cannot be understood without CONAIE and its regional and provincial structures, decisive for the proliferation of the social outburst, such as, for example, CONFENIAE or the Indigenous and Peasant Movement of Cotopaxi (MICC). However, in October there were several problems in terms of the relation of forces, given that their enemies were the IMF, the state and the ruling classes. There were also internal tensions; since the 1990s, several processes of economic, social and political differentiation took place within the Indigenous world and, as a result, factions developed. The Indigenous movement is not ideologically homogeneous and October served to strain these forces and promote an anti-capitalist stance.

2.1 'WE HAVE NOT COME ALONE; WE ARE ACCOMPANIED BY THE PEOPLE'

The discourse of the powerful insisted on minimizing the representativeness of CONAIE. It claimed that the percentage of the Indigenous population in the country is 7% and that its agenda did not represent the aspirations of the majority of Ecuadoreans. On the other hand, according to data from some pollsters, 85% of the population disapproved of the elimination of fuel subsidies (Córdova in *FM Mundo*, 2019). According to the survey conducted by CLICK, 68% of the population of Quito and Guayaquil supports the marches of the Indigenous Movement' (García and Soria, 2020, p. 400). Therefore, the demand for the repeal of Decree No. 883 was not sectoral, but a popular demand that, as Agustín Cueva thought, articulated the needs of the exploited.

According to leader Jaime Vargas, on 13 October, the day of the defeat of the Ecuadorean government, CONAIE became a sounding board for the needs of the population. In his words, 'Mr President [of the Republic], you are not talking to CONAIE [...] We have not come alone, we are accompanied by the people' (Herrera, 2019). In the same vein, Patricio Moncayo points out that 'at this juncture, the CONAIE has put aside its

Table 2: Factors that have led to changes in the Indigenous movement

Scope	Beginning of the 1990s	Present
Presence of the state	The weak and, in certain areas, non-existent presence of the state, both from the point of view of administrative agency in areas such as education, health, etc., as well as the construction of a hegemonic project. Little presence of Non-governmental Organizations (NGOs) and international cooperation. Organizational presence of the church.	Strengthening of the state across the territory, both in terms of its institutional presence and its ideological capacity to interfere in civil society organizations. In addition, the presence of international cooperation deepens social stratification and the technocratic exercise, typical of the liberal vision. The party system penetrates rural areas with electoral structures. Constitution of Pachakutik, in principle, as a 'political arm' of CONAIE, which became an electoral party that at many moments displaced itself from the initiative, orientation and political leadership of the Indigenous movement. Church concentrating mainly on evangelizing.
Social stratification	More or less similar economic conditions of existence among the population as a whole, i.e. few economic and class differences. The vast majority of the population was affected by a form of material reproduction of life characterized by exploitation. Weak original accumulation of capital in Indigenous families.	Existence of Indigenous bourgeoisie in the circuits of commercial, financial, industrial and bureaucratic capital turnover. Growth of a small bourgeoisie linked to the state, NGOs and professional work. Nevertheless, precarious conditions are maintained for the great majority. The poorest economic quintiles are made up of the Indigenous population.
Diversification of the labour force	Existence of a labour force mainly made up of poor peasants. There was a low level of proletarianization of peasant labour, which meant the demands of the Indigenous organisations centred on questions of land, as well as the struggles against discrimination and for education in Indigenous languages, among other aspects.	Diversification of the labour force within the communities due to the advance of capital in the rural zone, such as agro-industry, subsidiary work in industry, construction and precarious self-employed workers. Increasing difficulty for small UPAS (Agricultural Production Units) to sustain the family economy. Expansion of demands to other socio-economic spheres, such as labour rights, territorial labour rights, territorial dispossession, extractivism and disputes with the State.

Elaboration: own

ethnic demands to prioritise a class agenda' (in *DemocraciaTV*, 2019). The emergence of new leaders, charged with the memory of the *taytas* and *mamas*, as well as contemporary reflections, overcame corporative and ethnocentric positions in October to deal with the welfare of the majority from a class and anti-colonial viewpoint.

This new generation of intellectuals emerged from the struggle on the streets against neoliberalism and neo-developmentalism; they were born of renewed processes of political formation, of the rediscovery of the past-present, and of the dispute for the inclusion of disruptive demands in their organizations. They call themselves 'the children of the first uprising', they represent high-level structures, they are national, provincial and local leaders. Their political action requires thinking about the new economic realities of the Indigenous population which, as a result of migration processes, now also finds itself in the city, agro-industry and precarious self-employment. These new conditions also require a new form of organization.

In spite of internal problems, CONAIE and popular solidarity responded to the enormous challenges posed by the rebellion, above all, by the large influx from the provinces to Quito, which brought together tens of thousands of its members. National coordination, discipline of organizational structures and renewal of its leadership cadres were demonstrated.

The huge uprising also allowed the resolution of two problems that had been dragging on for years. On the one hand, the previous government had applied a demobilization strategy to the popular camp – particularly to the CONAIE – and which consisted of undermining its structure through the creation of the 'Indigenous Alliance', a body made up of public officials, government assembly members and FENOCIN leaders, former members of CONAIE, headed by the Ministry of Economic and Social Inclusion (MIES) (*El Universo*, 2015). This weakened historical bonds, as seen in Chimborazo province.

Secondly, there was the issue of the division of Evangelical and Catholic religious identities, exacerbated by electoral interests. In such a way, 'the reestablishment of second degree organizations in Tungurahua and Chimborazo show that they are moving forward overcoming the divisions that were sown during the government of Rafael Correa and have the capacity to reconcile their religious differences again' (Herrera, 2019). Even those who distorted the events of October by stating that 'the strike had been taken over by Correa supporters' (Tibán in Visión 360) ended up admitting that 'this was the largest uprising in the last 20 years' (*Plan V*, 2019).

Strictly speaking, CONAIE's presence was only possible in combination with the population as a whole, especially the popular sector that contributed to the struggle at various levels, while participating directly on the front line and building its own history as part of the process.

> The organizations maintained the self-organization and the national strike, the protests multiplied in the territories and in the neighbourhoods, some parts of the transport union who did not feel represented in the negotiations [with the government] also joined, the grassroots organizations of CONAIE began marching towards the capital ahead of schedule, and on 7 October, when the Indigenous people began to arrive in Quito, students, women, workers and neighbourhoods had been protesting for several days (Herrera, 2019).

On the coast, in the Highlands and Amazon millions of people from the city and the countryside took to the streets and to the main and secondary interprovincial routes, as well as to the city squares, markets, public and private institutions. With the political legitimacy granted by mass action, they confronted the IMF, the government and the rich. This situation undermined the doubts about achieving a powerful demonstration. 'The leadership of the Confederation of Indigenous Nationalities of Ecuador (CONAIE) itself did not expect it and we all had doubts about achieving an effective march' (Herrera, 2019).

2.2 CHANGES IN THE CHARACTER AND WAYS OF WORKING OF THE ANTI-CAPITALISTS

In the nineties – in the period of emergence of the Indigenous struggle, especially after the Inti Raymi uprising and the Amazonian Kawsaymanta Allpamanta Jatarishun march – the Indigenous movement enjoyed homogeneity, both from the point of view of the reproduction of their material life and ideologically. This has changed in the course of the almost three decades that have followed.

The presence of the state, the diversification of the labour force and its social stratification led to gradual changes in the character of Indigenous organizations. The strengthening of the state, international development and the party system, as well as the deployment of repressive and ideological apparatuses; the changes from a peasant to proletarian and sub-proletarian labour force; and the development of social classes and greater stratification of Indigenous society allowed the emergence of different perspectives and interpretations of reality.

Likewise, the fundamental political programme, such as land for those who work it, defence of community territories, recognition of Indigenous communities, education, health and criticism of the monocultural state, are not enough to respond to the later reality, since it is shaped by other socioeconomic problems such as labour rights, dispossession of territory by agro-industry and extractivism, the institutionalization of organizations for the project of the bourgeoisie and the hegemonic use of multiculturalism. This led to the differentiation of tendencies, which push a project according to their understanding of reality and, in some cases, to pursue their particular interests and not those of the whole.[7]

The structure of the Indigenous movement has a powerful organizational backbone. Its logic is communitarian democracy, ranging from the basic structures at the local level (communes, community centres, associations) to the coordinating structures at the zonal, provincial, regional and national levels (unions, federations, movements, confederations). Ideologically, however, the Indigenous movement is not homogeneous, a factor that responds to changes in its material structure. On the one hand, there is a consciousness tied to the party system and the institutions of bourgeois democracy, which oscillates between the institutional left and the right; and, on the other hand, one that challenges the state of things, constituting itself as an anti-capitalist tendency.

We consider that in the October rebellion the anti-capitalist tendency prevailed (over the institutionalist left and right tendencies), motivated, among other things, by the emergence of new leaderships. As Machado points out:

> However, today Ecuador is experiencing a moment of political renewal framed in the context of transitions. With the development of the current struggle, new leaders replaced historical leaders of the Indigenous movement who were politically exhausted.

---

[7] In the context of the October rebellion, we can see an overemphasis from some on the role of particular personalities, disregarding the action of the collective in favour of that of the individual. For example, believing that the popular response is due to the arrest of a 'leader': 'The first error occurred from the State … I think it was a very important trigger because a leader was arrested, the reaction was immediate, the reaction was at the national level, which then became a national agenda, and the national leadership of CONAIE had to align and give guidelines'. (Santi, 2020, pp. 35–36)

> In recent days, a renewed CONAIE was seen in the different territories where it is present: provinces of the Central Highlands and the Amazonian territory. This is a combative CONAIE with a strong capacity for popular mobilization (Machado, 2019a).

Some versions pointed out that 'what happened in the Agora of the Casa de la Cultura was the political displacement of a moderate leadership by a radical leadership, younger and willing to keep going to the bitter end' (*Plan V*, 2019). However, the renewal of the leaders is not merely a process of age or generational dispute, but rather it implies the interpretation of a specific reality that capitalism in Ecuador and the Indigenous organization are going through.

On the contrary, one of the slogans that was raised within the mobilization by the youth is to 'fight with the wisdom of the grandparents and the strength of the youth'. Unity is possible from an anti-capitalist philosophy, a total intolerance of all forms of exploitation and oppression, including criticism of the state and the party system and is resolved in action: 'The engine of the Indigenous struggle agenda is action'. The slogan says it clearly: 'How do the peoples of Ecuador fight? Words and deeds, words and deeds, words and deeds, damn it!' (Arana, 2019).

The October rebellion challenged methods such as 'citizens' consultation', 'citizens' laws', 'round tables', 'national dialogue', 'complaints of unconstitutionality', which are essential to the institutional left and defend the idea of 'using the state'. For Herrera (2019), '[...] at the same time, it was well known that the elected authorities of Pachakutik and great figures of the last period such as Yaku Pérez or Salvador Quishpe had a secondary role; and that the parliamentary parties had little political initiative to get involved in the movement'.

In practice, October meant the radical criticism of the actually existing power; it removed apparently central tensions of the political from the logic of the party system, an idea that is expressed in the phrase: 'I prefer a banker to a dictator'.[8] Certain leaders and those at the base that were driving the struggle consistently criticized such approaches: 'Before finishing his speech [Jaime Vargas] said that there were opportunist leaders who were taking the name of CONAIE in vain and threatened

---

8   This was Yaku Pérez's phrase when referring to the second round of the 2017 presidential elections in which Lasso and Correa were standing. In the context of the coup d'état against Evo Morales in Bolivia in November 2019, he denounced the alleged dictatorial 'practice' of the former Bolivian indigenous ruler, failing to acknowledge the context of the US siege of the South American country.

to take strong decisions against those Indigenous people who have sought the limelight. He called them traitors. Yaku Pérez, former president of Ecuarunari and prefect of Azuay, is one of those he challenges' (*Plan V*, 2019).

The critical opinions expressed towards certain characters from the Indigenous movement who have become integrated into the superstructure of the state (pointed out by an increasing number of the population, through social networks and in rallies) contrasted with the defence made of these by representatives of the right wing such as Ramiro Rivera, ex-Democracia Popular, a Christian democratic party – and Carlos Vera, a pro-Social Christian journalist. There were also racists such as Andersson Boscán – an irrational anti-communist with clear alignment with the right – who argued: 'There is a high standard in the Indigenous movement: such as Yaku Pérez, Lourdes Tibán' (Boscán, 2019).

Finally, the accusation of infiltration by 'external groups' as an argument to explain the growth of the anti-capitalist position in the Indigenous movement is a flawed argument that ignores the changes that have taken place in the country and in the performance of CONAIE in the last decades. To think that the 'design of what the leadership says and does not say' comes from 'outside', from 'infiltration', from 'ventriloquism', only causes the depoliticization of reality, the impoverishment of debate and the displacement of events to extra-political spheres. 'In light of the uprising we can affirm that in the Indigenous movement as a whole, consistent ideas are affirmed that privilege struggle before conciliation, that assume the need for the unity of the popular camp, that reject any understanding with the right and Correism' (Almeida, 2019, p. 82).

3   OCTOBER'S ACTORS: PESSIMISM OF REASON AND OPTIMISM OF THE WILL

The October rebellion demonstrates that the unity of the popular sectors can only be achieved in action. Potentially, the participation of the exploited classes opens the way for the strengthening of the organizational fabric, raising the level of political discussion, the construction of new reflections and practices from below and to the left without compromises and consequently for those most in need.

The October actors came together in opposition to Decree No. 883, which threatened to make the already impoverished living standards of the majority of Ecuadorean society even more precarious. From the poorest classes to the middle-income sectors, they came together with determination to stop one of the main requirements of the Letter of Intent agreed by the Moreno government with the International Monetary Fund: the elimination of hydrocarbon subsidies.

It is necessary to look at the range of actors who were part of the rebellion in order to establish the degrees of participation and involvement, the proportion between self-organization and organic adhesion; that is, to go beyond the list of participating collectives so as not to overestimate their political capacity, and to dissociate oneself from the undifferentiated generalization of the people as an explanation of the subjects involved in the mobilization.[9]

We address the participation of the trade union movement and the proletariat, of neighbourhoods and urban spaces, middle-income sectors, women and youth, as well as other peasant and Indigenous organizations such as FEINE and FENOCIN. Finally, we deal with the intervention of the institutional left and the ruling classes.

3.1 GROWTH OF THE PROLETARIAT AND WEAKNESS OF THE TRADE UNION MOVEMENT

In the context of the consolidation by US imperialism of a unipolar world in the 1990s, the Ecuadorean Indigenous movement led the struggle, together with other sectors, against the expansion of neoliberalism as the prevailing form of world capital. This meant the defence of territories against oil, mining and forestry extractive activities, and against the dispossession by agribusiness and the precariousness of labour. In short, they organized to counteract misery, inequality and poverty. The uprising of the 1990s was a turning point in the alternative struggle against modern capitalism, especially at a time when those forms of struggle, in line with trade unionism, were hard hit.

Despite the high level of mobilization, there were changes in the dynamics of economic reproduction, due to the loss of territory and productive sovereignty of poor peasant units. The result was the growth of a mass Indigenous population, pushed into precarious conditions in the movement of commercial, industrial and agro-industrial capital, as a cheap labour force in the market.

---

9 Listed as participating subjects: 'The Unitary Collective of Social Organizations, workers and trade unionists grouped in the FUT and the Popular Front, peasants, organizations of poor settlers, small merchants, teachers, youth and women, indigenous peoples and nationalities led by CONAIE were ready to respond with mobilizations and struggles against the neoliberal package. The leftist political parties and organizations, legal and not, prepared their forces for the popular struggle against neoliberalism' (2019, p. 14).

Graph 8: Trade union membership by decade

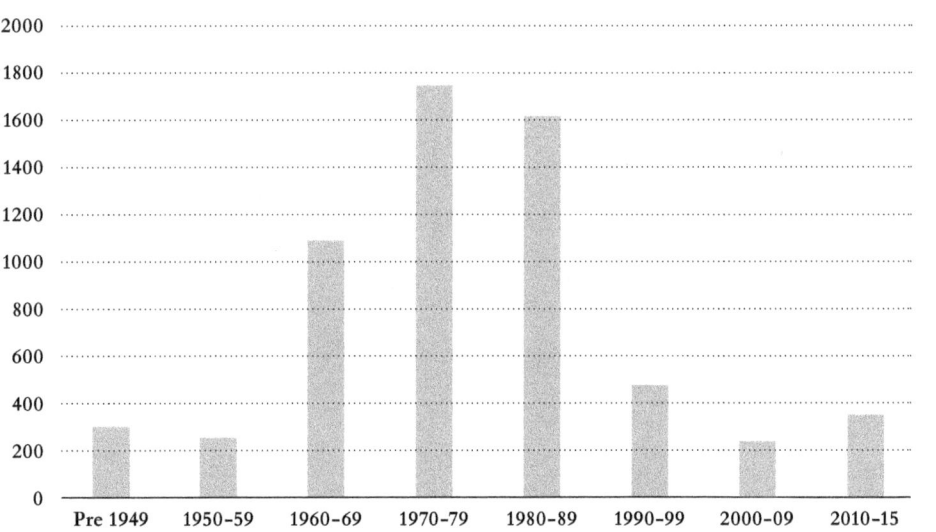

Source: Madrid, 2018b.

The Latin American Marxist José Carlos Mariátegui (2008) stated in the 1920s that the problem of Indigenous peoples is socioeconomic and, fundamentally – not only – revolved around the land question, in a context of the region's dependence on the global reproduction of capital. In 2020, we can add that the problem of Indigenous peoples and nationalities is the dispossession of communal territories, wage labour and the persistence of a mono-national and colonialist organization of society. This is another of the phenomena that drives the importance of understanding the role of the working class in the rebellion.

Prior to October, overcoming various difficulties, the social organizations had already proposed a response to the offensive of the government and the right wing, as can be seen in the resolutions of CONAIE and in the meetings of the Collective of

10 'On 4 October 2019 the Collective of Social Organizations which brings together CONAIE and the FUT, the Popular Front proclaimed the Indigenous uprising and the national strike for 9 October, and the call was issued for mobilizations to begin immediately, declaring October as the 'Month of Resistance and Struggle' (Miranda, 2019, p. 17).

Social Organizations – which included the FUT – where it was agreed to push for the 'The Programme of Escalating Struggle'. This was expressed in a call for mobilization on 14 October, but the speed of events led several organizations, including the trade unions, to call for joint action on 4 October.[10]

However, the participation of the organized working class in October was moderate. This is due to the weakness of the union movement, due to the small number of member organizations and the absence of an autonomous class programme. According to IFA,[11] in 2014, out of 512 flower companies, only four unions were formed. In the banana sector, out of 500 companies there are only five unions; this reality is similar in other branches of the economy. In addition, it should be noted that more than half of the country's workers, who work in precarious conditions, do not have a relationship of dependence with the employers, and are unorganized.

The trade union movement is going through a crisis of strategy, programme and identity, which is reflected in reduced membership and a weak representation among young people, precarious workers, agro-industrial proletarians and migrants from the countryside. This atomization prevents a real process of unity and limits the social influence and legitimacy of the workers' organization.

In the context of the October struggle, the Frente Unitario de Trabajadores (FUT), despite its limitations, joined the mobilization together with the forces that make it up: CEDOCUT, CEOSL and UGTE.[12] But its position hardly went beyond a symbolic act in the face of the dizzying development of events. As a result, their representativeness was diminished. Hence, one of the most 'agile' approaches of the FUT was to convene, only on 19 October, an assembly to define what to do,[13] demonstrating the weakness of a stagnant, bureaucratic leadership.

Nelson Erazo, President of the Popular Front, spoke of calling for a new national strike after 9 October (Pichincha Universal, 2019); but in practice this did not happen. As a result, the October

---

11   Ecuadorean-Swedish institution dedicated to research in the field of labour organisation, occupational and environmental health.

12   The members of the FUT are the Confederación de Organizaciones Clasistas Unitarias de Trabajadores (CEDOCUT), the Confederación de Ecuatoriana de Organizaciones Sindicales Libres (CEOSL), the Unión General de Trabajadores del Ecuador (UGTE) and the Confederación de Trabajadores del Ecuador (CTE). However, the latter dissociated itself from the popular struggle for political calculations and personal interest, alien to the working class which, apparently, it claims to represent.

13   Another example of this weakness was the FUT Assembly, held in Cuenca on Saturday 16 November, where it took a stand against the Economic Growth Bill just one day before the bill was debated in parliament.

struggle evolved independently of the decisions of this sector. Added to this is the distancing of the CTE from the rest of the FUT (Sarango in Jairala, 2019), since it is the most hesitant part and has become accustomed to pacts with the governments in office[14] – led by the Communist Party of Ecuador.

At present, the trade union centres do not have the strength to overcome the power of the ruling class; their current weakness is a far cry from what it had been in previous decades. It became evident that it was impossible for them to mobilize their scarce ranks; even the FUT march announced for 30 October was suspended, and the post-strike meeting held with the government ended with no practical result whatsoever.[15]

The Labour Parliament which includes CEDOCLAT, CSE, CTSP, CTOS and the CUT[16] is weaker still. None of these organizations participated in the mobilizations. Moreover, Richard Gómez, President of the CUT, said that the October struggle 'tarnished' the image of social organizations with 'too radical a logic', and tried to justify violence against the people by describing a member of the repressive forces 'as a human being who reacts' (Jairala, 2019). In this case, it is evident that the participation of certain grassroots organizations which are part of these federations went against the directives of their leadership.

Despite the large number of trade union federations, the number of unionized workers remains numerically and qualitatively unchanged. Moreover, the fragmentation of union representation increases the competition over recruitment between the existing unions. As a reference, no federation has more than 50 affiliated and active unions on its payroll.

> Organizations are weakened if they are not surrounded by a more or less solid social fabric; therefore, they expand their space for action

---

[14] On 21 October a meeting was held between the government and CTE, without the participation of the rest of the FUT.

[15] In this way, we answer the suspicious questions of the President of the General Confederation of Peruvian Workers, CGTP, who said: 'There are questions that need to be answered: Why did the government meet only with the leadership of CONAIE? Why were the trade union federations in the Unitary Workers Front and other social organisations participating in the protest excluded? Why did the CONAIE leadership not ask the government that the other organisations that fought together with the indigenous people also participate in the negotiation? Neither the government nor CONAIE leaders have responded' (Pacho, 2019).

[16] The Ecuadorean Labour Parliament (PLE) is made up of the Ecuadorean Confederation of Class Organisations (CEDOC CLAT), the Trade Union Confederation of Ecuador (CSE), the Confederation of Public Sector Workers (CTSP) and the Confederation of Social Security Workers and Organisations (CTOSS). The third 'coordinator' is the Central Unitaria de Trabajadores (CUT) which was created as a divisive strategy by the Correa government.

beyond organized individuals and seek ways to maintain permanent contacts with the general population, especially with young people. (Unda, 2020)

In spite of the dubious and autocratic behaviour of the bureaucracy, the rank and file of the union movement were present in October, despite the absence of a call by its national leaders. The exception was the call for the national strike of 9 October by the FUT. Although it had few practical results in the workplaces, the statement of action had a symbolic impact as a mechanism to rally the unorganized sectors of the population that joined the activities. Nevertheless, the union movement lost the historic opportunity to legitimize itself in front of the whole working class, with or without a dependency relationship, especially where it is dispersed. There is still a question hanging in the air: what would have happened, both for the events in general and for the project of strengthening the workers' movement, if the FUT had called for an active and indefinite national strike in the midst of the October rebellion?

After the call for the last national strike by the FUT, in March 2005, a press headline pointed out: '25 years later: the national strike is a weapon with damp powder'. This statement contrasts with the growth and worsening of the conditions of exploitation of the proletariat in Ecuador. Therefore, the reason for demobilization does not lie in the lack of objective conditions, but in the imperative need to renew trade unionism. This implies expanding its organizational fabric, criticizing the collective contract as a union principle and end, rejuvenating the leadership, understanding the modern forms of exploitation of capital, 'building more lasting meeting spaces in which links are being strengthened and prepared in order to move forward together' (Unda, 2020).

Finally, the traditional call for the unity of the people makes sense only if it is demonstrated in practice that this is possible; otherwise, it will remain empty words, in spite of the efforts at self-criticism made by the most committed forces, swimming against the tide. A collaborationist trade union movement, fragmented and déclassé, only confirms Henri Lefebvre's warning when he criticized, in the middle of the last century, the worker–management pact of European trade unionism: 'the trade unions against the revolution'.

We will deal with the participation of transport workers. The unions in this sector, due to their semi-individual productive condition and link with the party system (PSC, ID), have traditionally tended towards and been reluctant to take up a programme that goes beyond union demands. In general, they have a utilitarian stigma attached to them; hence, they play the role of heroes and villains.[17] Their behaviour was evaluated by 71% of the population as negative after the October events (CEDATOS, 2019). This is the result of leadership practices, which in recent years have been co-opted by 'institutional channels such as the Assembly – (the union leaders were parliamentary representatives of Alianza País (AP)), – the Executive Function (regular meetings between the cabinet and the leadership) and for the creation by the union of its own political movement, which saw the light of day in 2012 (Movimiento CONDUCE – Construyendo el Desarrollo de la Unidad Clasista Ecuatoriana), which supported AP candidacies in 2013 and 2016' (Stoessel and Iturriza, 2020, p. 256). In addition, in October they negotiated with the government the reduction of tariffs for the importation of tyres and failed to call for the repeal of the elimination of the fuel subsidy.

It is noteworthy that despite the limits of the transport union, at the beginning all the cooperatives (interprovincial and interparish, urban service, freight and taxis) participated in the strike and, after the surrender of part of their leadership, still carried on. However, public transport did not participate, despite the fact that in Quito they have union representation affiliated to CEOSL.[18] The transport leadership is also heterogeneous. The resignation of some of its representatives – in the context of the prosecution of several of its members – did not imply the repeal of the stoppage.[19] The grassroots transport workers maintained the stoppage, despite the government's threat of seizure of units and withdrawal of circulation permits. This holds out the hope of the emergence of a consistent position – with prior work – as in countries such as France and Portugal where the transport unions have carried out important stoppages that go beyond the demands of the unions.

---

17   Thus, in the province of Los Ríos, the transport union reached agreements with the Prefecture on 4 October. The 'end of the transport strike was welcomed, but even so, no one wants them to raise the fares' (Jairala, 2019).

18   The former president of CEOSL, Pablo Serrano, and the current president, Angel Sanchez, are members and leaders of the Trolleybus Union and were even former presidents of the FUT.

19   The unions represent the different modalities of transportation at the national and local levels. 'The National Federation of Taxi Transport Operators of Ecuador (FEDOTAXIS), of Tourist Transport (FENATTURE), of Light, Mixed and Medium Transport (FENACOTRALI), of Urban Transport (FENATU), of School and Institutional Transport (FENATEI), of Cranes (FENAGRUAS), of the National Chamber of Heavy Transport (CANATRAPE)' (Stoessel and Iturriza, 2020, p. 256). Eleven transport federations converge in the Federación Nacional de Cooperativas de Transporte Público de Pasajeros del Ecuador (FENACOTIP).

The national transport strike stimulated the Ecuadorean people to take to the streets and forced the mobilization to be brought forward by two weeks. The paralysis of this service is vital to limit the movement of capital.

3.2 URBAN UPRISING AND SOLIDARITY LINKS BETWEEN CITY AND COUNTRYSIDE

The shortcomings in the organization of the Ecuadorean working class translate into a lack of organization of popular urban sectors. This reality is more acute on the coast, due to the repression exercised in the last century against any semblance of autonomous organization, which eliminated them or reduced them to a shell. If we compare the dictatorships of the Southern Cone and the application of Plan Condor in Ecuador, their political, civilian and military systems of the 1970s and 1980s can be characterized as low-impact dictatorships. However, from the quantitative point of view (number of extrajudicial executions, forced disappearances, imprisonment of popular leaders and left-wing militants), the attacks in a similar way undermined the ability of the left and the autonomous popular organizations to involve people and strengthen their will to fight. From the qualitative point of view, the state devastated its opponents on the coast, particularly in Guayaquil.

The situation in several cities of the sierra is in stark contrast. Quito is one of the most outstanding cases, not only because of the correlation of organized forces but also because of its capacity for autonomous mobilization. The students of the universities, colleges and the youth of the popular neighbourhoods, who were determined to sustain the mobilization, shouting '*Quito no se ahueva carajo!*' (Quito will not give in damn you!) were one of the first targets of the repressive forces. By contrast, the students of the San Francisco de Quito University were determined to extinguish the tyres set on fire by the transport workers, in one of the wealthiest areas of the capital: Cumbayá.

Quito's spontaneous mobilization capacity was triggered by the cry: 'the Indigenous people are coming'. This was not just a question of 'support'. The struggle brought together the popular and middle-income sectors in the capital with the peasant and Indigenous mobilization from the provinces, in a beautiful historical conjuncture. The bonds of solidarity between the countryside and the city reinforced the idea of their indispensible alliance. In order for living conditions to change, this country needs an organization of the exploited classes with a more organic capacity to mobilize, both in the city and in the countryside.

There were several road closures, clashes, takeovers and unrest in the urban areas. The barrios and the urban-marginal areas and conurbations were where most of the actions of struggle took place in October. At the beginning of the rebellion, Quito and the surrounding areas were full of demonstrations. Among the main closures to traffic, in the north, were Simón Bolívar avenue, Carapungo, 6 de Diciembre and Ramón Borja avenues, Guayllabamba traffic circle, Carcelén, Oyacoto, Calderón, Comité del Pueblo, La Bota, Pomasqui, La Prensa and Vaca de Castro avenues, Collas road, República avenue and Mitad del Mundo traffic circle. In the south: Guajaló, Quitumbe, Caupicho, Tambillo, Uyumbicho, Santa Rosa, Teniente Ortiz, La Atahualpa traffic circle, Dos Puentes, El Pintado, Morán Valverde, La Ecuatoriana, Guamaní, Quicentro Sur, Maldonado, Mariscal Sucre and Michelena avenues, Marco Albornoz and Mariscal Sucre and La Loma de Puengasí. In downtown from La Marín to Patria Avenue (in neighbourhoods such as La Vicentina, La Floresta, La Tola and El Dorado), Universidad Central, La Comuna, Venezuela and Buenos Aires streets, as well as the toll booths at El Valle and Monjas. In the valleys: Cumbayá, Yaruquí, Pifo, Puembo, Tumbaco (Ruta Viva), Chiche bridge, Intervalles road, El Colibrí traffic circle (Sangolquí) and Conocoto.

Despite the difficulties, from the first day, in the city of Guayaquil, important road closures were reported, including Machala and Cuenca streets, Via Casuarina at the entrance of Balerio Estacio and Monte Sinai, in the Maritime Port, Pedro Moncayo and 6 de Marzo, 25 de Julio in front of Mall del Río (south centre), Quito and General Gómez, Domingo Comín and Pendola (Jairala, 2019). The action in the cities, mostly spontaneous, confirms the need for the construction of spaces of representation for the working class in the *barrios.*

In addition to this, dozens of premises, houses and community centres have been set up; as well as households and self-organized families to provide direct solidarity in the supply centres of food, medicines, clothing and logistics; the elaboration of food delivered directly to the demonstrators in the rear or who were resting – which met the material demands to sustain the struggle. There was the spontaneous elaboration of shields and defensive material, tools that tipped the unbalanced relationship of forces during the street and barricade struggles, when the government increased the use of violence.

An important phenomenon of the October rebellion was the link of the popular camp with the so-called 'middle class' (to a large extent a working class with a medium level of income), raised against the most conservative and reactionary sectors of the capitalist class and its servants in Quito (Patricio Moncayo on *DemocraciaTV*, 2019). Such a link had been absent during the period of mobilizations in the years 2014–2015. Thanks to this positioning, October counted on countless efforts that supplied the eleven days of the rebellion.

A sector of particular importance were the intellectuals – academics, artists, students and others – without whom the course of October would not have been the same. We believe that the challenge for the intelligentsia is to remain integrated or, at least, to stand close to the interests of the popular organizations. Not because 'practical' work is morally superior to 'intellectual' work – if such a separation of human labour exists – but because, as Walter Benjamin thought, the construction of history which goes against the grain cannot be done from a desk, because this living narrative inhabits the dynamics of the subject classes themselves. Consequently, unless the intelligentsia is integrated into the struggle, its observations will be speculative, far from being air in the lungs.

Perhaps the most eloquent example is the counterpoint between the depth of the reflections of one of the main leftist inorganic intellectuals of Ecuador, Bolívar Echeverría, and the praxis of the main intellectual and organic militant of the Indigenous and trade union movement, Dolores Cacuango. The former had, in his exile in Mexican universities, an adequate space to process his ideas and live in peace; the latter, an illiterate comrade, from whom only a few ideas were collected, lived struggling in the midst of poverty. Echeverría, with the exception of small academic circles, is, unfortunately, unknown. Mama Dulu has become the symbol of inspiration for every Indigenous uprising and workers' strike. What makes one thought so 'harmless' and another so subversive? It is essential to transform ideas into material forces.

3.3 WARMI TAKI:[20] THE STRUGGLE OF WOMEN IN THE REBELLION

It is important to highlight the leadership and struggle of women within the Indigenous movement and the Ecuadorean popular movement. They were an important part of the strategy of the Indigenous movement, were at the forefront of the

---

[20] Quecha – means 'The song of the women'.

marches, and acted as doctors and nurses to help the wounded on streets transformed into battlefields. Middle-income women workers together with those from the popular sectors; 'leaving their kitchens', reporting from alternative media. Women from all parts of Ecuador arrived in Quito on 7 October, *en masse*, with their sons and daughters. Decades ago, communists of the stature of Tránsito Amaguaña, Dolores Cacuango, María Luisa Gómez de la Torre or Nela Martínez did the same, at the dawn of the first agricultural unions, the basis of the modern Ecuadorean Indigenous movement:

> In order to effect profound changes in the system of land ownership in Ecuador, the Indigenous leaders would have to take their demands directly to the government [...] they would walk to Quito, barefoot and carrying their small children on their backs. They would first arrive in the town of Cayambe, where they would spend the night and leave for Quito at three in the morning. At noon they took a rest in Guayllabamba and continued on to Calderón, where they arrived at nightfall. The next morning they would arrive in Quito, where they would spend several days or even weeks until they were able to present their demands to the government. Tránsito Amaguaña, one of the Kayambi leaders, made twenty-six such treks on foot to Quito [Becker and Tutillo, 2009, p. 113].

In the face of uniformed men in imported armour, a dignified block with its own armour was constructed. Despite the asymmetrical relationship, they firmly and courageously opposed the violence of the repressive forces, which, paradoxically, were led by another woman, the Minister of 'War' and liberal feminist María Paula Romo; street graffiti called her 'María Bala Plomo' (María lead bullet). Patriarchal violence is still intact and brutal, although it has adopted the feminine figure in a liberal and petty-bourgeois frame.

They set up camps in the spaces provided by universities, institutions and cultural centres to take care of the babies who arrived with their mothers. From there they proposed policies to guide the actions; they supported the demands of the rebellion, demanded the protection of the rights of their people and defended their territories. El Arbolito Park and the Agora of the Casa de la Cultura were the places of assembly, rest and struggle where day care centres, medical brigades, sanitation, dozens of kitchens and collection centres were installed; sites that were indiscriminately bombarded with tear gas.

The rebellion was swollen by an important contingent of women who were deployed in several battle lines, including the front line. The participation of women in the organization, care, political agitation and fighting with the repressive bodies positioned them as protagonists of the October insurrection.

> The distribution centres and humanitarian shelters were a real political school where, from the deployment of dynamics of care, solidarity and reciprocity, we were able to reaffirm what feminist theory has shown us with absolute clarity: the work of care and support, historically devalued because they are seen as being in the private sphere, are as important as the vanguard of the struggle in the streets, in what is seen as the public sphere. Without this work, our existence is impossible (Noriega and Criollo, 2020, p. 144).

Efforts were concentrated in logistics and supply networks, which were being set up as the rebellion progressed, as well as in the struggle against the repressive forces. The same women who in the countryside promoted the defence of territories, health, education and resistance to the neo-colonial and extractivist development model that objectifies and exploits nature, joined forces with women from the city, who have sustained and fought for the right to food, decent housing, basic works and services through *mingas* for water in the peripheral neighbourhoods, for work in order to support their families and the maintenance of their children.

The October struggle is linked to a whole programme of action built by popular and feminist organizations. They confronted the advance of reactionary and mainstream patriarchal views that the governments – including the progressive ones – were unable to challenge. In the programme of the Progressive Days of Struggle, that called for the mobilizations driven then by the excitement of the rebellion. Multiple demands were put forward, including:

- Respect the agenda of struggle for women's rights:
- End the campaign of misrepresentation and attack on the rights of women of the popular sector.

- Approval of the right to abortion in case of rape, as a matter of public health.
- A comprehensive policy, not only legal measures, against femicide and patriarchal capitalism (Annex 1).

The cumulative struggles of women, in the months prior to October, focused particularly on demanding the decriminalization of abortion. This led to the fact that, during the October rebellion, Indigenous, popular and young women, women from the markets and popular neighbourhoods and organized feminists called a march denouncing institutional violence and the murder of their comrades, demanding the repeal of Decree No. 883, pointing out the role of the IMF and also in remembrance and repudiation of 12 October, the day of the invasion of *Abya-Yala*. 'In the morning, a women's march was held, promoted by several feminist collectives and women's sectors of CONAIE, as part of the mobilization against the '*paquetazo*' and with the objective of denouncing the repression and having a presence in other parts of the city of Quito' (Le Quang, Chávez and Vizuete, 2020, p. 73).

This was not just about economic demands; there is also an essential political challenge. The women denounced the patriarchal, racist and colonialist character of the government's measures. 'Nothing for the Indians alone', the slogan of the first Indigenous uprising of 1990, is still valid thirty years later. In the march a chant was repeated in a high-pitched voice: 'To the struggle, comrades, to the struggle and union, we are many and the boss is only one'.

As has historically been the case, women of all ages took part in the mobilization, with their children on their backs and their dignity to the fore. They made use of a community practice that criticizes the individualization of social life and the 'biologizing' version of women, constructed from the patriarchal narrative that annuls their political subject.

For eleven days the women fought without ceasing to be carers. They walked, retreated and advanced in the street struggle, in the countryside and in the city. They spoke in public, to guide, to fight and to say goodbye to the fallen comrades. Young women who took up historical leadership in the struggles, such as Nayra Chalán, a Kichwa from Saraguro, Vice President of ECUARUNARI, who in addition to being a powerful spokesperson for women's rights, was one of the main organizers of the rally in Quito. In the negotiations Miriam

Cisneros, a Kichwa woman representing Amazonian women, emphasized that: 'It hurts my soul when our little ones have had to give their lives choking to death with tear gas bombs. Our brothers have died, meaning that our President sends armed men to attack us, when we have come with a peaceful struggle. Mr President, what is happening in a plurinational state?' Feminism, as the October experience has shown, only makes sense in political and community practice.

3.4 YOUTH: POLITICIZATION AND GENERATIONAL RENEWAL

Youth in the Latin American region have played a leading role in the liberation struggles. Che won the Revolution at the age of 31, Fernando Daquilema and Manuela León Guamán commanded the uprising in the central Ecuadorean sierra against the landlord state at 22 and 26 respectively, Olga Benario internationalized her struggle to Brazil at 26, Arturo Jarrín organized Alfaro Vive Carajo at 23, Fausto Vargas Cortés, first President of FESE, was declared a danger to the state at 20, Tránsito Amaguaña began his communist militancy in his teens ... The same is true overseas: Palestinian icon Ahed Tamimi, at 16, slapped an Israeli Zionist soldier and was sentenced to eight months in jail.

In October, the participation of the youth was crucial, just as it was in the Chilean revolt that started the same month, orchestrated by 'the generation that lost its fear of the curfew, one of the symbols of the Pinochet era' (BBC, 2019b). The emergence of the Chilean youth struggle has antecedents in the massive mobilizations of high school (2006) and university (2011) students (*La Izquierda Diario*, 2019).

The *chapa* – as the policeman is called in Ecuadorean slang – is a symbol of social control, especially for young people. Confronting him constitutes a profound critique, which transcends specific economic demands; it is a challenge to the regime that sustains the current unbearable existence; it is the repudiation of the imposed and undemocratic authority of the modern social contract, and the point of injustice and inequity. 'Those young people lost their fear of the forces of order, whom they consider their assassins' (Alarcón, 2019), as the slogan warns: 'Police and military in the service of the rich'.

In October, a significant proportion of detainees, wounded and extrajudicial executions were of young people. Young women and men held the supply corridors, confronting the army and police on the front line. An important part of the community, Indigenous and popular guard was young.

The presence of youth in Indigenous and peasant organizations is not a recent phenomenon. One of the driving forces of FEINE, FENOCIN and CONAIE has been young people, who have taken charge of sustaining the street struggle and the leadership of some federations, communities and regions. It is estimated that in the national organizations young people under thirty years of age make up 45%, and in the regional leaderships 70% (El Telégrafo, 2019). This situation contrasts with the reality of the trade union movement, where the leadership has remained almost unchanged for half a century and there is little participation of youth in general, especially in decision-making (El Telégrafo, 2019).

Although the student federations FEUE, FEUPE, FEPE and FESE[21] joined the mobilization, most of the young people who joined did so regardless of their affiliation to these unions, since a large part of this sector does not have access to tertiary education. The mobilization can be explained by the stimulus of the political fronts which, although embryonic, have sustained the work in the poorest areas of the city[22] and, above all, due to the explosive potential of this age group, which was outraged by the effects of Decree No. 883.

The intimate link with the struggle, especially in the streets, led the youth to politicize their objectives and agendas on two levels. One comes from their class and the other from ethnicity. This political subjectivity comes from concrete experience that is lived out physically on a daily basis. Class is experienced as a place of exclusion – excluded from university, from a dignified life, from the possibility of a future, from the labour market – and racial identity which is reinforced by bullets and felt as discrimination, produce reflections that, in a context of struggle, acquire political form. This was aggravated by the class hatred and racism of the ruling class, which exudes hatred towards Indigenous and poor people because they do not reproduce a white ethic. The response of several young people was to make use of their ethnic origins in a political sense. In the face of the attack and vituperation of the Indian, affirming ethnic origin is a political act.

---

21 These are: Federation of University Students of Ecuador (FEUE), Federation of Students of Private Universities of Ecuador (FEUPE), Federation of Polytechnic Students of Ecuador (FEPE) and Federation of Secondary Students of Ecuador (FESE).

22 Such as La Juntada, Bloque Proletario y Vientos del Pueblo, Acción Antifascista Ecuador, Movimiento de Barrios en Lucha, Movimiento Guevarista, Colectivo Popular, cultural centres and other organizations of the autonomous anti-capitalist left. In addition to cultural and neighbourhood groups linked to the institutionalist left.

The integration of the youth into the street struggle in the countryside and the city made it possible to bring together the past and the present. The younger generation did not have the opportunity to forge itself in a struggle on the barricades when Correism was hegemonic, because it criminalized social protest (through legal measures, administrative measures, expulsions from educational centres and extrajudicial executions – such as the killing of Edison Cosíos). It also took over several student and youth organizations, transforming them into groups that function to ideologically reproduce modern capital. They censored and persecuted, a situation similar to other expressions of the institutional left which, in past decades, club in hand, denied any type of dissent that questioned their electoralist dogma.

A phenomenon of October was the consistent objection of youth to the presence of those who made their relationship with the state a way of life, who were physically thrown out of the places of assembly in Quito. The condemnation of various figures who claim to represent popular organizations but who have electoral aspirations was clear. This was strengthened by the growth of different anti-capitalist organizations composed mainly of young people, who focused on grassroots work and at the same time criticized the useless drivel of the 'analysts of political economy' bogged down in Byzantine debates.

The constant search, exploration and innovation of young people gives them easy access to technology, through the circulation of audiovisual material suited to the pace of the modern world. This strengthened the visibility of the struggle, and contributed to the counter-hegemonic work of alternative and community media, in the face of the stranglehold of media promoting the interests of the bosses.

Another important contribution came from urban cultures. Despite the fact that several of its members are very young, they were actively involved in the youth cultural movement. In turn, a generation that identifies with hardcore, punk, rock, hip-hop, rap, cumbia, chicha or Andean music genres coalesced into class unity through action, as did the members of several cultural centres and alternative spaces. In addition, feminist fronts advocating for the right to abortion, animal rights groups, football supporters, cyclists and those seeking the legalization of marijuana were also actors in the October struggle. This led to the coexistence of diverse narratives, captured in graffiti on city walls. Some had more political elaboration, such as: 'Capital, surplus value, die with the bourgeoisie'; others economic: 'Down with the *paquetazo*', and there were even those who trivialised the representative political system: 'Great shit to be President [of the Republic]'.

3.5 RANGE OF PEASANT AND INDIGENOUS ORGANIZATIONS

Despite difficulties, the Ecuadorean Federation of Evangelical Indigenous People (FEINE), the Ecuadorean Federation of Indigenous and Black Peasant Organizations (FENOCIN) and CONAIE forged the most important convergence between peasant and Indigenous organizations. The presence of organizations such as the Union of Peasant Organizations of Cotacachi (UNORCAC), an affiliate of FENOCIN in the Province of Imbabura, contradicted the positions of a sector of its national leadership by militantly joining actions against the government.

In Andino's terms, 'another important factor was the presence of Catholics and Evangelicals marching together [...] from the second day [...] everything was united in a single cry of protest, courage and anger pent up during many years of marginalisation and humiliation' (2020, p. 45). This process has historical antecedents, especially in the 1990s; then, in more recent times, in February 2001 due to the increase in fuel prices and, in 2012, on the occasion of the approval of the agrarian legislation. This link, however, gradually frayed during the periods of Gutiérrez, Correa and Moreno. The distance between these Indigenous and peasant organizations can be explained by the divisive politics of the governments, the electoral party system, the differences in religious identities and the inability to generate solid bridges of unity among the left – because of the strength of the electoral illusion. That is why the reopening of this relationship, in the context of the mobilization, was important.

Mariátegui was convinced that an 'a priori anticlericalism' in the popular camp did not promote the revolutionary organization of society and was sterile and fruitless. It only succeeded in building new dogmas, from a rationalist viewpoint, without understanding the religious context of Latin American society (Mariátegui, 2008, p. 163). Mariátegui focused on the understanding developed by the native peoples of *Abya-Yala*, which constitute cohesive practices and feelings (intimate connection with nature, the sacredness of everyday spaces, symbiosis between political and religious notions, and the use of psychoactive substances in ritual). The relationship developed during October between evangelical and Catholic Indigenous communities should be rethought from a political and anti-capitalist perspective, with the purpose of stimulating the strengthening of organizational structures in both cultural and religious contexts. In the words of Pedro Guasango Morales, Guancavilca leader and evangelical leader of Puerto del Morro, 'there are two sides here: those who are with the landowner and the rich, and those who are with God'.

The politicisation of the religious component, from an emancipatory point of view, is another of the challenges thrown up by October. Ecumenism projected as a dialogue of diverse religious and spiritual perspectives, outside the straitjacket of institutions, puts hegemony under tension and – looking forward – can contribute to breaking the pre-existing divisions of domination, bringing emotionality, pleasure and spirituality closer to the left, and distancing them from the grassroots structures of the right built on reactionary, conservative and fascist narratives.

Correa's influence in the context of the mobilization was peripheral. The former president sought demobilization and division, persisting in his discourse against CONAIE. His marginal role is evidenced in the rejection of the presence of the former president of the Council for Citizen Participation and Social Control (CPCCS) José Carlos Tuárez and the former president of the National Council of Rural Parochial Governments of Ecuador (CONACOPARE) Bolívar Armijos, as well as in the limited mobilization in provinces where they enjoyed electoral support. An apparent strength at the polls is not mechanically transferred to a street fight and, vice versa: the capacity of popular mobilization does not automatically lead to electoral growth. Moreover, there was an absence of Correístas' slogans and symbols in the October demonstrations (Ruiz and García, 2019).

The Citizens' 'Revolution' (CR) operated through the National Citizen Assembly (ANC), a body constituted in January 2019 that brought together organizations and collectives.[23] They carried out some marches in the city of Quito – devoid of CR symbols – towards the Carondelet Palace, which was prevented by the

---

[23] In the peasant sector, the most important organizations are the Confederación Unitaria de Afiliados al Seguro Social Campesino (CONFEUNASSC); the Coordinadora Nacional Campesina 'Eloy Alfaro' (CNC-EA); the Federación de Campesinos y Organizaciones del Litoral (FECAOL); the Unión de Organizaciones Campesinas Beneficiadas por el Plan Tierras and the Confederación Ecuatoriana de Pueblos y Nacionalidades Indígenas (FEI). On the union side are: OSUNTRAMSA, the Network of Teachers for the Educational Revolution and a segment of electrical and oil workers. Some neighbourhood organizations (such as the Colectivo Plaza del Teatro), women's organizations, Christian communities and the remnants of the so-called Comités de Defensa de la Revolución Ciudadana (Committees for the Defense of the Citizen Revolution) promoted in 2012 complete this coordination.

police siege. In Guayas 'a group of demonstrators blocked the National Unity Bridge in the section connecting Durán with Samborondón in protest at the economic measures' (Le Quang, Chávez and Vizuete, 2020, p. 56).

However, they are not homogenous. The Coordinadora de Movimientos Sociales por la Democracia y el Socialismo (CMS-DS), whose main components are the CONFEUNASSC and the CNC-EA – which are part of the ANC – reappeared issuing communiqués critical of corruption and closed ranks with the demands and actions of the strikes (*TVC El Comercio TV*, 2019). This was unlike the FEI, which played a most shameful role. Despite being part of the ANC, it did not join the mobilization even though the government announced the withdrawal of the minimal amount of land awarded to it by the previous government (Pichincha Universal, 2019).[24]

The mapping of peasant actors in the October rebellion would be incomplete without the action developed by the Assembly of the Peoples of the South that activated in the Ecuadorean South together with the Popular Peasant Coordination (CCP). There was also the FEUNASSC,[25] which closed off some areas of the Sierra and the Coast (Miranda, 2019, p. 56).

3.6 INSTITUTIONAL LEFT, LIBERAL PERFORMANCE AND THE SOCIETY OF THE SPECTACLE

When we talk about the institutional 'left' we mean the bureaucratic apparatuses that use leftist rhetoric as a tool for social validation, while following the rules of the game of the electoral party system – under the guise of 'democracy' – and that, consciously or unconsciously, contribute to strengthening the bourgeois order. Characterising them as institutional is indicative of their central link with state institutions, particularly the electoral system, which moulds a normative, legalistic and disciplinary consciousness. The relationship with the electoral party system 'shifted the idea of politics as a revolutionary rupture of history, to that of participation under conditions of legal equality (one citizen, one vote) in the electoral race for government' (Madrid, 2018a, p. 88). To this extent, the institutional left has a liberal interpretation of Marxism (Madrid, 2018a, p. 92). As the militant Fernando Velasco argued:

---

24 Despite the grandiose discourse about redistribution, the handover of state-owned land during the Correa administration was less than 0.01% of Ecuador's agricultural land.

25 Federación Única Nacional de Afiliados al Seguro Social Campesino (Single National Federation of Farmers' Social Security Affiliates).

> The Ecuadorean left has been developing from the second decade of the present century [twentieth century] based on liberal conceptions in many ways. From them it draws not only its tradition of struggle, but also its methodological and analytical frameworks, which were assimilated by the growing movement without benefit of memory and appealing to the baptism of ideological conceptions with Marxist names which, as is obvious, were nothing more than window dressing for bourgeois contents (Velasco 1979, p. 62).

The most important and relevant parties of this current are Pachakutik, then Popular Unity (ex MPD-PCMLE)[26] and, to a much lesser extent, the Socialist Party (PSE-FA);[27] the first case we dealt with earlier, so we will now tackle the smaller then the larger.

The position of the PSE-FA on the events can be explained from the reflections of Enrique Ayala Mora (who ultimately represents the leadership of the party),[28] which came to light through the leaked audio of a meeting.[29] We do not seek to respond to Ayala's position in his scurrilous terms, but to show him as a prototype of the reflection of the leadership of the institutional left.

His analysis of the events lacks a reading in terms of the relation of forces between social classes, the situation of the process of capital accumulation, the racist composition of the state, the place of the conflict within the process of globalization of capitalism, and the possibilities opened up by one of the most important days of mobilization in the history of Ecuador. There is not a single observation that starts from the place of socialism. On the contrary, applying the neologism of leftist jargon, it seems to be the analysis of 'sociologism', in view of its formally socialist position, but based on pragmatism and compromise.

> The time you spend negotiating with the heads [leaders of the Indigenous, social trade union

---

26 Movimiento Popular Democrático, Partido Comunista Marxista Leninista del Ecuador (Popular Democratic Movement, Marxist Leninist Communist Party of Ecuador).

27 Ecuadorean Socialist Party.

28 Enrique Ayala Mora is Ecuador's most respected Marxist historian. He is also the central leader of one of the main factions of the Ecuadorean Socialist Party (PSE), which was one of the main parties of the left in Ecuador from the 1920s, located ideologically somewhere between social democracy and the traditional communist movement.

29 Ayala Mora claims the accuracy of a notarised report of an audio of 01 minute.42 seconds. But, as the same document of Art House Estudio (2019) shows, the complete 44 minutes of material that circulated on social networks was never analysed. Consequently, the shorter version is adulterated.

> movements], the long weekends are useful for dismantling all that [together with the government leadership]. If you negotiate with the two strong ones [CONAIE, FUT], that leaves only the Correístas, whom you can accuse of being criminals.
>
> If the President calls them and tells them that he will repeal the decree tomorrow, they will suspend the strike, but you have to convince certain people, whom the Correístas have already convinced that the President must be overthrown, that this is a victory, you have to retrace that path, you have to talk with the MPD, with Messias [Tatamuez, leader of the FUT trade union], with CONAIE. We have to tell them that the strategic objective is to overthrow the decree. (Transcription of a leaked audio recording of Enrique Ayala Mora, leader of the Ecuadorean Socialist Party, speaking in an internal meeting and apparently outlining advice on how the government of Lenin Moreno should respond to the uprising).

The institutionalist spirit and the ventriloquist aspiration are present throughout this discourse. Behind the language used by Ayala in the audio there is a deep patriarchal streak in his way of conducting things. The insults and the reactionary posture, which pretend to offer salvation in a conflict observed from the distance of the university faculty, are not the only problems. The central issue is the permanence of a 'political' analysis, predominant in the institutional left, and which has not the slightest relation to the study of the unity of multiple factors which is the method of the left.

> Do not negotiate anything, do not give anything for free, because they will only ask for more [...] Every measure has to be negotiated, If the President announces now, for example, that he will suspend the measures or repeal the decree, tomorrow they will ask for his resignation. On the other hand, if he speaks in front of the press, they will be an ally; they do not want to overthrow the President [...]. What the President has to do is to call them for talks, while I can work to get them to go to dialogue. (Transcription of a leaked audio recording of Enrique Ayala Mora, leader of the Ecuadorean

Socialist Party, speaking in an internal meeting and apparently outlining advice on how the government of Lenin Moreno should respond to the uprising).

In the case of UP-PCMLE there is a similar story, but with a greater capacity for manoeuvre and mobilization. The UGTE, which is under their influence and control, did not put pressure on the FUT to call for a national strike.

We conclude that the delay in a combative response to the government was due to the fact that some of its members have connections in government. It was probably influenced by the fact that the legal status, assets and financial resources of the National Union of Educators (UNE), also controlled by the UP-PCMLE, had been restored.[30]

The mobilization of the student sectors they control was also limited and was less well supported than the mobilization generated by other youth organizations – such as the Community, Indigenous and Popular Guard or the youth cultural collectives – since they lack standing in this community or the capacity to organize because of their own errors. Thus, the participation of this party in the mobilization was reduced to handshakes, press conferences and – most significantly – the participation of courageous grassroots militants in the streets.

Two examples will suffice. During the funeral of the hero Inocencio Tucumbi, its leaders suddenly moved to the front of the funeral; they chanted slogans, carried party banners, and delivered a wreath before the gathering. It was simply self-promotion. In the same way, it is common to find the most humble of their militants carrying a flag during press conferences or protest actions; although their mobilization capacity does not correspond to the number of banners they bring to these events.

The second case was the placement of the *wipala*, the flag of Ecuador and the red flag – the symbols of that party after the reform of its statutes at its VIII Congress – in some public space, as well as other propaganda actions. All of these were an attempt to position its image in order to present itself as a revolutionary, that is to say, a non-institutional force. The refusal to call for more combative acts of struggle – despite having trade union structures that could have contributed – and the insistence on giving prominence to media actions that made its party structure visible, are manifestations of Guy Debord's concept

30 There is a contrast. In the case of CONAIE, after the 2015 strike when there was an attempt to evict them from their headquarters, there was a process of legitimate resistance and defence to keep the space, despite the fact that they do not own the property. The pressure generated massive national and international solidarity.

of 'society of the spectacle', which is the imitation of objective reality through images emptied of content that influence the relationship between people. The problem is that the left is supposed to seek the transformation of this type of alienated human relations, and not their reproduction.

3.7 THE RULING CLASSES: A SICK, DEFEATED LINEAGE

The initiative gives people the capacity to design and steer political phenomena. This is what the ruling classes lost during the October rebellion. They limited themselves to: 1) pressuring for mediation, through the group of mayors of the Association of Municipalities of Ecuador (AME); 2) issuing statements, as did some legislative bodies, as well as the OAS, UN, the Church and other institutions that offered to mediate in the dialogue; 3) intervening in the media, with the intention of supporting Moreno and disqualifying the strike, as did the representatives of the Chambers; 4) the sit-ins carried out (8 and 9 October) in the Shyris tribune in Quito, under the slogan: 'Against violence not one step back, all for peace';[31] 5) the 9 October march in Guayaquil that did not cover more than three blocks,[32] and 6) the blockade of the accesses to this city with municipal machinery.

Paradoxically, the state of emergency was flouted by its very proponents. Jaime Nebot Saadi, together with various business sectors supporting the increase in fuel prices, called for a counter-march, obstructing the free movement of citizens. The Social-Christian leader expressed his warmongering position on 9 October, the day of the protest, 'sometimes you have to make war to achieve peace. And I repeat it today. Peace is not achieved by calling for it, nor is it won by holding marches to beg for peace, it is won by doing things and having attitudes that can achieve peace and if one of those is war, war must be waged' (Nebot, 2019b). However, it was evident that the support for the Social-Christian rally was limited and that, although the party enjoys strength, it does not have sufficient capacity to carry out a massive march in a short time.

The state learned lessons from the cycle of the fall of presidents of the Republic (1996–2007). On this occasion it decided to evacuate the Carondelet Palace in Quito before the arrival of demonstrators, and barricaded the government headquarters in

---

31 Among other things, on the second day of the sit-in 'For Peace' in the Shyris Tribune, the former President of the PRE, Rosalía Arteaga, dismissed in the midst of the accusations of the National Congress against her partner Abdalá Bucaram for corruption, intervened.

32 The low turnout for the march happened despite the fact that, for example, people from Guayaquil's markets were forced to go by the city council (Jairala, 2019), as has been reported on other occasions.

Guayaquil to ensure the protection of the ruling classes of the coast, whose representatives shouted: 'Democracy will not fall in the streets of Guayaquil' (Cynthia Viteri, Mayor of Guayaquil, on TVC *El Comercio TV*, 2019); 'We will defend the freedom of the 24 provinces of Ecuador from here' (Jaime Nebot on TVC *El Comercio TV*, 2019).

The flight of the Executive raised the question 'Where is the President? We don't know where he is' (Jairala, 2019). The institutional capacity of the State to manoeuvre was annulled. The National Assembly, which ceased to be in session eleven days earlier, limited itself to issuing official letters to call for dialogue, and then issued a report whose conclusion was the need to investigate the facts. The crisis was resolved outside the Assembly, which only managed to meet on 16 October. Several of the country's municipalities decided not to pay for the increase in urban transport fares and handed over the responsibility to the central government.

In the first four days of the mobilization, the political calculation led the Democratic Left (ID), the Democratic Centre (CD) and the Social-Christian Party (PSC) to criticize the government's package. However, as events unfolded, the first party to align itself with the escalating repression was Creando Oportunidades (CREO), despite initially expressing 'understanding' towards the poor, solidarity with Quito and even disagreeing with mining (Guillermo Lasso, FM *Mundo*, 2019). Then the discourse of the 'defence of democracy' was raised by Fuerza Ecuador (ex-PRE) and the PSC, parties that requested an iron fist against the 'attempted coup d'état', as mentioned by the Social-Christian assemblyman Henry Kronfle.

At the other extreme, the 'Citizens' Revolution' called for the fall of Moreno by constitutional means, Juntos Podemos called for the construction of a 'coalition government', and the Mayor of Quito – formally neutral – morally supported the refugee centres.[33] The debate between the institutionalist factions was used as a way to try to solve an organic crisis. Hence, the accusation of an attempted coup d'état is untenable, because for this to happen there must be an actor who claims the government for themselves, as happened in November 2019 with Jeanine Añez, Carlos Mesa and Luis Camacho in Bolivia.

The slogan: 'Out Moreno, out!' was part of the popular repertoire, as a result of the legacy of questioning institutionalism

---

[33] On 9 October the Mayor of Quito obtained the support of 50 institutions and 1,500 signatures of personalities for the declaration of the refugee centres as a peace zone.

that has antecedents in 'Out Correa, out', or the destructive 'Everybody out!' In spite of everything, it was far from being a plan to seize power; and the government – the usual aspiration of the institutional left. This common mistake of the left is exposed, in a self-critical manner, in the section on the three most important difficulties of rebel October.

Therefore, Lourdes Tibán's hypothesis regarding an alleged manipulation by Correism in October is absurd (Machado, 2019), since it objectifies sectors that were part of the mobilization, which, on the contrary, made their own destiny. Under Correa, any autonomous popular struggle was labelled a 'plot promoted by imperialism'; for the Moreno government, while according to both the institutionalist right and left, it is a 'strategy that plays into Correa's hands'. It was the same reductionism in different periods.

It is worth pointing out that Correa's arrival in government was a historical defeat; he did not manage to channel the capacity for struggle of the popular camp, gained in the confrontation with neoliberal capitalism, towards the construction of a strategy that could challenge actually existing power. On the contrary, it dissolved in the '21st century illusion'. Using leftist language, it pushed for the reassembly of the nation-state via constitutional reform, remaining subservient to the interests of the reproduction of capital, albeit with redistributive and welfare nuances.

The autonomous organizations and anti-capitalist tendencies confronted the model of the bureaucratic bourgeoisie of Correa through mobilizations, just as we are now opposing the project of the comprador bourgeoisie of his former friend Moreno. Both yesterday and today, this has meant persecution, imprisonment and assassinations. The attacks on the popular camp and the defence of bourgeois democracy were ratified by Correa after the strike, from his home in Brussels:

> They don't convince me that they are also leftists. Being progressive is not only ideology, it is principles, values, and those people who sold themselves to the highest bidder – Jaime Vargas – deceived their own people because he gave Moreno a life raft. He thinks he is emperor in those territories, contradicting everything they say elsewhere. What they do with their hands they erase with their elbow, for example, this economic plan they have presented. They want to apply their

economic plan, so let them win elections, we are in a democracy. With those people it is impossible to go anywhere (Correa, 2019a) [Emphasis added].

The Portuguese writer José Saramago said that real power is economic and it makes no sense to talk about democracy. This reflection does not exist in the institutionalist way of looking at things. Rather it reduces the concept of 'democracy' to the vote and the party system, ignoring its restrictive character in a society marked by the existence of social classes. The traditional Latin American slogan: 'Our dreams are not enough at the ballot box', is alien to Correism and to the various fractions of the neoliberal and statist right wing that lost support in the context of October.[34] The rebellion advanced against the will of the dominant classes, which reacted with hatred and racism, typical of a defeated lineage.

If love is a pendulum between death and death that reveals the courage of the human spirit, the advance of hatred strips opaque souls bare. The bourgeois intelligentsia presented itself with first and last name,[35] with the futile aspiration of stigmatizing one of the most resounding events in the history of Ecuador.

4   THE STATE: FROM CONSENSUAL NETWORK TO COERCIVE MACHINE

October produced a conjunctural crisis that challenged the assumptions of domination in Ecuador. The collapse had been brewing due to the combination of the economic crisis – whose most dramatic expression was the collapse of commodity prices – the progressive deterioration of legality in state institutions, and the constant popular struggle, which grew with the increasing discontent with the impoverishment and dispossession of different sectors.

In this interpretation we will use Gramscian concepts: hegemony and crisis. Hegemony, following Gramsci (1975), makes it possible to universalize the particular interest of the dominant classes towards the lower strata as a whole, through the active consent of the dominated themselves, which is achieved through culture, ideology and common sense, without

---

34   For sample, 'those who obtained particularly negative ratings are mainly the Correa assemblies and the 'Correístas' with 88.8% (31.5% bad and 57.3% very bad) followed by Rafael Correa with 85% bad/very bad rating (33.5% and 51.4% respectively)' (CEDATOS, 2019).

35   The following stand out: Andersson Boscán and Eduardo Vivanco (*La Posta*), Roberto Aguilar (*El Expresso*), Fausto Cobo (PSP), Mario Pazmiño (former SENAIN), Jaime Nebot, Cinthya Viteri and César Ron (PSC), Martín Pallares (4 Pelagatos), Fidel Egas (owner of Banco del Pichincha), Alberto Dahik (former vice president, fugitive from justice for corruption), Fabricio Villamar (CREO).

the direct and visible intervention of coercion in normal circumstances. This scheme of domination is possible as long as there are minimal conditions to satisfy the basic needs of the population. Hegemony is feasible in specific periods such as in Ecuador, recently, during the second oil boom. However, if compliance cannot be achieved through consensus, force is unleashed, as happened in October.

The October rebellion revealed one of the conditions for the crisis of hegemony: that the subordinated become conscious of their condition and are in a position to confront it. However, the second condition for the worsening of the crisis was not fulfilled: namely the dissolution of the historic power bloc and its loss of the leadership of society, as a consequence among other things of the fracturing of the ruling class. In October, on the contrary, those forces, including the armed forces, supported the President. The ruling classes were was not in a situation of weakness and the crisis did not provoke a revolutionary situation, despite the fact that the elites lost the consent of the subalterns.

The successful hegemonic project of the ruling classes, in the context of the second oil boom, reached its watershed after 2014, a period in which, as we reviewed in Chapter One, the decline of the economic bonanza and of political stability converged. Prior to the unleashing of the rebellion, the cultural project of the elites was questioned from various social spaces, criticisms that constituted one of the reasons for the advocacy of united action, which was synthesised in the programme of 'The Programme of Escalating Struggle'.

The warning about the 'advance of a reactionary bourgeois culture (common sense)' was clear. Its demands can be summarized in the following points:

- The use of slogans against poor migrants, criminalizing the presence of foreigners, especially Venezuelans.
- The organization of demonstrations around conservative demands: such as so-called 'pro-life' led by the Church, 'white' marches against violence, 'Don't mess with my children' parades, and marches called by Christian Socialists.
- Campaigns to discredit communism, confusing it with regulatory state intervention.
- Popularizing talk of 'law and order' to increase the presence of police repression and leave unresolved the country's serious social and economic situation.

- Criminalization, misrepresentation and vicious attacks on the agenda of women's struggles, especially those of the popular sector, in relation to their fundamental rights on issues such as abortion in the case of rape, femicide and, in general, the struggle against patriarchal capitalism (See Appendix).

The effectiveness of the devices that reproduce hegemony diminishes when the crisis becomes dynamic and discontent is transformed into direct and autonomous action by the masses. In October, the deterioration of hegemony produced a situation where the devices of coercion and the administration of violence were strengthened and consolidated, acting where hegemony lost control.

However, the strengthening of the repressive dimension does not always prevent the erosion of consensus; there may even be a strengthening of authoritarian beliefs that validate authoritarian processes.[36] According to the Bolivian Marxist René Zavaleta (2013), negative hegemony implies an enforced construction of beliefs where the coercive has more and more relevance. Although hegemony still exists, it is very weak. Zavaleta also speaks of negative stability, insofar as a political regime is maintained without the widespread consent of the population, coercive systems expand and ideology withdraws, although it does not disappear. Some clear examples of this tension, in which some ideological devices lose effectiveness and others are strengthened, are the 'Venezuelanization' of the employment problem; another when patriarchal practices allow cohesion to be broken from below. Also in this category are the efforts to reintroduce, within the dynamics of popular struggle, an appeal to institutionalization as a mechanism for conflict resolution.

However, given the majority support for the uprising, and the rejection by the popular sectors of the manoeuvres of the powerful to restore their rate of profit, the coercive state machinery underwent an accelerated process of reconstruction, which was strategically conducted to confront the rebellion, as part of a movement to unify the state as a whole.

The repressive strategy had two moments; the first (from 3–9 October) through the criminalization of politics; arbitrary

---

36   As in the case of Colombia, where there is a bureaucratic-military repressive apparatus that is an expression of class domination, with relative support from the popular sectors that allows the state to act with greater impunity.

and illegal arrests were made of more than a thousand demonstrators, most of whom were released after 24 hours. In the second (9–13 October), the number of detainees flattened out, but the number of injured and the number of extrajudicial executions increased dramatically. Logically, this change in strategic disposition allowed the state to tip the balance.

The following section will analyse the strengthening of the chain of command and the application of the concept of total war; the aggravated use of force; the re-equipment and modernization of operational methods; the increase in income and other benefits for commanders and troops; and the frequent use of states of emergency.

4.1 STRENGTHENING THE CHAIN OF COMMAND AND THE CONCEPTION OF TOTAL WARFARE

For classical war theorists, discipline and morale are essential to military logic. Discipline is based on a hierarchical relationship between commander and subordinates, and is based on obedience, not deliberation. For the modern army there is no discipline if the hierarchical structure is called into question. In presidential republics such as Ecuador, the President of the Republic (Commander in Chief) is the pinnacle of the pinnacle, and is in a close relationship with the Joint Command of the Armed Forces; in practice, they direct the Command Headquarters.

Since the return to the party system in 1978, the relationship between formal and practical command has gone through ups and downs. In periods of social unrest, the armed forces and police have been forced to re-establish the terms of the bourgeois social contract, to participate in the overthrow of some presidents, or to rebel against policies contrary to the interests of their commanders (Vargas Pazzos) and the troops (30s)[37]. Similarly, when there have been tensions between officers and representatives of political power, the former have been removed from their posts. This scenario did not occur during the October rebellion, apart from the fact that, a few days after the end of the outbreak, Roque Moreira and Javier Perez[38] were removed from their positions by the government; the bulk of the officers aligned themselves with Lenin Moreno. This situation is evidence of the improvement in discipline achieved in recent years.

On the other hand, morale is vital for the strengthening of the chain of command and fighting capacity; Napoleon said that

---

[37] 30s is the name given in Ecuador to a police revolt against President Rafael Correa on 30 September, 2010.

[38] Former Chief of the Joint Command of the Armed Forces and General of the Army, respectively.

it comprised three quarters of an army. The ideas of 'patriotism' and 'commitment to the institution' are fundamental elements from which the military term *esprit de corps* derives. During the rebellion, videos circulated on social networks reflecting military rhetoric – as when the commanders exhorted their troops during some clashes with pickets on the Pan-American Highway – or collective prayers; their objective was to increase the morale of their subordinates. The tributes paid by the government to the national police and the armed forces were filmed by the Secretariat of Communication. They turned out to be a propaganda operation, in the tone of a victim.

Discipline and morale, typical of modern armies, were central to the total war strategy orchestrated by the Minister of Defence, Osvaldo Jarrín.[39] The political, financial, psychological, institutional and constitutional resources of the state and the elites were subordinated to the military order. For example, smear campaigns were mounted branding the demonstrators as terrorists, saboteurs or insurgents; the demonstrators' sense of terror in the face of repression was generalised; there were acts of public humiliation; arrested people were taken to unauthorized places, such as in the Command of the Intervention and Rescue Group (GIR) in Pomasqui;[40] representatives of social organizations, including Jorge Calderón (FEDOTAXIS),[41] Marlon Vargas (CONFENIAE) or Paola Pabón (*Revolución Ciudadana*), were surgically arrested with the complicity of the judiciary. The government headquarters were moved to Guayaquil, following the suggestions of military intelligence; a media siege was orchestrated by agreement between private and public media companies; access to information from the public health system was limited and the medical reports on the wounded and deceased were altered; and extrajudicial executions were carried out. These actions were part of a mixed strategy of psychological

[39] Jarrín's arrival as Minister of Defence marks the return of military relations with the US after 12 years, the reintegration into Southern Command exercises and the training of Ecuadorean special forces in Israel (Ramos, 2019).

[40] On 7 and 8 October journalists alerted a group of human rights lawyers that police had detained and taken 83 protesters from the National Assembly building. One of the lawyers told Human Rights Watch that they went to look for the detained protesters at several police units in Quito, where they routinely take people who are detained. Their whereabouts only became known on 9 October, when the lawyers learned that they were at the headquarters of the National Police's Intervention and Rescue Group (GIR) (HRW, 2020).

[41] President of the National Federation of Taxi Transport Operators of Ecuador. In addition 'the secretary general of the Azuay Drivers Union and the president of the Cuenca Chamber of Transport were arrested' (Le Quang, Chávez and Vizuete, 2020, pp. 59–60).

warfare, political persecution and state terrorism, which was applied to undermine the popular will to resist in the streets. The criminalization of protest initiated in Ecuador by previous governments was used by Moreno's government.

> The use of the law and the entire legal apparatus of the state to annihilate its political adversary [...] a method of unconventional warfare by which the law is used as a means to achieve a military objective. The success of the mechanism lies in its ability to use the legitimacy of the justice system and a discourse promoted by the media that justifies the legal annihilation of those already condemned by the media (Guamán, 2020, p. 157).

To reinforce some things, we have already pointed out, let us look at the withholding of information in hospitals. According to *Plan V* digital magazine (2019), in Legal Medicine of the Eugenio Espejo and Carlos Andrade Marín hospitals 'there was a great reluctance to give information', 'the silence from the Ministry of Health has been implacable', a view corroborated by other international media (GK, 2019), human rights organizations (Alianza de Organizaciones por los Derechos Humanos, 2019, p. 79) and by the injured themselves and their families, who complained that they had not received medico-legal reports, given that there were serious suspicions that the deaths were extrajudicial executions committed by the police (Luis Tipantuña and Jhajaira Urresta in *El Comercio*, 2019).

> Official statistics indicate that there were a total of 1,507 patients treated in the public health system for injuries during the protests. The ombudsman's office told Human Rights Watch that the number of people injured was higher and that at least some injuries had not been properly recorded. Several witnesses reported irregularities to the ombudsman's office, including cases in which health personnel changed data on emergency admission forms to conceal that these were injuries caused in the protests [HRW, 2020].

The concealment of information was also practised by public and private media, which are subservient to government; as analysed by the *Colectivo de Geografía Crítica del Ecuador* (2019), the operations of repressive forces against the protesters were timed until after the evening edition was published, thus avoiding coverage.

> [One could hear] in El Arbolito and other humanitarian peace zones [...] the constant sound of tear gas bombs, which was maintained, at least, in Quito, during the five days of the Indigenous uprising and at almost defined times (at noon and from 17h00, approximately) (Alianza de Organizaciones por los Derechos Humanos, 2019, p. 67).

4.2 AGGRAVATED USE OF FORCE

According to CONAIE, the repressive escalation left a toll of 11 dead, 1,700 injured, 1,250 detained and hundreds persecuted, 90% of whom were arbitrarily and illegally detained. This took place in the midst of a general context of militarization, police abuse, loss of civil and collective rights, aggression against journalists, fake ceasefires truces, house raids, prosecution of leaders and a policy of criminalization of social organizations.

> The Attorney General's office is currently investigating 9 of the 11 deaths. The ombudsman's office told Human Rights Watch that at least four of the deaths were allegedly caused by excessive use of force by the police. While authorities counted 1,507 people injured, the ombudsman's office indicated that not all cases were recorded, so the total is likely higher (HRW, 2020).

The National Assembly's own report (2019) on the events of October acknowledges that 1,508 people were treated in the public health system, 71% in the province of Pichincha and almost 80% if Azuay is included. In addition to these cases, medical brigades of the Pontificia Universidad Católica del Ecuador provided medical care to 1,249, 'most of them [...] due to complications from tear gas'; those carried out by volunteers from the Central University of Ecuador, 747 attended by the Ecuadorean Red Cross (48% in Pichincha and Azuay), and the 4,050 treated by the Socorristas de Paz 'in the so-called 'ground zero' for asphyxia, dehydration, blows, broken heads, burns' (Asamblea Nacional, 2019, pp. 108–109). The rescuers' account alone is enlightening:

On 11 October, the day on which Mr Toroche lost his left eye due to the impact of a teargas bomb in his face, he was coordinating the paediatric and psychology brigades to provide recreational spaces for children, as well as nursing mothers, inside the El Arbolito park. But at that moment a crowd of people began to arrive and run towards El Arbolito, to the grassy area, everyone on the ground, we and the brigades were running from one side to the other. There was a lot of blood on the grass, blood on the sidewalks from injured people. We had to improvise sheets to move injured people, because we no longer had boards and we proceeded to move them on the sheets to the tents; there were about 4 brigades inside the Arbolito. Within 15 minutes we had about 70 medical cases. (National Assembly, 2019, pp. 75–76)

Regarding the types of injuries he mentions 23 patients with various contusions: to thighs, knees, eyeballs, legs, thorax, ankle, wrists. 27 patients with fractures: nose, skull, ribs, legs, lower jaw, upper jaw, teeth, patella and tibia. There were 43 patients with injuries to scalp, thigh, knee, head, neck, thorax, abdomen, ear, shoulder, arm, eyeballs and legs. They dealt with 24 cases of trauma, contusions or penetrating injuries to the eyes, according to information reported specifically by the Eugenio Espejo hospital. 1 person with second and third degree burns was discharged from the ICU of the Andrade Marin Hospital. 2 people underwent neurosurgery for projectile impact to the thorax.

In terms of permanent injuries, there are a total of 11 people who have lost an eye, 1 person who lost 90% of visibility in one eye and completely lost the other eye, and 1 person who is deaf because he was apparently hit in one ear by a tear gas bomb (National Assembly, 2019, p. 61).

The quantitative assessment alone is not enough to measure the magnitude of the attack. The testimonies of victims also provide a picture of the seriousness of the police action:

> My name is Héctor Cañar. I am 26 years old. I am a technologist and was working as an electrical technician …

I was wearing a motorcycle helmet. I didn't see what they shot me with. The helmet protected me. But in less than two minutes I was wounded by metal pellets. The shot was at close range. I felt the impact in my chest. At first I thought it was a tear gas bomb. I stepped back and began to lose consciousness. I lifted up my shirt and saw blood gushing out. 'They hit him, they hit him,' my comrades shouted. I walked a few metres and fell. I couldn't speak. I felt short of breath, I felt like I was drowning. They covered me with shields. My girlfriend called the paramedics and they were the ones who gave me first aid.

I went in as an emergency. The chest specialist came down and said my condition was critical. The pellet that hit me had a diameter of 4 cm and a depth of 1.5 cm. I was hooked up to machines and given oxygen. They put a drain in my right side to drain the blood that was accumulating in my lung. They gave me pints of blood. They sutured my wound without removing the pellet. The cartridge exploded inside me and the pellets spread in my right lung. I was operated on Tuesday 22nd. They could not remove all the pellets from me. They left me 8 which did not compromise the lung. They also removed the cartridge I had in my chest. They are still evaluating my lung. They discovered that I have a haematoma. I don't know if they removed part of my lung or if it is all there.

I was hospitalized for 28 days. I left on Monday when the IACHR delegation arrived. I could not go to give my testimony. I have been off sick from work. I estimate that I will be able to work in about three months. I have no medical insurance. The repression was very strong. Just using tear gas bombs was enough to disperse us. I expect the state to tell the truth, to speak clearly and assume their responsibilities. The government says that they have not admitted people injured by firearms to hospital. But I am a real case. They were effectively shooting to kill. They treated me like a terrorist, because criminals at least are given the option to raise their hands or get down on the ground. In my case they were shooting to kill (*Plan V,* 2019).

The repressive forces definitely have impunity because 'those who investigate are police officers, officers who may or may not have been involved in these very events, '(National Assembly, 2019, p. 72). Even Human Rights Watch states:

> A reliable source, who asked to remain anonymous, told Human Rights Watch that results have been limited and that investigations of abuses linked to the protests have been hampered by a lack of cooperation among government agencies involved, such as the police, the Ministry of Government, and the security forces. The source argued that asking the National Police to investigate events involving police officers was in itself a conflict of interest (HRW, 2020).

The government justified the police actions through a variety of rhetorical arguments. The Minister of Government, María Paula Romo, went so far as to state that the protesters knew they were at risk and that officers were also injured (*El Comercio*, 2019). Reports from the Inter-American Commission on Human Rights (IACHR) and humanitarian organizations (Alianza de Organizaciones por los Derechos Humanos, 2019) agreed with CONAIE about the disproportionate use of force by the state. Despite this, President Lenin Moreno considered them biased. All in all, not even the National Assembly has managed to hide the overwhelming inequality of figures presented by both sides: no police or military personnel died and only one policeman suffered an eye injury (Asamblea Nacional, 2019, p. 126) while there are at least eleven extrajudicial executions, dozens of permanent eye mutilations and thousands of injured protesters.

This leads to two observations. First, the repressive apparatus increased its capacity to attack the people. Terror became the mechanism used by the state to try to maintain order by intensifying violence. Second, the balance of the wounded and dead on each side is dissimilar: the state's version is far from reality; it states that the deaths occurred outside the protest, and that the repressive forces complied with the law. Such nonsense only reinforces the certainty that, in the face of the state and the interests of the ruling classes, we are being divided by the material form of reproduction of life, and also by the interpretation of it.

4.3 RE-EQUIPMENT AND OPERATIONAL MODERNIZATION

During the October rebellion, the government used a wide range of weapons and anti-riot tactics to contain the popular forces, as part of a total war strategy. During the Correa administration, several changes were promoted through the Ministry of the Interior, many intended to 'humanize' the repressive system. For example, 'friendly' slogans were placed on the shields of the National Police, human rights courses were given, the strategy of hand-to-hand combat was applied, motorcycles, horses and dogs were deployed to demobilize demonstrators, among other dissuasive tactics that tried to project a benevolent image, despite the existence of extrajudicial executions, such as those of José Tendetza, Bosco Wisum, Freddy Taish or Iván Muela.

During the events of October the police and the army used a large number of tear gas bombs; 'in several cases, according to witnesses and the ombudsman's office, the police fired tear gas at demonstrators from very close range' (HRW, 2020). The Minister of Government, María Paula Romo, admitted they used 'bombs that were out of date' (Pichincha Universal, 2019), 'so that their chemical composition can be unstable and are more likely to cause suffocation' (HRW, 2020). In addition, stun bombs, pepper spray, rubber bullets and blanks, horses and police dogs, anti-riot units and armoured tanks were used; weapons such as 12 mm calibre Mossberg shotguns were also included.

In recent years investment in the armed forces has increased fivefold. It went from 307.31 million USD from 2000–2006, to 1,718.86 million USD from 2007–2014 (Ordóñez, 2016, p. 68). This exponential growth is related to a change in the approach, which 'defines a new area of coordination of state security around the Council of Public and State Security (COSEPE)' (Pontón and Rivera, 2016, p. 223); at the same time it required a process of institutional reengineering, and the mainstreaming of repression across society as a whole.

The number of troops also increased. In the case of the army, reservists increased by 20% during the period 2003–2016 (Cedeño, 2018), a striking situation due to the fact that there were no open armed confrontations or underground conflicts with any neighbouring country. The number of police officers increased from 38,472 in 2009, to 57,000 in 2017 (Pontón and Rivera, 2016, p. 234), an increase of 48.16%. Paradoxically this expansion of the state has not been contested by the 'anti-statist' ruling classes, despite the fact that they put forward the doctrine of reducing fiscal expenditure.

The inclusion of more sophisticated operational methods, the economic investment and the official number of officers in the protests – in addition to those who infiltrated the demonstrations – accounts for the warlike situation to which the majority of the Ecuadorean people were subjected in October: '13,658 police: Guayas 1,640; Azuay 600; Pichincha 2,278; plus 36,530 preventive and operational support police' (National Assembly, 2019, p. 68, p. 147). Beyond the debate on weapons, economic investment and the number of troops, the result of the re-equipment and operational modernization is seen through the unlawful killings carried out, directly or indirectly, by the state.

4.4 IMPROVING THE PAY OF OFFICERS AND LOWER RANKS

If the state learned anything from 30 September 2010 (30s), it is that reducing the spending power of members of the police can generate disaffection in the armed forces towards the government. The October 2019 package did not affect the interests of the security forces; the obligation to deliver one day's salary per month was waived and their holidays were not halved, as happened to other public sector workers. After that, the position of law enforcement was never touched.

Since 2006 the salary of the national police has significantly increased. In 2014 the income of the lowest rank reached $1,020 (second corporal), and that of second lieutenant $1,462 (Pontón and Rivera, 2016, p. 244). The first case is equivalent to more than double the salary of a factory worker, and exceeds the cost of the basic family basket, a 'luxury' that most of the Ecuadorean working class lacks.

At the same time, the police enjoy a greater margin of autonomy: 'A special feature [of the national police] is that, despite being attached to the Ministry of Government, it had legal status and administrative and financial autonomy [...]' (Espinel, 2015, p. 30). This regime provides institutional shielding and prevents it from being supervised in the same way as other state agencies. After 2006 defence spending began to be audited, not as a daily and transparent activity, but only when there were allegations of negligence in the accounts, such as weapons overpriced or in poor condition (Romero, 2010).

In the case of the armed forces, their benefits increased due to their relationship with productive and financial capital, particularly Holding Dine SA, which is among the 12 strongest companies in Ecuador. As Romero points out, from the mid-1970s until 2008, the military and enterprises were promoted and legalized as public companies (Romero, 2010). The armed forces wield both military and economic power; several of the senior commanders are both officers and members of the bourgeoisie at the same time.

The increase in economic benefits for the armed forces is complemented by the creation of a democratic institutional image, respectful of human rights, in an attempt to overcome the negative perception of the population. The New Internal and External Security Agenda, developed in 2002, put forward new arguments to justify public security interventions: 'The new approach is based on a reformulated vision of 'security, sovereignty and democracy', articulated within a comprehensive pro-human rights perspective' (Romero, 2010, p. 23). At the same time it seeks an alignment with the 'hemispheric security promoted by the OAS [and] the strategy of foresight, prevention and provision of resources, in order to avoid or neutralize the emergence or expansion of conflicts' (Romero, 2010, p. 38). This opens the option of 'preventive' police intervention and allows for an increase in the budget for operational activities, considering that the margin of resources allocated to spending on personnel in the armed forces is 81%. As detailed below, during periods of popular mobilization it is clear that the untainted image of the 'forces of order' is illusory.

4.5 THE STATE OF EMERGENCY: MORE FREQUENT AND HABITUAL THAN EXCEPTIONAL

The state of emergency (Decree No. 884) issued a few hours after the *paquetazo* (Decree No. 883) – which triggered the uprising – should not be read as a desperate measure or as an alibi for repression but as a decision that demonstrated the character of the state as a formation that (re)produces domination. According to the father of contemporary constitutionalism, Carl Schmitt, the exception is the very nature of the state and is evident when the law ceases to be functional for the survival of order (Schmitt, 2014). By virtue of this, the state of emergency and democracy are separated by only a thin line that can be broken in order for the former to assume monopolistic sovereignty, understood as the ability to make the ultimate decision on behalf of society as a whole (Schmitt, 2009).

In the legal sense, the state of emergency is the power of the President of the Republic, in the name of reasons of state, to limit the civil rights of modern democratic systems: freedom of association and thought, freedom of the press, inviolability of the home, among others. In this regard, the formulation of the Minister of Defence, Oswaldo Jarrín, regarding Decree No. 884 becomes eloquent: 'A state of emergency is established when the social order or the legal order that the state has are not sufficient to control, to prevent the increase of threats that arise' (*Teleamazonas*, 2019).

In response, national and international organizations stated that the decree violated and disregarded protocols. For example, the national police abuse of supposedly 'non-lethal' weapons was 'an excess that would have caused some people to lose eyes or be in danger of dying' (GK, 2019). An account that is in line with the approach of the ombudsman's office, in questioning the integrity with which the officers handled themselves, reports: 'I can confirm that it is clear that on some occasions the National Police used excessive force' (Morán, 2019). One can also add the allegations made around the unregulated use of weapons, which caused some demonstrators to lose their eyes, given that tear gas bombs were fired in the face from close range – as in the cases of Jhajaira Urresta or Luis Tipantuña – or the illegal detention of 71 demonstrators after the symbolic seizure of the National Assembly, who were transferred to the facilities of the elite group of the national police GIR of Pomasqui, and not to the police stations. (*TVC El Comercio TV*, 2019).

It is necessary to make a critical reading of the 'excessive use of force' – which emerges from a normative humanism – in order to expose the core of democratic legitimization. The state of emergency runs counter to the elementary freedom of liberal society, but at the same time it is an ace up the sleeve that liberalism itself has at its disposal, for maintaining the order of bourgeois society. Liberal democracies are willing – if necessary – to sacrifice themselves to guarantee their power and prevent sovereignty from being transferred to the people, a fact that was admitted by the liberal María Paula Romo: 'the state is empowered to use force' (Romo, 2019; *El Comercio*, 2019); its 'excess' is a prerogative in the regular dynamics of its functioning. Therefore, the state of emergency coexists with the rule of law, a link made possible due to the development of the state machine.

Graph 9: Number of people injured and detained during the demonstrations
Dark line; numbers injured. Light line; numbers detained

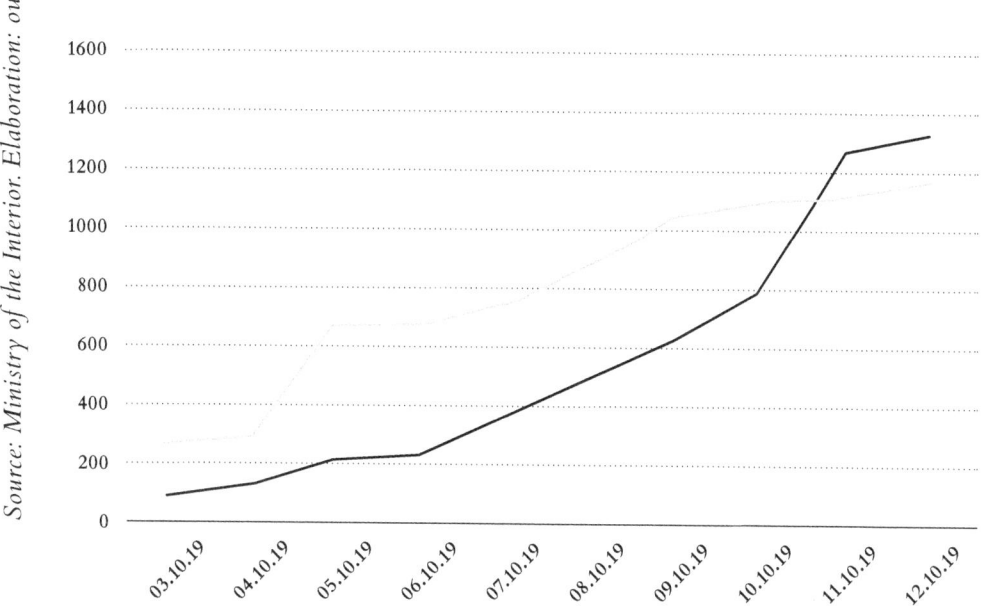

Statistics make it possible to appreciate the true purpose of the state of emergency, if one analyses the escalation of arrests over the course of the days. From 3–13 October detentions increased by 305.43%, which is equivalent to one person every 20 minutes. Decree No. 884 was not intended as a tool of deterrence, but as an operation to criminalize social protest: state terrorism.

Two moments of the repressive strategy stand out. The first, from 3–9 October, when the criminalization of politics – not the electoral game as happened in the post-rebellion moment – was the central instrument to combat the popular initiative. Most of those arrested were arbitrarily and illegally detained, which is why they were released after 24 hours. Of those finally prosecuted, most were concentrated in Guayas, accused of common crimes such as theft, attempted robbery and possession of weapons. Political charges followed, such as paralysing public services, terrorism, illicit association, attack and resistance, damage to the property of others, failure to comply with a decision of authority, incitement to rebellion and assault (Borja, 2019a; Alianza de Organizaciones por los Derechos Humanos, 2019, pp. 30–33).

Table 3: Criminalization of Social Protest

Alleged offense	Reported	Status of the process
Shutdown of a public service	8 people, including the Prefect of Sucumbíos	Sentence between 4 months and 1 year 4 months each, and fine of US$6,000 per person.
Formation of subversive groups	Leaders of different Indigenous organizations	Previous investigation
Instigation	Indigenous leaders	Previous investigation 14 proceedings 3 suspects
Shutdown of public services	Cab driver leader	Prosecutorial Instruction 75 proceedings Forbidden to leave the country and periodical presentation before the competent authority
Rebellion	4 persons, including the Prefect of Pichincha	3 persons with preventive detention and one with periodic presentation
Terrorism for the fire at *Teleamazonas* (charges were reformulated to damage to property of others).	4 persons prosecuted	Prosecutorial Instruction 33 proceedings

Source: Borja, Basantes and Castro, 2019. Elaboration: own

It should be added, as *Plan V* (2019) points out, that 'the vast majority of detainees were beaten, [something] highly irregular'. In theory, the state of emergency does not annul legal principles of necessity, proportionality, legality, temporality, territoriality and reasonableness; however, in the events of October these rules were all violated. This was aggravated due to the bias with which criminal prosecutions were taken forward, where only demonstrators were pursued and members of the repressive forces, as well as those intellectually and politically responsible for torture, confinement, mistreatment and extrajudicial executions like Oswaldo Jarrín and María Paula Romo, were left unpunished.

However, the use of the state of emergency has not only been a prerogative of the Moreno government, but also of previous administrations. As Basabe points out, 'it is actually very common, it is not exceptional at all, rather it is a measure that different governments have applied with relative frequency' (*La República*, 2019). The number is high; more than 100 states of emergency have been declared in the last decade (*La República*, 2019); however, the great novelty of the moment is the return

Table 4: Illegal killings during the October rebellion

Names	Date	Cause	Location
Arrival in Quito			
Ángel Raúl Chilpe	6	Hit by private vehicle	Molleturo
Marco Humberto Oto Rivera	7	Falling off a pedestrian bridge	San Roque (Quito)
José Daniel Chaluisa Cusco	7	Falling off a pedestrian bridge	San Roque (Quito)
Édison Mosquera Amagua	7	Gunshot	Cumandá (Quito)
Gabriel Angulo Bone	7	Tear gas bomb shot in the chest	Durán
Change of arrangements			
Segundo Inocencio Tucumbi Vega	9	Falling from height	Salesiana University (Quito)
José Rodrigo Chaluisa	9	Choking and crushing	*El Arbolito* Park (Quito)
Silvia Mera Navarrete	11	Motorcycle accident	Malchinguí
Abelardo Vega Caisaguano	12	Run over by a patrol car	Historical Centre (Quito)
Édgar Yucailla Álvarez	12	Gunshot	El Arbolito Park (Quito)
Francisco Quiñonez Montaño	unknown	Hit by military car	unknown

Source: Luque, Poveda and Hernández, 2020, p. 35. Elaboration: own

of the curfew 'for the first time since the return to democracy' (Luque, Poveda and Hernández, 2020, p. 19).

The second repressive moment goes from the national strike of 9 October to the moment of the negotiation, when it is evident that the number of detainees dropped (79% of the arrests took place before that time) and, at the same time, the number of wounded and injured increased enormously as a consequence of a change in the official behaviour of the repressive forces (between 9–12 October 62% and 45% of the wounded and murdered were registered respectively; a third of the murders took place on 7 October). From this it can be inferred that the strategic order was not to detain, but to inflict physical harm as a repeated mechanism of state terrorism. In the same way, the extrajudicial executions were not intended, but in line with a new plan and logic of violence. Two stages can be identified: 1) during the arrival of the Indigenous movement to the capital (on 7 October), and 2) with the change of dispositions to privilege the use of open violence over criminalization.

The negotiations took place, within this framework, on 13 October. Therefore a solution to the conflict was considered impossible without pressure in the streets; in fact, this was one of the conditions of the popular camp. However, it was not realistic that the state would accept paralysis indefinitely because it clashed with their strategy of an exponential use of violence, sustained and systematic aggression against the population in asymmetrical conditions of force, in the face of the steamroller of violence called the state.

5   CONTROL OF OFFICIAL DISCOURSE: IF BUSINESS LOSES, DO WE ALL LOSE?

The dispute of discourses – the battle of ideas – is ultimately a struggle for the reading of history. One person cannot replace the action of millions; not even an individual genius can be understood without the historical context in which they act. However, the understanding of objective social reality is determined by the added force of an interpretation of history. In certain circumstances, the uprisings of past history saw majorities as the protagonists, but they were written about by the minority interested in recounting the facts according to their convenience, thus tearing reality apart. The exploited classes provided the dead, but it was their adversaries who, in the midst of their disputes, recorded the outcome of those battles.

The October conjuncture was different. The ruling class had little capacity to distort reality, to interfere in the will of others and, above all, to affect the outcome of the conflict. Instead it concentrated on disseminating the idea that 'we have all lost'; in this respect we will make two observations:

The first is about language. When it comes to sustaining or improving the rate of profit and undermining the struggle of the lower classes, the representatives of the ruling class speak in the plural, trying to disguise their own interest, identifying it with the 'national interest', as does Pablo Arosemena, President of the Chamber of Commerce of Guayaquil:

> Carlos Vera: I was surprised by your initial presentation because it seems to agree with the workers who paint the businessmen as entrepreneurs. What worries you are the losses in sales, not even the human losses [in the strike]. Why?
> Pablo Arosemena: Well, at the time we called for calm and we said that ...

> CV: I did not say that. Why in your initial intervention were you more concerned about the losses in sales than the human losses, why?
> PA: Well, we are essentially concerned about the human part, if the human capital is not ...
> CV: You said: without sales there is no work, without work there is no employment. But you give me to understand that it is not important that eight individuals died.
> PA: No, not at all. What we want is to move the country forward by working. That is our role
> (In *Veraz*, 2019).[42]

The statements of Juan Carlos Díaz, President of the Guayaquil Chamber of Commerce, contained in the report of the Legislative Commission on the October national strike are along the same lines. According to his reflection, if competitiveness is lost by lowering positions in the rankings, and if foreign investment drops due to the increase in risk, then we all lose (National Assembly, 2019, p. 95). So, on the face of it, when business wins, 'we all win', but when they lose, 'we all lose'. How distressing!

The second observation focuses on the reading of history. When the ruling class cannot reposition itself as the political leadership of society, it argues that history will stand still or regress to the times of barbarism, displaying the colonialism that characterizes power relations in Ecuador. The demonstrators – poor, irrational, Indians and blacks or their descendants – are the barbarians, and the ruling class, of course, represents civilization. This is what the banker Guillermo Lasso said: 'We must be on the side of democracy, the Republic and civilization [which] is represented by the national government' (on *DemocraciaTV*, 2019). The omnipresence of the category of race is a device for their reading: history only advances when it is controlled by a bourgeois-white-heteronormative subject.

The version of the ruling class is not the only one that interprets history as paralysed or regressive. In their confusion, well-meaning authors, who are distant from the popular struggle like Ruiz and García (2019), convinced social democrats like

---

42 Another example of indolence is the statement of Juan Carlos Díaz, President of the Chamber of Commerce of Guayaquil in the report of the Legislative Commission on October, where he mentions as a context that 'in 2018 as a country we were ranked 123 in the Doing Business and that we are currently ranked 129, which evidences an affectation in relation to competitiveness, in turn, reiterates that due to the protests and the events occurred in the national strike the country risk went from 640 to more than 800 points, which [from his criteria] drives away tourism and foreign investment' (Asamblea Nacional, 2019, p. 95).

Borón (2019)⁴³ and union bureaucrats like Valentín Pacho (2019) speak of 'crumbs', 'nothing concrete' or 'defeat' as the result of the days of mobilization. As long as intellectuals measure history by four-year terms, that is, from a vision of politics through the lens of governments, they will not understand the transcendence that these events have for the liberation process. Consequently, they produce opinions incapable of fertilizing the field of the organization and popular struggle against capitalism.

Who won? For the exploited classes and their vanguard sectors, the October rebellion represented a massive development at many levels. In the immediate sense, the main victories were the repeal of Decree No. 883 and the blow struck against the IMF. Structurally, the historical experience was to understand and propel the tendencies of the revolutionary struggle in Ecuador. In turn, the vindication of the sacred right to protest⁴⁴ and rebellion, as a right of rights, insofar as all human rights were created as a consequence of these principles: to protest and rebel.

Of course, in the face of this perspective, there are opposing interpretations, such as those of Minister Romo (in Vélez, 2019) who spoke of 'social media warfare' and 'unprecedented violence', forgetting that the hosts of Attila in modern times are reincarnated in the state and the ruling class. Ecuador is no exception: 15 November 1922 in Guayaquil (2,000 workers murdered), at the beginning of 1930 in Columbe (3,000 Indigenous people killed), 2 and 3 June in Guayaquil in 1959 (500 massacred), 18 October 1977 in Aztra (120 sugar cane workers martyred), 29 May 1969 in the Casona Universitaria (50 high school students massacred), in addition to those murdered during the uprisings, general strikes and national strikes, among other events. When the ruling classes kill, they call it justice, chance, an isolated act or, *in extremis*, the use of force; when the poor fight, they call it barbarism, premeditated acts, organized terrorism or, in general, violence.

There was no shortage of people who tried to condemn 'violence wherever it comes from', but who condemns the state, an institution that is doomed to the systematic administration of violence? To unravel the problem, it is necessary to concentrate on the dispute for power, and not on the quarrels over government. For this reason, we point out two parallel ideological

---

43 Borón stated that: 'To conclude: far from having triumphed, what really happened was the consummation of a defeat of the popular insurgency, whose enormous sacrifice was offered without anything concrete in return and to top it all off at a false negotiating table' (Borón, 2019). We suppose that he longed for the struggle to end in the call for elections, neo-developmentalism and state capitalism.

44 In addition, it is a human right recognized in Article 21 of the Covenant on Civil and Political Rights of the Inter-American Commission on Human Rights.

facts arising from the sharpening of the class struggle: the radicalization of the right-wing discourse in public opinion and the loss of ideological-cultural hegemony of the ruling class.

5.1 'TELL THEM TO STAY IN THE WILDERNESS': THE MEDIA CORPORATIONS

The horizon of the ruling class's analysis of October was marked by their feeling of helplessness, a fact that, as we mentioned, was related to the impossibility of their directing the protest. The loss of control was perceived by some representatives of these sectors with panic, as 'a night of terror', as stated by the President of the Association of Private Banks of Ecuador (Julio Prado on *DemocraciaTV*, 2019), or at the height of the protests, when the President of the Ecuadorean Business Committee stated: 'I still cannot get over the perplexity and trauma I experienced here in Quito on Saturday [12 October], where I felt that at any moment in the place where I live a mob could break in to assault me, to harass me, to loot, and that I think that was the common denominator of what those of us who live in this city experienced' (Roberto Aspiazu in FM *Mundo*, 2019).

It is likely that, as Aspiazu points out, the feeling of fear was the common denominator of the small part of society that lives in the wealthy areas; the same that insisted on branding the majority of the Ecuadorean people demonstrating as drug traffickers, gang members, vandals, terrorists and uncivilized (Paz and Miño, 2019; Quishpe in FM *Mundo*, 2019). The bourgeoisie, when it cannot treat the poor as its means of production, reduces them to potential delinquents, a fact that was evidenced, for example, in the anxiety that was unleashed in the Cumbayá Shopping Centre – one of the most elitist in Quito – in the face of the possibility of shortages (Pichincha Universal, 2019), or in the defamation of the second fighter killed in October, Marco Oto, who 'was accused of being a delinquent' (Marco's mother in Asamblea Nacional, 2019, p. 72). With more words or less, the entrepreneurial logic establishes a comparison between protest and theft. But this reflection is not based on an outburst or prejudice, but on belonging to a privileged stratum, and its hateful impulses manifested in moments of danger. Thus the confrontation escalated on all fronts. In residential areas there were attempts to organize neighbourhood patrols (Morán, 2019), despite the fact that the exclusive citadels do not need them because they already have private security and, in several cases, are gated communities.

> The 'patriotic armies', to which the former mayor of Guayaquil alluded days before, took shape in certain elite neighbourhoods of Quito through the organization of neighbourhood patrols and the arming with golf clubs, baseball bats, tennis rackets and other clothing that gave away their extensive wealth (Díaz and Mejía, 2020, p. 281).

The alignment of the media to the narratives produced by the ruling class was undeniable; its purpose was to distort the general anger derived from the enactment of Decree No. 883; according to Gustavo Vega, Rector of the International University of Ecuador, 'These days Ecuador and especially Quito, became a city and a country not only barbaric, but savage. The horde, the mob, replaced the civilizing social coexistence of solidarity'. (Vega, 2020, p. 4). Or the version of the businessman Nebot Saadi: 'When you summon vandals, to vandalize, guided by a vandal, vandalism is produced' (Nebot, 2019b). Among the images privileged by the corporate media were the looting that took place, in particular, in the city of Guayaquil, and which they tried to position as 'evidence' of the vandalism of the mobilizations.

Shrouded in uncertainty, the tripartite alliance that sustained Moreno composed of the state, the media and the ruling classes faced enormous limits in directing the government's communication (Machado, 2019b).[45] This deepened the loss of credibility of the Executive. The approval of the President's administration was in sharp decline; in the month of October, it reached 83% of rejection and 8% of approval (CEDATOS, 2019).

In the experience of mathematician Polibio Córdova (in *FM Mundo*, 2019), 'popularity [...] has only been seen to fall in this way with those presidents who left power [the government, he means] and were forced to leave'. In times of crisis it becomes evident that, within capitalism, the ultimate factor that puts in place and removes rulers is not the people, or their votes, but the bloc in power. In the case of October, the government was

---

45 The rapprochement between the government and the big media began on 12 July 2017 when the President met, behind closed doors, with the owners and directors of: newspaper *El Universo*, Carlos Pérez Barriga; newspaper *Expreso*, Galo Martínez Leisker; the General Manager of *Teleamazonas*, Sebastián Corral; newspaper *El Comercio*, Carlos Mantilla; the directors of RTS, Xavier and Raúl Gómez Amador; Director of Radio Democracia, Gonzalo Rosero; Director of Radio Visión, Diego Oquendo. The annulment of the public contest for the awarding of transmissions by the Agency of Regulation and Control of Telecommunications (ARCOTEL), on 21 September 2018 and the reforms to the Communication Law approved to the liking of said media on 20 February 2019, sealed the pact between Moreno and the private media, which worked during the days of the unprecedented insurrectional mobilisation of the popular classes and continues to work after it, as we shall see' (Bedón, 2019).

sustained solely and exclusively because the ruling classes, the armed forces and ideological apparatuses closed ranks.

The discourse of the bloc that defended Moreno metamorphosed into a request for 'understanding' from the people, an attempt to minimize the scope of the protest,[46] a call for pacification and, finally, the unleashing of a witch-hunt. One of the most notable positions, not so much for its erudition as for its stupidity, was that of Jaime Bayly, a journalist notorious for endorsing the crimes of the state against the Indigenous population in Peru:

> If they are 'so Indigenous' and live in the forests, they should not be affected by the increase in gasoline prices. I don't know in what way it hurts them because, if they are really Indigenous, and live in caves or in the forests, I don't think they drive an Audi or use public transport. So, I say, if you are an indigenous person, a native one, how does it affect you when gasoline and diesel go up? (Bayly, 2019).

In this approach, the use of language shows a shift to the right. Expressions such as 'we call for social peace', 'guarantee democracy', 'subversive cells', 'supply centres' became common; at the same time, the press systematically spread a message of incitement to hatred:

> These new facts are added to those already known months ago and which have endured in the popular imagination, such as the racist expressions of Jaime Nebot, 'Tell them [the Indians] to stay in the wilderness,' or of the mayor of Guayaquil Cynthia Viteri during the days of the strike, as well as others of the Guayaquil aristocracy with the 'joke' 'Put a feather on the Indian Jaime Vargas,' and that together with the racist expressions of Boscán himself generated the reaction of the Council for Equality of Nationalities and Peoples, a governmental body that has called for an investigation and punishment of those responsible (Castro and Tapia, 2019).

---

46   Until Monday 7 October 2019, the Minister of the Interior, María Paula Romo, insisted on disseminating an alleged weakening of the mobilizations and that 'normality is gradually imposing itself' (in Machado, 2019). Even on Friday 11 October, two days after the round table, the government announced that the mobilisations were ending.

In fact, from the beginning of the protest to its final days and indeed in the aftermath, the editorials of the media were riddled with calls for greater use of violence. Radio Quito/Platinum host Miguel Rivadeneira called for 'shooting bullets at the rioters' (in Bedón, 2019); the President of the Chamber of Commerce, Patricio Alarcón, called for the 'defence of Quito' against the protesters (on *DemocraciaTV*, 2019); the former Assemblyman of the CREO Movement, Fabricio Villamar, called for 'not being afraid of violence'(on *DemocraciaTV*, 2019).

To this clamour was added a repertoire of contempt for the Indigenous and black peoples and nationalities of Ecuador. Villamar (in *Ecuavisa*, 2019) asserted, explicitly, that the state has historically delivered gifts exclusively to these sectors of society. Others, in a more guarded way, defended the racist idea of the 'manipulation' of the Indigenous movement by an electoral party or by a continental 'plot', an aberration that ruled out any possibility of autonomous initiatives by the Indigenous movement. The eagerness to 'distinguish between the peaceful Indigenous movement and external actors' (Paz and Miño, 2019) also surfaced. This is a form of rewriting, in a new situation, Rousseau's discourse of the noble savage, which concludes that, due to their natural or social condition, oppressed peoples and nationalities are incapable of rebelling.

The stories cited above affirm a vision of the poor as ungrateful, powerless and docile. What bothers power is not the 'destruction' of heritage, but the irruption into the bleached space of whiteness, where the imaginary Nation resides:

> They never complain about the communities surrounding Quito being dispossessed of their territories by construction companies in complicity with the municipality. They did not cry when they destroyed the archaeological heritage to build the Quito subway tunnel. No, it does not hurt their city, it bothers them that the ancestral owners of these lands come to 'dirty' their whitening process, it bothers them to be reminded that they are not in Europe or the United States that they are not citizens of the first world that they want so much to be because of their aspirations (Sierra, 2019).

There was a bias in the dissemination of information. Images that supported the discourse of violence were privileged. The exercise of self-defence of the population against state violence was omitted.

The pattern of behaviour of the repressive forces was only presented in a marginal way. The police operations, in a premeditated manner, were executed after the closing of the night edition of the television media (17:00 hours), so that the most serious cases of aggression would not be exposed during prime time.

Additionally, why did the hegemonic media not question the systematic calls of the right wing to subversion and its recourse to violence? For example, the Christian-Socialist businessman Nebot Saadi said at a rally:

> If those who should protect the citizen, if those who should maintain order do not do so, with the harshness that is requited, within the law of course, *then it is up to us to replace the state* and punish them as they have to be punished'. (TVC *El Comercio TV*, 2019) [Emphasis added].

Or look at the xenophobia of the presenter of *La Posta*, Andersson Boscán, who criminalized Indigenous people: 'Indian found, Indian imprisoned, is what the country deserves... we imprison another 200 and if this is not enough we imprison another 200 and when they run out there is no one else to imprison' (in Castro and Tapia, 2019).

On the other hand, there was increasing censorship of the media that transmitted the events more thoroughly or took account of the point of view of the demonstrators. For example, people who spoke against the government were taken away from the microphone and what the official media called 'demonstrators for peace' were given time to speak. Some of them expressed a fierce rejection of the 'rude and impolite Indians' *(RT en Español*, 2019). Or the 'constructive' television schedule of 12 October: *SpongeBob* was broadcast for 4 hours and 35 minutes on *Teleamazonas*, while *Ecuavisa* preferred a soap opera. One more indicator, recurrent in the interviews: how many times is a leader of the Indigenous and popular movement interrupted live, and how many times are the words of interviewees representing the ruling class cut off?

Radio Pichincha Universal[47] was raided, after the electric power was cut by persons unknown. In addition, the pages of digital media such as Zángano Press and Wambra Radio were tapped. Telesur was taken off cable television; the RT and Hispan

---

47 Radio Pichincha Universal was one of the few media that openly aligned itself with the protest. In this context, its audience grew exponentially, reaching 6.5 million on Twitter and 5.8 million on Facebook.

TV channels were censored, as well as three columnists and three journalists of the public newspaper El Tiempo de Cuenca. There were no guarantees that people would be able carry out their journalistic work, especially in the case of community communicators. The indiscriminate blocking, hacks and temporary suspensions of accounts of leaders and popular organizations in social networks, attacks from trolls and the installation of mobile signal inhibitors to reduce connectivity in the concourse of the Casa de la Cultura Ecuatoriana were part of the state of emergency's controls on the media initiated by the ideological apparatuses of the state (Castro and Tapia, 2019).

The central role of this campaign consisted of systematic defamation in the media, for example in the stellar news program 24 Horas of *Teleamazonas*.[48] The portal 4 Pelagatos stated 'CONAIE sees racism in everything' and 'Violence: CONAIE unpunished for everything', and the newspaper *El Expreso de Guayaquil* said: 'The country moves towards calm, the Indigenous people towards violence', and 'Vandalism leads the Indigenous uprising'.

Their discourse belonged to a model of wartime communication, which forms part of the total war doctrine – as Cobo (in Veraz, 2019) recognizes – included in the White Book, a manual that set the national defence policy of the Ecuadorean state. The communication strategy of the hegemonic media was part of a vociferous and hidden programme to combat the autonomy of the subordinate classes.

October 2019 has left behind a great lesson: the so-called 'freedom of expression' does not exist. Beyond the legal formality, freedom of expression is, in real terms, a dispute for the recognition of the legitimacy of ideas through force. The different arguments are, in general, issued within a debate over truth and power, in which the ideas that have more resources and capital – in the Bourdieusian sense – are likely to be victorious. In this sense, what are the legal and *de facto* criteria for guaranteeing the right of opinion of the social classes that do not have the assets and ties to present their ideas publicly?

In spite of all the media encirclement of the power bloc, October won some victories in the battle of ideas. First, the government's communication strategy did not succeed in positioning its image: the average acceptance rate was 15.4%, reaching at its lowest levels 8%. This allows us, in addition to looking at the percentage of

---

48 This occurred on 24 October: 'The attack included disqualifying phrases such as "They contribute very little or nothing in taxes" and immediately after, "Where? if they contribute it is in the claim and protest in the streets"' (Castro and Tapia, 2019).

49 Among numerous other examples, during the fall of President Bucaram in 1997, *Teleamazonas* presenter Diego Oquendo launched a long report divided into two chapters to denounce the government in power.

acceptance, to identify the margin of society which, in times of high confrontation, tends to align itself with the preservation of the status quo and conservatism.

Second, in spite of the cover-up of the news, the growth of the mass mobilization affected for eleven days mass consciousness which, as Gramsci argued, is the habitat of the ideas of the ruling class. Thus, according to CEDATOS, from 5 October the vast majority of people disagreed with the elimination of fuel subsidies and, despite the surprise of the measure, by 11 October 92% of households were aware of the conflict and 76% considered a solution urgent (Córdova in *FM Mundo*, 2019).

Third, unlike other social conflicts, the biased editorial position of the mainstream media was evident to most of them. The result was that 86% of the population believed that, during the mobilizations, the facts were hidden by the communication empires (Perfiles de Opinión en *Kolectivoz*, 2019), which led to profound questioning of the hegemonic media.

6 STORIES THAT SILENCED THE NOISE OF THE OFFICIAL MEDIA

The protest questioned the mainstream media's practice of presenting reality according to the interests of its shareholders. As a result, their supposed 'unquestionable credibility' was questioned. One of the ways was the proliferation of slogans such as 'What you are not going to see in the media' (Visión 360, 2019), 'The media do not say what is happening in the country' (Jairala, 2019).

One of the fetishes for political legitimacy in the 21st century is the 'defence of democracy'. This is a discourse that the capitalist media uses as a shield – because corporations also manufacture shields – not to transmit information coming from the popular sectors, despite the fact that, in theory, the idea of democracy is associated with popular sovereignty. If in the media's version, the concept of democracy is dissociated from mass social mobilization, should we consider that the major media in Ecuador were 'against' democracy during the fall of the presidents of the 1997–2005 period, by positioning themselves on the side of the protests that deposed them from their posts?[49]

According to CEDATOS (2019) the media corporations were rejected by the majority: 'The media obtained a positive rating of 43.4% [...] and 47.8% negative'. In turn, international press agencies had to circumvent the media siege to access information on the events directly. 'They went to the national territory and verified the information and facts, among them Russia Today, DW, Reuters, EFE, the BBC, the *Guardian*, CNN, Telesur and others' (Castro and Tapia, 2019).

> One of the demands we saw during the demonstrations to journalists was: why don't they broadcast, why don't they report what is really happening? This is a super logical request, worthy of a society that feels desperate about what is happening (Gisella Bayona in FM *Mundo*, 2019).

In order to break the siege by officialdom, social networks became, for the first time in Ecuador, a resource with significant media influence that reproduced the version of reality in line with the needs of the majority that was part of the October rebellion. Community and alternative media were the first to use them, but after the extension and intensification of the mobilizations, their use multiplied among the unorganized population. According to Castro and Tapia (2019), more than 50% of the sources of information during the strike came from social networks: 31% on Facebook, 13% on digital media, 4% on WhatsApp and 1% on Twitter. Meanwhile, 47% were 'informed' by television (Opinion Profiles in *Kolectivoz*, 2019). Digital media, as a whole, surpassed television as an information medium.

> The press is not pristine. We journalists are not infallible. We can fail. We can get it wrong [...] And it is good that they demand balance from us. And it's good that they demand fairness from us. And it is right that they demand quality from us. And it is also right that, if we do not give it to them, they do not consume our content (Borja, 2019).

Another way used to reverse the informative bias was the pressure on the hegemonic media to transmit the facts without an editorial filter. This arose after the first illegal murders during the demonstrations. On Thursday 10 October, by decision of a mass assembly, the press was kept for more than seven hours in the Casa de la Cultura in Quito, obliged to broadcast live the funeral service of Inocencio Tucumbi, an Indigenous leader murdered by the police the night before. As reported by *Plan V* magazine (2019):

> Some teams reported leaving and entering the place without a problem [and that ...] Inside the enclosure, journalists were given water, a sandwich, cola, hard-boiled eggs, they were given facilities to recharge their equipment for the transmission and their safety was guaranteed, and so it was. But they were required to transmit 'everything' that happened inside. They especially monitored the coverage of private and public channels. 'Yes, it is happening', it is not happening', were the insistent messages from the Indigenous monitors.

The corollary of this process was the televised dialogue between CONAIE and the national government, under two conditions: it had to be direct and transmitted live. In this framework, the result was that October put on one side all state officials[50] and, on the other, the leadership of the Indigenous movement representing the majority of the population in rebellion. The confrontation left two sensations. It was 'a deep breath of fresh air' (Herrera, 2019); according to CEDATOS (2019) 76% of the population supported the dialogue on 13 October and the repeal of Decree No. 883 was demanded by 71%. The event was the biggest thrashing in the history of the country that the representatives of the popular organizations could give to the highest officials of the government.

> While the dialogue was taking place, social media networks were set on fire with memes and someone said 'It looks like a reality show, on one side; people who can barely express themselves, they have a bad command of Spanish and can hardly be understood; on the other side, the Indigenous people'; others pointed to a 5 to 0 match and an own goal by the government (Herrera, 2019).

The momentary elimination of competition between media companies, evidenced in the homogeneity of editorial lines, is another lesson learned during October. The differences between the fractions of the ruling class turned out to be secondary to

---

50 Among the representatives of the state were: the presidents of the Legislative, Executive, Judicial, Electoral, Citizen Participation and Social Control functions, the Prosecutor, the Comptroller General and several Ministers.

Table 5: Presence of demonstrators in Quito and Guayaquil

	In favour of protests	Against protests
Went out to demonstrate	24%–30% Quito	5.7% Quito
	16% Guayaquil	
Did not go out, but supported	39% Quito	19% Quito
Declared neutral	17% Quito	

Source: Social Climate in Pichincha Universal, 2019. Elaboration: own

guarantee, as Buñuel satirized, the discreet charms of the bourgeoisie. However, the war logic of the official media and the censorship of the autonomous platforms strained the relations with the population that questioned their behaviour.[51] In contrast, there were no reports of aggressions or criticisms of the journalistic work developed in neighbourhoods and communities. Moreover, several alternative and community media reported feeling safe in the midst of the demonstrators. In addition, is it not an aggression not to have freedom of expression as well as the use of war communications against the protests of the exploited classes?

The events and stories produced by the alternative and community media tipped the balance in the battle of ideas, counteracting the official media noise. Thus the questioning of neoliberalism was very broad; between 60% and 70% of the population considered that the agreement between the government and the IMF was detrimental (Perfiles de Opinión en *Kolectivoz*, 2019; Clima Social en Pichincha Universal, 2019). According to Perfiles de Opinión, 87% of the population thought that the mobilizations were very necessary or at least necessary and only 12% said they were not (in *Kolectivoz*, 2019).[52] A similar trend is seen in the social climate data:

The legitimacy of the days of mobilization, on a national scale, led to a broad and militant participation of the exploited classes. In Quito, about one million people participated directly in the protests, and about one and a half million supported them. The decision to push for a process of struggle against the government by popular organizations broke with a centuries old trend of disinterest in political participation by the population, as seen in previous periods (Latinobarómetro, 2019).

When analysing the population's perception of the actors in the protests[53] and the unions involved,[54] the involvement of the

Table 6: Reasons for attending/not attending demonstrations in Quito and Guayaquil

Reasons to attend		Reasons not to attend	
Against government measures	65%	Insecurity, fear of state repression	47%
Government mismanagement	34%	Believes it is useless	17%
Increase in fares	37%	They had to work and other reasons	36%
Bad economic situation	25%		
Unemployment	10%		
Elimination of subsidies	9%		
By Decree No. 883	1%		

Source: Opinion Profiles in Kolectivoz, 2019. Elaboration: own

Indigenous movement and social organizations is confirmed. In other words, the image of the organizational references that had been battered in recent years was elevated. Such was the sympathy for the de facto measures. According to Perfiles de Opinión, 84% of the population in Quito and Guayaquil thought that the Indigenous movement defended the interests of the people in general, and only 16% that it defended their own (in *Kolectivoz*, 2019). When broken down by socioeconomic status, among the population with medium and high economic income levels, 50% thought the former and 50% the latter; while, among the population with medium-low and low economic income levels, the perception that the Indigenous movement defended the general interests of the people was a majority. Therefore, it is concluded that political identities are built among the poor through the processes of struggle.

51 Among the strongest demonstrations against the mass media were the protests against the editorial line of the *Teleamazonas* channel – not the workers – which took place in Quito on 7 and 12 October, involving the burning of vehicles and the destruction of part of the façade, as well as a minor raid on the newspaper *El Comercio*.

52 There was no lack of those who tried to evaluate the protest actions in a Manichean way with questions such as 'Did the national strike benefit or harm the population?', with the objective of obtaining data that would censure the popular struggle and delight the ears of the real losers of October (CEDATOS, 2019).

53 Responses on the presence of social and political actors during the protest yielded the following results: 90% recognized the indigenous movement, 46% the transport workers, 25% the Corrientes, 16% the students, 16% the workers, 7% women's organizations and 2% the people (Opinion Profiles in *Kolectivoz*, 2019).

54 Regarding the perception of who called for the mobilizations, the following responses were obtained from the population in Quito and Guayaquil: 73% think that it was called by social movements, 27% by Correa and Maduro. Among the population with medium and high economic income levels 52% think the former and 49% the latter; on the contrary, among the population with medium-low and low economic income levels the former is in the majority (Opinion Profiles in *Kolectivoz*, 2019).

On the other hand, only 17% of those who did not participate directly in the mobilizations did so because they believed that they were useless, and the rest did so because of the restrictions their employers placed them under or because of state repression.

In the ideological battle, the main concern for the ruling classes is not the conditions of those who work in communication – long working hours, occupational hazards and, frequently, precarious working conditions – but the questioning of hegemony. People who declared having little or no trust towards media such as television, distrust that had been growing for years, lost it even more during the October rebellion (Latinobarómetro, 2019).

Despite the fact that opinion statistics in the context of October express a high level of rejection of the order of things, it would be wrong to argue that common sense was completely transformed and a far-reaching counter-hegemonic proposal was consolidated. For this reason, the objective planned in the CONAIE manifesto prior to October, of 'advancing to an action that will permit the achievement of great victories for the dominated classes, the majority of workers, peasants, popular, women, students, youth, artists, peoples and nationalities of Ecuador' (Annex 1) was partially fulfilled, insofar as the medium-term agenda of the popular organizations could not be established, nor a long-term one either.

The majority consciousness of the population, in general, continues to be conservative, a characteristic that has deepened in the post-neoliberal period, as recognized by the ideologist of Andean capitalism Álvaro García Linera. The core of ideas that are part of the popular repertoire still reproduce hegemony. Reviewing the debates during and after the October rebellion, for the most part, it seems that the problems of the country's economy are reduced to the deficit of the general state budget – the famous 'fiscal crisis'. These discussions ignore the direct interference of the bourgeoisie in most of the economy, and make few references to the structural, integral and civilizational crisis of capitalist modernity.

The true hegemonic nucleus of Ecuador is not anti-Correism, as some believe; an idea that is just a slogan for the next electoral juncture. To break the ideological and cultural patterns that allow the reproduction of domination demands overcoming an understanding of reality limited by the dichotomy between statism and neoliberalism. ★

Demonstrators throw a burning tyre at repressive forces near the National Assembly building Quito, 8 October 2019 (Photo: Alejandro Ramírez Anderson).

Police confront the people (aya uma) (Photo: Alejandro Ramirez Anderson).

Students, youth, women and popular sectors resist in Quito's Theatre Square, 3 October 2019 (Photo: Fluxus Foto).

People in the popular sector supply materials to the barricades and the front line
(Photo: Luis Herrera/Audiovisual Cooperative).

A line from the song 'Aguanta' (Hold the Line) by the Quito rock group
Sal y Mileto (Photo: Andrés León/Kapucha Communications).

Member of the Community, Indigenous and People's Guards carries a shield and an acial, 8 October 2019 (Photo: Axel Naranjo).

Members of the Community, Indigenous and People's Guards use hand-made masks in Quito, 8 October 2019 (Photo: Emilia Narvaez).

Indigenous peoples block the Trans Amazon Highway, 7 October 2019 (Photo: CONFENIAE Communications).

March by Kichwa women of the Chibuleo people against state violence and the Day of the Race, 12 October 2019 (Photo: Axel Villacís).

Occupation of the Town Hall of Tungurahua by the Indigenous movement, 10 October 2019 (Photo: Axel Villacis).

A Minga, or community gathering of Indigenous peoples – to build barricade in El Arbolito park in Quito, 10 October 2019 (Photo: Luis Herrera/Audio visual Cooperative).

A Kichwa Panzaleo family from the province of Cotopaxi arrive for the occupation of Quito, 7 October 2019 (Photo: Luis Herrera/Audiovisual Cooperative)

Arbitrary arrest of a demonstrator in the centre of Quito
(Photo: Luis Herrera/Audiovisual Cooperative).

The struggle at the barricades in El Arbolito park Quito
(Photo: Bryan Garcés).

Demonstrators in resistance at one of Quito's barricades, 9 October 2019 (Photo: Fluxus Foto).

Handmade shields arrive from the provinces (Photo: Luis Herrera/Audiovisual Cooperative).

An Indigenous woman from the Kichwa Panzaleo people of Cotopaxi province, during the occupation of Quito (Photo: David Diaz Arce/Fluxus Foto).

Group of emergency brigades – doctors, paramedics, auxiliaries and students in the centre of Quito (Photo: Kevin Armendariz).

Mama Rosa Elvira and Tayta José María: Your struggle against *huasipungo servitude* bears fruit in our struggle against capitalism.

Popular slogan, Cotopaxi 2019

The mould of our words we will fill with our actions.

Popular slogan from the October Rebellion

Impact: lessons, debates and perspectives

In the crucible of October, several struggles merged – struggles that had been developing, in adverse conditions, for several years. Above all, it was an accelerator of history. It condensed into days what would have taken years. As V.I. Lenin put it: 'There are decades in which nothing happens, and there are weeks in which decades pass'. For eleven days the actually existing structures of power were put in question. The majority of the population went from being objects to becoming political subjects. The stage was cleared and it suddenly became possible to understand the trends, how people behaved, what was missing, their mistakes, their positions, their strengths. These were the actors who, potentially, could begin to change the course of history.

The rebellion combined memory and initiative, the old and the new, the past and the present. The whole repertoire of collective action was created and recreated with unbelievable ingenuity. This epic brought together an Indigenous and peasant uprising with a revolt of the urban poor. The forms of popular power that unfolded in October are a hinge between reality and utopia. They coalesced, as Moreano suggests, in what may well be called the 'Quito Commune' (2020, p. 76). The countryside and the city connected in an atypical way: the city fed the countryside. Spontaneous, improvised forms of organization developed against the current, under pressure, beset with urgency and difficulty. Solidarity networks flowed over the borders of the nation state and built proletarian internationalism.

The October uprising teaches us that without pressure from the streets no government will respond to the needs of the people.[1] Beneath the semblance of democracy, projected through the meetings held with '80 organizations and different groups' after the rebellion (*El Comercio*, 2019), the state resorted to its essential, tyrannical logic when central aspects of the reproduction of capital were questioned. Apparently, for the people to have their

---

[1] Thus, after the repeal of Decree No. 883 and the end of the protests, the few rounds of talks that took place didn't go anywhere, because the UN delegation was biased in favour of the government side, which sent lower level negotiators and advisers.

voices heard and their demands debated, an uprising of at least eleven days is required.

October demonstrated that the combativity and size of a mobilization are decisive factors in the balance and imbalance of forces. In the circumstances described in this book, it is possible to force some of the people's demands to be met, and to trap the interests of capital between a rock and a hard place, by spreading the demands on a mass scale throughout the country. Once again, we see the panic of liberalism when confronted by the majority, the cruelty of the repressive forces, and the mantra of the mainstream media that 'the revolution will not be televised', at least if they can help it.

In this chapter, in answer to the question, 'Where does October leave us?', we bring together the main lessons of the uprising under four headings: 1) we review the new forms and tactics for popular struggle; 2) we identify the most important internal and external difficulties that arose during the mobilization; 3) we reflect on the question of violence; and 4) we outline the key tasks to guide the anti-capitalist left in the coming period.

1 THE MEMORY OF HISTORY AND NEW FORMS OF STRUGGLE

The creativity of October produced a leap that would have taken decades if the conflict had not occurred. The repertoire of collective action was enriched as the Indigenous and peasant uprising combined with the revolt of the urban poor; the result was the development of a historic event for the exploited of the countryside and the city. The process allowed the development of a powerful mode of struggle against capitalism that constitutes, *in itself*, a major contribution to the transformation of Ecuador and Latin America.

The last three decades have seen two important peaks of struggle in Ecuador: the Indigenous uprisings and the overthrow of presidents. In both cases, forms of popular power were created. October inherited and strengthened this repertoire. New situations of autonomous mobilization appeared, breaking the barriers imposed by liberal democracy.

Those in power developed a sensationalist myth that foreign agitators and troublemakers were giving military training to groups of 'Taliban' to sow terror. At best, this cartoon account might serve as part of a farce. Putting aside this absurd narrative, however, how does one explain the spontaneous deployment of techniques and strategies that allowed the building of barricades and defensive systems, and the definition of security structures (the front line, supply lines, a rearguard)? At what point did the people learn to master the battlefield to sustain life in the face of death? Apparently, the people did not know that they already knew.

Collective and individual memory is constituted by social experience, transmitted through tradition, custom and lived experience (Thompson, 1981, pp. 16–22). Memory is engraved almost genetically; it is the collective knowledge that manifests itself at certain moments. Historical events such as the Rebellion of the Barrios of Quito (1765), the Liberal Revolution (1895), the Four Days War (1932), the Glorious May (1944), the April Days (1978), the national strikes (1970s and 1980s), the Indigenous uprisings, (particularly that of 1990) and the overthrow of presidents (in the 1990s and early 2000s) were transmitted through oral accounts, affectivities (family relationships, neighbourhood friendships) and through iconic slogans such as: 'Quito the light of America', 'We are fighting peoples' and 'We are the children of the uprising'. In the October uprising the past was magically recomposed. The accumulated experience of struggle at the barricades across the ages was reinvented in the present.

In October different modes of struggle were combined to resist the onslaught of the repressive forces. Various instances of popular power were created, such as: the Community, Indigenous and People's Guards, the struggle in the streets against the police and army, the detention of members of the repressive forces and the occupation of public spaces, the development of techniques of street fighting and mass mobilization, the deployment of popular solidarity as a source of supplies, the proliferation of symbolic and artistic expressions; expressions of discontent through pot-banging and Twitter storms; declarations by the movement of our own states of emergency, roadblocks and closures; the holding of marches, sit-ins and interprovincial mobilizations, among many others.

All the above were interwoven with community practices coming from popular ideology and culture and non-monetary economic and social institutions such as the *minga* (collective work by the community), *randi-randi* ('giving and giving') and the *ayni* ('lending a hand'). These are part of the community spirit expressed in popular festive and funeral rites and of the way Indigenous and peasant organizations manage their own territories in the forests, moorlands and water protection zones. They are present in the administration of Indigenous justice, in the traditional health systems, in the bodies of self-organization and representation of the popular sectors, and in the community defence bodies. All these community practices have been developed through complex organisational structures and the practice of grassroots community democracy.

This whole web of experiences, of a traditional, contemporary and proto-socialist character, has been the starting point for imagining the organisation of a new society – one based on people's power, beyond the nation state and capitalist modernity.

1.1 THE COMMUNITY, INDIGENOUS AND PEOPLE'S GUARDS

In the October uprising the guards made it possible to confront 'the precarious state of people's rights and develop a process of resistance' (*El Comercio*, 2019). This experience has its roots in the warrior traditions of Amerindian societies; the experiences of Wio, Erash, Arutam and Etsa guards, mythical and sacred figures of the Shuar tradition; the peasant patrols; the administration of Indigenous justice, as recognized in the Ecuadorean constitution of 2008; the neighbourhood brigades and committees; the techniques for organizing mass street protests. These have been present in the different territories, communities and organizations of the Indigenous, peasant and popular movements, including in the fight against territorial dispossession by the extractive industries.

Such self-defence guards have served to maintain order at assemblies and congresses, provide security for combative leaders and protect columns of demonstrators on marches. They have led clashes with the police and the army when these attack demonstrations, combated cattle theft, robbery and drug trafficking, as well as domestic and patriarchal violence, and helped to conduct community health campaigns against diseases, infections and epidemics. In neglected rural areas and city neighbourhoods, where the permanent presence of the state is reduced to very poor health and education services, the abusive behaviour of the police and the occasional visit or publicity from some candidate standing in the next elections, taking care of the area and defending it falls to the people themselves.

The existence of the community guards triggered a debate about the right of the Indigenous and other peoples and nationalities to self-determination – an issue which generally only comes up when there is a deliberate attempt to show the supposed 'violence of Indigenous justice' while ignoring the brutality of the modern state. The Minister of Defence, Oswaldo Jarrín, criticized this right because he said it risked creating a 'proto-State'. In this regard, it should be remembered that self-determination is the right of oppressed nations to exercise their own sovereignty when the existing state does not guarantee it.[2] This controversy deserves a digression.

Many of the community self-defence organizations now being questioned were integrated into the armed forces during the last border conflicts with Peru. In that context, these organizations were given recognition and even strengthened as military structures. The Iwia army, for example, was formed by the Shuar and Kichwa people out of their community structures. But when these same structures stand against the system that oppresses the Indigenous population, the state slanders, persecutes and criminalizes them.

In that war the governments of Ecuador and Peru, both in the service of imperialism, were supposedly defending the sovereignty of their respective countries. In reality, they were in fact the puppets of mining transnationals which had their sights set on the underground wealth of the Amazon region. In the end, the territory was handed over to foreign companies that control the mineral resources, the lives of the workers and the surrounding communities, and have the power to make decisions over the territory given to them in concessions. They are indeed an informal state within the state, but nobody complains here. In the same way, during the COVID-19 pandemic, the care of certain rural areas of the Ecuadorean highlands, the *sierra* and the Amazon was taken on by the community guards and other local structures, whose functions included sending food to the cities in solidarity. These are the same bodies that, in October 2019, were attacked and their members branded as terrorists.

During the mobilizations, the need for defence was evident to millions of people involved. In the face of mounting repression by the state, the community, Indigenous and people's guards gained in legitimacy. However, their action was limited. Indeed, in the future it may seem irresponsible on the part of the movement's leaders not to prepare clearer means of self-defence, when the brutality of the repressive forces is unleashed on working people, as dozens of reports show it was in October.

Here is one first-hand account of an arrest in Quito, as recorded by the Alliance of Human Rights Organizations:

---

[2] After the October rebellion, Jaime Vargas, the president of CONAIE, talked about 'building our own army'. (*El Comercio*)

> I arrived at 5 o'clock in the afternoon. I was with my girlfriend. They began firing tear gas bombs and I started to run. I was near my house and they were grabbing whoever they found. [...] They took us to the yard at the back of the checkpoint and made us do exercises (squatting and push-ups, running and carrying each other). They asked us: Are you an adult or under age? They were separating us; in total there were 9 of us. 5 adults were detained and the other 4 were minors; one was a girl. [...] They pushed us all down on the ground, tied us up and threw a tear gas bomb at us. Whoever fell over was kicked or beaten. The kids were crying and rolling on the floor and those who couldn't do the exercises were kicked and beaten with truncheons. They even used a plank. There were about 15 policemen, 4 women, they all came out laughing, they made fun of me ... Arévalo was the one who arrested me, I saw his name tag. Most of us who were beaten had blood on us. They made us wash our faces and dry our clothes, or throw them away, so that when we were taken out they wouldn't realize we'd been beaten. They told us not to say anything, to keep silent because that way we would get out faster, or they would give us 5 days in jail. We did not say anything at the medical check-ups. That is why they did the check-ups again, because the wounds did not come out in the first check-up (2019, pp. 39–40).

And here is another from the coastal city of Guayaquil:

> When I saw the attack on my friend, I told the policeman that he was hurting her [...], and then I was hit on the back with a truncheon, while I heard the other policeman say: 'Catch that son of a bitch, he was filming us,' I started to run but I was surrounded by many policemen. When I saw that I raised my hands to show that I was not resisting and I asked them not to attack me, because I wasn't doing anything. In spite of this, they began to hit me with their truncheons and kick me. One policeman took out his pepper spray and sprayed me. I felt a motorcycle run over my legs. I still have the

marks and I am only just beginning to be able to walk properly again. In the process, my cell phone, which I was using to record, fell on the ground, and in another video [filmed by someone else] you can see that a policeman picked it up and put it in his pocket [...] At that point in the attack I started to feel dizzy and I don't remember what happened after that. When I recovered, I saw a group of people who were there trying to help me. It turns out that I'd had a seizure, which I hadn't had for many years. I suffer from epilepsy; I even have my disability card but I hadn't had an attack for a long time (2019, p.62).

These testimonies are not 'isolated cases', nor do they reveal 'rogue elements', 'bad apples' or 'failures to follow the regulations' within the police force. We can find the same thing in any other country in Latin America. We only need to recall the cases of extrajudicial executions, widespread eye injuries (as a result of the security forces firing gas canisters and other munitions directly into the faces of protesters) and other forms of cruel treatment that spread across the region in the last quarter of 2019, to confirm the violent character of the state. In the Ecuadorean case, the United Nations identified what it called a 'disturbing pattern' (*El Comercio*, 2019), and reiterated the definition of a crime of state; as the Minister of the Interior herself put it, 'It has the characteristic of being a systematic practice. If the police have a systematic practice of going out and shooting at demonstrators that could be [a state crime]' (Romo, 2019).

There are several indications that there were secret orders to step up the repression against the people in revolt, and to spread terror and panic through injuries, arrests, fake news[3] and extrajudicial executions. Political systems may be formally defined as 'democracies', even though they behave more like modern dictatorships, not in the sense of government by the military, but as the exercise of power by the rich. The murders, arrests, injuries and anxiety caused by state repression contrast with the complete inaction of the state in confronting 'common' and 'elite' crime. The community, Indigenous and people's guards filled the empty space left by those in power, and developed it anew, from below and towards the left.

---

3 The national police issued false alerts of looting in some neighbourhoods of Quito, for example at La Ecuatoriana, Guajaló and Solanda, so that shops would close, thereby causing panic among the population (Pichincha Universal, 2019). The same happened with the media reporting water cuts in Ambato, which caused the panic hoarding of water (7,400 litres per second out of a total capacity of 8,000 litres per second) even though there was nothing wrong with the supply of drinking water in the city.

1.2 STREET STRUGGLE, POPULAR INVENTIVENESS AND GRASSROOTS POWER

Class struggle often follows a logic of action and reaction, a process in which we may know where it began, but it can be difficult to see where it will end. As one news anchor put it, 'The Indigenous movement will give as good as it gets' (Jairala, 2019). Faced with mounting repression, the people developed new forms and instruments of struggle and adapted familiar techniques to the needs of the moment, although they could never make up for the asymmetry of resources used by the protesters and the police. For example, 'The Indigenous guards covered themselves with rudimentary shields made from boards' (*Plan V*, 2019), while the state forces had equipment designed by the arms industry. The people's ingenuity knew no limits, creatively devising defensive equipment through the re-signification of public space:

> Home-made shields were also fashioned out of tin drums, decked out as if by ancient warriors, with rectangular metal sheets obtained from a building site, and even with the round dishes of cable TV aerials, taken off some roofs (Vaca, 2019).

There was also a diversification of street fighting techniques and the tools of mass deployment, such as masks to protect people from tear gas, shields, barricades against the riot police, traps for police motorbikes, the use of fireworks and Molotov cocktails, the detention of policemen and soldiers by the people, and so on.

> When the police began to use large quantities of tear gas, the demonstrators began to use masks, goggles, vinegar and bicarbonate of soda; when the bombs began to produce casualties, shields were made (and the bombs were plunged into drums of water); when the anti-riot vehicles and motorcycles lashed out violently, the people set up their barricades (or blocked the mounted police with systems of ropes strung between trees); when they began to throw stun grenades and fire buckshot cartridges or bullets, stones, fireworks and the occasional fire bomb were thrown back; when the police and military began to force their way into local communities and other places, some of them were captured and detained (Alarcón, 2019).

The number of protests in Quito went from 293 on 3 October to 272 on the 9th and 220 on the 12th (Zapata, 2019; *TVC El Comercio TV*, 2019). We estimate that's about one road block per kilometre on the city's main avenues, in addition to countless others on side streets, as shown by the traces of burnt tyres on the tarmac.[4] There were countless fires (*TVC El Comercio TV*, 2019). On 12 October, nationwide, 392 highways were closed, along with 1,228 secondary roads in rural and urban areas (*DemocraciaTV*, 2019). In all, '1,800 affected sites were registered on GPS' (Asamblea Nacional, 2019, p. 58). For its part, the ECU 911 emergency service recorded 471,000 calls in 10 days (Zapata, 2019).[5]

The country was totally paralysed and a hundred highways remained closed or only partially open even after the government repealed Decree No. 883, due to the magnitude of the blockades and the difficulty of removing the obstacles (Jairala, 2019).[6] The cities of Ambato, Latacunga, Riobamba and Cuenca were under siege; in Cuenca, Guayaquil and the provinces of El Oro and Loja an air bridge was set up to fly in fuel. Social movements became the legitimate authorities in the territories where the protest gained strength. In the Province of Imbabura, 'the only legitimate pass was the one issued by the Indigenous and Peasant Federation of Imbabura (FICI). The only authority that everyone respected was that of the FICI […] [and the safe conduct] signed by the Federation and its Governing Council, with its logo and seal' (Chancosa, 2020, p. 26). We could call this a parallel power, or the growth of people's power, to the point of temporarily controlling several areas in the country. However, this did not manage to become, in the sense analysed by V.I. Lenin, a revolutionary situation of dual power.

When the repression intensified and the number of wounded multiplied, the population formed huge human chains that moved, in a collective effort, the cobblestones (Vision 360, 2019) to build barricades to hold back the violence of the state. The high point was the battle of the barricades in Quito and Cuenca; those images remind us of the Liberal Revolution, the national workers' strikes and even the barricades of the Russian Revolution. The dynamics of the confrontation made it necessary to organize a supply system with vans and trucks, ferrying tyres and other materials for the barricades (El Comercio, 2019).

---

4   Despite this, there was an underreporting of mobilisation. For example, on the Quito-Valle de los Chillos highway alone, there were around 25 blockades in 30 kilometres.

5   For reference, nationwide, during a 4-day long holiday, there are approximately 170,000 emergency calls.

6   For example, in Morona Santiago 2 roads were closed until October 15 (Jairala, 2019).

> It was the day when Quito armed itself. The marchers, including people from the local community and others from further afield, carried sticks, baseball bats, iron rods and even machetes. They moved in groups on foot, on motorcycles or in pick-up trucks, shouting combative slogans. [...] In the neighbourhoods, there were very few or no soldiers or police (Morán, 2019b).

The popular outburst against the savage repression spread like foam. Twenty-seven small police posts were destroyed, mostly in Quito (*El Comercio*, 2019) along with four military installations;[7] 128 police vehicles were attacked, either burned, stoned, smashed or destroyed; the same happened to 101 armed forces vehicles, including armoured cars, trucks and vans, 100 motorcycles of the Quito Metropolitan Police and 80 surveillance cameras were damaged during the protests,[8] 36 of them being totally destroyed (*Ecuavisa*, 2019; Zapata, 2019; TVC *El Comercio TV*, 2019; Borja, Basantes and Castro, 2019). The situation caused the Director of the National Police to give orders to evacuate the installations and facilities that were in most immediate danger (Pazmiño in *La Posta*, 2019). The mood of the oppressed classes reached boiling point and was described by the Ecuadorean Collective of Critical Geography as one of 'civil disobedience' (2019, p. 24).

In short, given the logic of action and reaction, what was the key factor in this mounting spiral of confrontation? Despite the unequal correlation of forces, the Indigenous and popular movement responded in proportion to what it received; this was not a whimsical or exaggerated reaction. Beyond the immediate circumstances, there are two basic arguments to explain it: (a) the cycle of capital accumulation, where the illusion of a pacified society makes it hard to distinguish the reality of the anarchy of production and the capitalists' insatiable search for profits; and (b) the balance of forces in the class struggle which, although deprecated by postmodern academia, is far and away the most important organizing principle of human relations – whether consciously or unconsciously – and which is exacerbated by the structures of colonialist and patriarchal domination. Finally, confrontation is the sphere of action where human beings are

---

7   In the vicinity of Quito, according to Luis Lara, Head of the Joint Command of the Armed Forces, there were sit-ins outside the Telecommunications Group, the Logistics Command Centre in 'La Balvina', the 'San Jorge' Military Fort and the 'Marco Aurelio Subía' Fort (*El Comercio*, 2019).

8   Nationwide there are about 4,630 cameras and in the Metropolitan District of Quito 900 (*DemocraciaTV*, 2019); so that is slightly less than 10% of the cameras in Quito.

transformed into the subjects of history. It is the chink through which the exploited and the oppressed can rebel and change the course of events, even if they are not fully aware of it.

1.3 THE INDIGENOUS 'STATE OF EMERGENCY', POPULAR JUSTICE AND THE WAVE OF OCCUPATIONS

One form of struggle that was rediscovered – it had been used in the Indigenous uprising of the 1990s – was the capture and detention of members of the state's repressive forces, including both regular policemen and soldiers and undercover agents. The same form was put into practice when CONAIE declared its own state of emergency on 5 October 2019, which read: 'In the face of the brutality of the armed forces […], those military and police personnel who encroach on our territories will be detained and submitted to Indigenous justice'.

A total of 202 police officers were detained. The list is as follows: 'Chimborazo (67), Quito (54) and Cotopaxi (44), according to the Ministry of the Interior' (Vaca, 2019), to which should be added the '255 military personnel arrested' (Borja, Basantes and Castro, 2019). The most important cases include the victory at Nisag (Chimborazo) where 47 military personnel were detained and the victory of Calderón Stadium (Pichincha) where 55 police officers and 21 soldiers were detained. The last detentions took place on 13 October, the same day that the government took a public beating on TV. Along with these members of the security forces, army buses, trucks and armoured cars, as well as police patrol cars, motorbikes and weapons were seized.

In some cases, the detainees were later flown out on helicopters, often with local governors and mayors, or institutions such as the UN, acting as intermediaries. There were also frequent cases of detainees being held for several days, due to the delay in the negotiations as the other side failed to address the most pressing demands of the local population. This happened in the case of the police officers detained at the Casa de la Cultura in Quito, the big cultural centre that the Indigenous movement was using as its base in the capital, when the authorities delayed handing over the body of the murdered comrade, Inocencio Tucumbi (Morán, 2019; TVC *El Comercio TV*, TVC2019), or in the case of the late exchange of a Shuar leader released by court order on 14 October – for two members of the armed forces and a policeman in Morona Santiago (*Ecuavisa*, 2019).

It wasn't that the repressive forces were constrained by their 'professionalism', as the Minister of the Interior Maria Paula Romo (2019) suggested. On the contrary, as she herself recognized on another occasion, it was that the massive participation of the people in the struggle went well beyond the state's capacity to respond. This was demonstrated in the sharp confrontations that occurred on 7 October, along the route taken by the Indigenous movement as it entered Quito from the south; the police and military checkpoints in Panzaleo, Machachi, Aloag and at the Santa Rosa bend, were simply overwhelmed by the strength of the mobilisation (*TVC El Comercio TV*, 2019; Jairala, 2019); it was also shown by the clashes in the historic centre of Quito that were triggered by the arrival of the Indigenous movement, while the installations of the Quito Regiment No. 2 (Manuela Sáenz Police District) were going up in flames and the members of the police found themselves surrounded, clearly outmanoeuvred and undermanned.

Another important component was the seizure of public institutions. These actions involved the occupation of seven governors' offices across the country[9] for a period of between 3 and 11 days; in Chimborazo, Imbabura, Loja and Azuay popular assemblies were launched (Herrera, 2019; Zibechi, 2019; Ministry of the Interior in National Assembly, 2019, p. 56). Four offices of the emergency calls service, ECU 911, were taken over in Macas, Ambato, Ibarra and Riobamba, forcing them to move their operations (Zapata, 2019; *TVC El Comercio TV*, 2019). The culmination of this form of struggle was the occupation of the National Assembly, questioning, momentarily, the legitimacy of those who claim to represent the people.[10] The last component of this form of struggle was the temporary seizure of the means of production of some large public and private capitalist enterprises. According to the trade body Expoflores (in Morán, 2019) 31 flower farms were taken over,[11] as well as four other dairy and broccoli agribusinesses; ATMs were burned; 18 supermarkets were looted in the coastal region; the water supply was cut off in Ambato (Tungurahua) and Antonio Ante (Imbabura) and water installations were occupied in Guaranda (Bolivar); electric power was cut in Pujilí (Cotopaxi) and the signal was blocked from the radio and television transmitters in Pilisurco (Tungurahua), which cover three provinces of

---

9   Governor's offices were taken over in the provinces of Napo, Tungurahua, Bolivar, Pastaza, Chimborazo, Morona Santiago and Cañar. In others, such as in Imbabura, some damage was done to their installations.

10 Demonstrators occupied the National Assembly after a truce by a group of soldiers who refused to repress them and held back the police; although, later, both forces brutally evicted the protesters from the parliamentary building.

the central highlands; fuel tankers were seized in Gualaquisa (Morona Santiago); and, in a move of huge importance in an economy so dependent on hydrocarbon resources, 12 oilfields belonging to transnational companies, and 14 fields belonging to the state-owned oil company, Petroamazonas, as well as a refinery in the Amazon (Orellana, Sucumbíos and Napo) were occupied, causing a significant reduction in oil production and export shipments. Even the Trans-Ecuadorean Oil Pipeline System (SOTE) – one of the two most important oil pipelines in the country – was shut down for more than two hours. The general dynamics of the country were disrupted.[12]

> For the last 10 days, Ecuador has been semi-paralysed, classes in educational establishments are suspended, food and other staple goods are running short at the distribution centres, there is no urban or inter-city transport, there is a lot of speculation and prices are increasing (Tamayo and Serrano, 2019).

The bourgeoisie linked to the dairy industry[13] declared an emergency on 12 October. At that stage they estimated they were losing 5 million litres of milk a day due to the lack of supplies which caused a shortage of dairy products. They claimed to represent one and a half million producers, but in the end they really only spoke for the interests of the big dairy producers. The October rebellion would not have ended if not for the pressure on all these sectors of production. They ended up 'requesting' that the government resolve their problems: 'For this reason we

---

[11] 'The Association of Flower Producers and Exporters of Ecuador (Expoflores) denounced looting on flower farms in the areas of Lasso and Latacunga (Cotopaxi) and Cotacachi (Imbabura)' (Le Quang, Chávez and Vizuete, 2020, p. 65).

[12] 'In the case of Petroamazonas, the 14 oil blocks affected were: Eden Yuturi, Indillana, Palo Azul, Yuralpa, Pucuna, Armadillo, Shushufindi, Libertador, Cuyabeno, Tipishca, Vinita, Sacha, Auca and Coca Payamino. Between 13 and 19 October Petroamazonas lost 1.5 million barrels of production (about half the country's normal output). In the case of the private companies, the twelve blocks reportedly affected were operated by the following companies: AGIP, Andes Petróleo, Consorcio Pegaso, Consorcio Palanda, Yuca Sur, Consorcio Petrosud Petroriva, ENAP PEG (two blocks), Gente Oil, Orion (two blocks), Pacifpetrol, Petrobell and Petroriental (two blocks). 373,000 barrels of oil production were lost' (Asamblea Nacional, 2019, p. 59).

[13] Centro de la Industria Láctea, Consejo Nacional Lechero, Cámara de Agricultura de la Zona I, Asociación Holstein del Ecuador, Manjar de Leche, Alimentos Ecuatorianos S.A., Fundación Latina de Alimentos, Parmalat S.A., IMPROLAC S.A., Asociación de Ganaderos de la Sierra y Oriente, Lácteos San Antonio, Club de Agricultores y Ganaderos, Federación Nacional de Productores de Leche, Asociación Nacional de Fabricantes de Alimentos y Bebidas de Ecuador.

ask – said the capitalists – that the parties involved in the conflict sit down and talk in order to overcome the problems, end the protest and allow us to restore the conditions where everyone can work safely and securely'.

In response to these demands, the government laid on 1,108 vehicles, and organized a total of '62 convoys, with escorts, to reach their destination and ensure supplies for the population' (Borja, Basantes and Castro, 2019). The efficiency of the police and the army in protecting the wealthy contrasts with the insecurity experienced in the poor urban communities.[14]

In the debates following the October rebellion, one figure was often repeated: US$2.8 billion in losses in 11 days (*El Comercio*, 2019; *FM Mundo*, 2019; *TVC El Comercio TV*, 2019; *Teleamazonas*, 2019). Even if we accept this exaggerated figure, obtained through the 'complex scientific procedure' of dividing the country's annual GDP by the number of days the stoppage lasted, we still have to ask: Who lost? Who lost 2.8 billion dollars in 11 days? There's no doubt the people lost part of their income due to the stoppage, but who actually controls the economy? Losses like this are borne, fundamentally, by the capitalists. For the exploited classes, a strike does not substantially change the already difficult living conditions of their households; for the rich, on the other hand, it means that their profits are reduced. What a tragedy that their bank accounts are not getting bigger!

The victory in October slowed down the squeeze on poor families' living standards, while they gained in dignity. For the ruling class, every second they are unable to exploit the labour of others is a burden on them, it hurts, it breaks the heart of their pocket. Evidently, the dominant approach emphasizes the loss of income by the big bourgeoisie, which seeks to turn the page on all those days of lost profits.[15] That's why this discourse inflated the size of the capitalists' 'losses' to around the mythical figure of US$ 3 billion (National Assembly, 2019). When the 2019 GDP figures were finally tallied, they showed that 'the national strike [...] caused losses of between US$ 700 and USD 800 million in terms of economic activity, according to the general manager of the Central Bank of Ecuador' (Tapia, 2019).

---

14   Thus '50.2% of people consider that their neighbourhood is unsafe, and this figure increases when asking, how unsafe the person feels in the city where they live, where the national average rises to 83.1%, followed by 77.3% of people who consider that crime increased in the city they live' (Espinel, 2015, p. 53).

15   The President of the Chamber of Industries of Production, Pablo Zambrano (in *FM Mundo*, 2019) said: 'We get ahead by working not striking'. Similar annoyance was shown through a complaint about paralysing production and 'hijacking the country' by Daniel Legarda, President of the Federation of Exporters of Ecuador (on *FM Mundo*, 2019).

Chart 9: Economic balance of the protest (millions of dollars per day)

	In favour of protests	Against protests
Went out to demonstrate	24%–30% Quito	5.7% Quito
	16% Guayaquil	
Did not go out, but supported	39% Quito	19% Quito
Declared neutral	17% Quito	

Source: our own estimates based on Varela, 2020, pp. 95–98

For the working class, the economic losses due to a possible implementation of the *paquetazo*, the IMF-inspired measures contained in Decree No. 883, would have been much greater than those caused by the stoppage. From Varela's study (2020) it can be concluded that for most of the people it was economically beneficial to mobilize and defend their rights. Not to do so would have meant a daily loss of 87.9 million dollars, and a total of 966.9 million dollars as a result of the loss of one day's pay a month, the reduction in wage levels, the surge in inflation caused by the elimination of fuel subsidies, and so on. Far from the fanciful accounting of the capitalists, the losses for the majority of the people would have been five times greater if they had not carried out the mobilization. Mobilizations result in better living conditions for the working class.

The losses from supplying the repressive forces are also greater than those 'caused' by the demonstrators. Let's make a simple comparison. The price of a cobblestone is estimated at US$1. If 100,000 cobblestones were removed to build barricades and protect the lives of thousands of people that is much less than the price of 5,000 tear gas bombs – the number used was in fact greater than that – at a cost of 50 US dollars each. The cost of the repression between 3 and 13 October 2019 includes: the logistics expenses (transport, wages and supplies for 13,658 police officers); the direct expenses of repression (tear gas bombs, pepper spray, stun grenades, rubber bullets and blanks, 12 and 16 calibre cartridges, 9mm calibre bullets, horses, dogs);[16] fuel for vehicles (armoured personnel carriers,

---

[16] Costs per horse total: $6,000 for each animal, $60,000 for training and $600 per month for maintenance. Sixty-six horses were used. In the case of dogs, the expenses are: US$15,000 per animal and US$200 per month for their food and care. Forty-two dogs were used (*El Comercio*, 2019).

anti-riot vehicles, patrol cars, motorcycles, helicopters); and the destruction caused by the repression (infrastructure such as windows, etc.); compensation for injuries such as loss of sight and other eye injuries, and for deaths involving compensation for loss of earnings. To this we can add what was very possibly the self-organized attack on the State Comptroller's Office.

Finally, there is something that cannot and should not be quantified in terms of money, something the rich will never make sense of, because it is not susceptible to exchange value and the laws of the market: the working class gained dignity.

1.4 PEOPLE'S SOLIDARITY AND SUPPORT FOR PROVISIONS

The sudden imposition of the government measures generated an instantaneous response. There was no time for planning. The administration of a large number of demonstrators, who came to the main areas of confrontation from other provinces and from other parts of the capital, had to develop and be perfected as things went on.

Consequently, in the first few days there were serious difficulties in the distribution of supplies among the organizations (food, medicine and other essentials), which caused some conflicts, but they were rectified as the days went by. Then there was a shortage of food cooked in the community soup kitchens, but this situation was remedied thanks to the massive arrival of food prepared by hundreds of families voluntarily. The experience gained in the process helped to rationalize the provision of food, which improved in both quantity and quality. The large numbers of people in one place led to sanitation problems, caused by the accumulation of garbage; disposing of this was a logistical task in itself. At the same time, the cleanliness of the bathrooms and the lack of water facilities caused stomach problems which required the support of medical brigades and, above all, the application of preventive health care.

Children also suffered from the long waits and the conflict, so it became necessary to organize spaces for play and education. Cases of misbehaviour in the requests for donations, and of disturbances in the collective spaces were dealt with by the organizations themselves, where necessary with the intervention of the Community, Indigenous and Popular Guards.

The popular struggle built new social relations based on solidarity; resources were distributed under the motto: 'To each according to their work' and tasks were assigned on the principle of: 'From each according to their ability'. The Quito Commune was being built in practice. The fight could not be conducted following the logic of individualism; the only way to stand firm was through a sense of community. This mini city-utopia encompassed a population of at least 30,000 people, equivalent to that of 80% of Ecuador's municipalities.

The importance of this is even greater if we remember that similar ways of managing public affairs were developed in various parts of Ecuador; for example, in the governors' offices taken over by demonstrators, in the branches of social movements and other organizations, and even at the blockades along the highways. It was, therefore, a palpable demonstration that the working class of the countryside and the city can run the country themselves, without any need for their exploiters.

The solidarity in Quito was broad. It was said that 'the city fed the countryside during the days of mobilization', a reversal of the historical relationship between town and country, where it is the peasant and Indigenous sector that delivers food to the cities. The support for the mobilization covered many spheres of people's daily lives. On the one hand, five large reception centres and countless smaller resting points were organized, housing about 30,000 people permanently, and hundreds of thousands who were coming and going.

> The Central University of Ecuador (UCE), one of the largest public institutions in the country, opened its doors just after the reception centres at the two Catholic universities, the PUCE and the UPS, opened on 8 October. The university's coliseum, with a capacity for 800 people, was open from Tuesday 8 October to Monday 14 October. However, given the number of people who needed to be accommodated, in addition to the Amazonian Indigenous people who joined the call to converge on the capital, on Friday 11 October three more spaces were opened at the Central University: at the Faculties of Communication, of Arts and of Architecture and Urbanism (Noriega and Criollo, 2020, p. 131).

These shelters withstood the attack of the repressive forces and, on occasion, were protected by human barriers formed by hundreds of people, who put themselves between the repressive battalions and the spaces where children and the elderly were located.

On the other hand, the foodstuffs, medical supplies, clothes and blankets – products stored in improvised deposits – were redistributed among those present according to their needs and militant work. 'Three classrooms filled with rice, toiletries, clothes, water and medicine. The solidarity of the people of Quito overflowed the initial capacities of the space, to the point of requesting more classrooms at the University' (Noriega and Criollo, 2020, pp. 134–135).

Donations came not only from the population of Quito (*TVC El Comercio TV*, 2019): 'The peasants of the Coast gathered supplies to send to Quito; the same actions were carried out from all the provinces of the country' (Chiliquinga, 2019); they even came from remote districts of the Amazon region. In more than one case, donations were paid for by migrants who, from the United States and Europe, sent remittances so their families in Ecuador could deliver the products.

Solidarity fostered a process of autonomous organization among people in local communities, cultural centres, schools and neighbourhood associations, family groups, groups of friends, LGBTQI collectives, open markets and others who joined together in the tasks of organizing, collecting, classifying and sending donations. Very often the same groups that brought the donations were in charge of distributing the prepared food. 'It was the people's food that we shared, a piece of bread, oatmeal, aniseed water' (Chancosa, 2020, p. 27), lunches, coffee, sugar water, *chicha* and so on. There were expressions of solidarity in poor urban neighbourhoods to ensure the supply of food and other products, given the prolongation of the struggle. This was the case, for example, with the barter fair in Puembo or the peace brigades created in some popular neighbourhoods.

The volunteer brigades that remained throughout the conflict in the hot zone numbered at least 3,000 people. The tasks were multiple and exhausting. Working groups were set up to deal with human rights, and teams of lawyers were formed to provide legal advice, detect possible violations, issue alerts and reports (Alianza de Organizaciones por los Derechos Humanos, 2019).[17] Networks of alternative, popular and community media disseminated more reliable information about the rebellion;[18] teams of doctors, nurses and paramedics provided free services, in the areas of both preventive health and emergency care;[19] psychologists, social workers and kindergarten staff attended to children who were with their families in the vicinity of the areas of confrontation. Performers, plastic and visual artists, writers, storytellers and musicians were involved in the mobilization, preparing spaces to receive the groups that arrived and entrusted with producing audiovisual, dramatic, plastic and musical works and performances.

A large group of volunteers, regardless of their level of education or their national or ethnic identity, contributed to the environmental sanitation services (the cleaning of bathrooms, garbage collection and recycling, cleaning of social areas and corridors), to unloading and transporting donations, food preparation in the community kitchens, among other tasks. A growing number of vehicles flew white or tricolour, national flags, with slogans such as: 'Because I love Ecuador, today we join the people'. In the Province of Azuay, according to the Assembly of the Peoples of the South, during a mass celebrated before thousands of demonstrators, the Church gave the money collected with the alms to the local strike committee. In the province of Tungurahua, players from the Club Deportivo Macará football team played ecuavolley (an Ecuadorean variant of volleyball, which may date back to pre-colonial times) with the demonstrators.

> In Guayaquil, Cuenca, Portoviejo, Machala and other cities, protest demonstrations proliferated, under the slogan '*Quito aguanta, el pueblo se levanta*' ['Quito stands firm, the people are rising up'] (Tamayo, 2019).

---

17 In addition to countless legal professionals who provided their services free of charge, the lawyers' offices and organizations that supported the victims of the repression were: the Ecumenical Human Rights Commission (CEDHU), the Permanent Committee for the Defense of Human Rights (CDH), the Regional Human Rights Advisory Foundation (INREDH), the Permanent Committee for the Defense of Human Rights, the SURKUNA organization, the Idea DIGNITY Foundation, and the Amazon Frontlines organization.

18 The network of alternative and community media that reported on the mobilisation consisted of: Kapari, *Crisis* Magazine, Cerco Mediático, Lanceros Digitales, Apak TV, Política con Manzanas, Radio Periférica, CORAPE, Radio Casa de la Cultura, Escuelas Radiofónicas, Radio Quimsacocha, Zángano Press, Coop Docs, RPP, Revista Conciencia Revolucionaria, Fluxus, Nina Radio, Radio Facso, Wambra Radio, Wasimedia, Infórmate Pueblo, Radio La Calle, Willer Radio, Radio Illumán, Radio Latacunga, TV MICC, Radio Voz de la CONFENIAE, Radio Parlante de Carcelén, Red de Voceros Comunitarios de Quito, Red de Comunicadores Comunicadores Comunitarios de Manabí, Hoja de Ruta.

19 The stories from two mobile medical centres set up for protesters in Quito bear witness to the level of solidarity. 'In the Arbolito Park there were about ten doctors and between 40 and 50 student volunteers providing care to the injured' (Cuvi, Arteaga, Cueva and Maldonado, 2019). 'Students from the PUCE turned out en masse as volunteers. At least 739 of them, of which 413 were women, signed up for various tasks on campus. 169 hours of continuous medical care was provided' (Vaca, 2019).

On the Coast, despite the regionalism on which part of the national identity is built, in El Oro, Quevedo, Manta and Guayas, organizations took to the streets to show solidarity with the Indigenous uprising and as a slogan they chanted '*Quito aguanta que Manta se levanta*', ['Quito stand firm, Manta is rising up'], [or 'Quito stands firm, Huaquillas rises up'] or 'Quito stands firm, Quevedo is rising up' (Herrera, 2019).

Solidarity knew no borders. Internationalist actions in solidarity with the struggle in Ecuador proliferated around the world. We heard of support demonstrations in Argentina,[20] Germany,[21] Italy, Portugal,[22] France,[23] Spain,[24] Mexico,[25] the United States[26] and Canada. This is what is needed to confront the closing of ranks among the exploiters of the world (such as the neoconservative Mike Pompeo of the United States) who expressed their support for Moreno.

Although there was some racism, the vast majority of the Ecuadorean people actively participated in the struggle alongside the Indigenous movement. The phrase 'Tell them [the Indians] to stay on the moors', or the game 'Pin the feathers on the Indian Vargas' (*Periodismo en buseta,* 2019), spoken or promoted respectively by Jaime Nebot in the Municipality of Guayaquil and by the ladies of the Junta de Beneficencia in Samborondón, show the deep roots of racism among the ruling class.

One of the crudest, most reactionary and recalcitrant forms of racism has been the insistence, in the media, that CONAIE is a minority group representing only 7% of the population. Of course, the same argument is never used to attack the bankers and businessmen responsible for the economic disasters experienced by poor families (e.g. the financial crisis of 1999, known

---

[20] Among the organizations that joined the actions of struggle in Argentina are: Frente de Organizaciones en Lucha (FOL); Partido Revolucionario Venceremos; Frente Popular Darío Santillán; Corriente Nacional, (CON); MTD Aníbal Verón; Frente de Organizaciones de Base (FOB); Autónoma, MTD Oscar Barrios; Movimiento por la Unidad Latinoamericana y el Cambio Social (MULCS); Izquierda Latinoamericana Socialista; Movimiento 8 de abril; MRP Frente Arde Rojo; COPA en Marabunta; MTR Por Democracia Directa e Igualdad Social; Movimiento de los Pueblos; Asamblea Plurinacional de Mujeres del Abya-Yala, al MST.

[21] Ecuadorean residents in Berlin carried out a series of events with the support of the Latin American bloc. On 9 October a sit-in was held in front of the Ecuadorean Embassy in Berlin, attended by different social sectors and an international denouncement was made against the repression of the Moreno government. On 17 October a rally was held again in front of the diplomatic headquarters in homage to the victims of the government. On 25 October a conference was held in Zielona Góra: 'Resistance against neoliberalism: Ecuador's current situation and perspectives'. On 6 December a cultural evening was held in Hamburg to raise funds for the victims of the repression, which were channelled through the Victims' Association 'Inocencio Tucumbi'.

as 'the bank holiday'). Why are Guillermo Lasso and Alvaro Noboa not constantly reminded that they only represent the 0.01% of the Ecuadorean population who own banks or banana companies? Talk of the 'minority' is a continuation of the Ecuadorean elites' attempt to 'whiten' the country, by denying the network of social and cultural relations developed by and around the Indigenous population, which goes well beyond statistics and genetics. To paraphrase Bonfil Batalla (1990), the dominant class has constructed an imaginary Ecuador, denying the existence of the deep Ecuador. However, during rebel October the vast majority of the population did not swallow this imaginary scheme.

The extraordinary arrival of the Indigenous movement in Quito on 7 October and the phenomenal support received during the days of the rebellion demonstrate the bankruptcy of the segregationist attempt of the elites. Apparently, the thesis of Manuel Espinosa Apolo (2010), that the *mestizo* is a derivation of the Kichwa nationality, turned out to be – in the context of the October struggle – a living, dynamic and thriving fact. The need to overthrow the IMF's anti-popular measures was transformed into a commonwealth of popular interests represented by the Indigenous movement and actively backed by a variety of social sectors. This challenged, in practice, the narrative of a nation built by the white-*mestizo* elites, and gave shape to a nation that, for eleven days, was constituted from the Indigenous-*mestizo* grassroots.

> As the days went by, however, the meaning of humanitarian aid was transformed. Collaboration ceased to be charitable and became political. Donations were no longer given out of compassion but through a sense of reciprocity with the comrades who were putting their bodies into this struggle against measures that affected everyone.

22 Demonstrations and sit-ins were held in Lisbon, on Avenida da Libertade, with the participation of Ecuadorean and Latin American migrants.
23 'In Paris, more than 300 people were reportedly present at the Trocadero to protest against IMF measures' (Le Quang, Chavez and Vizuete, 2020, p. 75).
24 'In Madrid, more than 500 people gathered to express their rejection of the decisions of the Ecuadorean government, the repression and the statements of the Ecuadorean ambassador in Spain, who had minimised the deaths of demonstrators' (Le Quang, Chávez and Vizuete, 2020, p. 75).

25 'On Thursday, 10 October 10, 2019, at the Ecuadorean embassy in Mexico City, a rally was held in solidarity with the Ecuadorean Indigenous movement, which continues with demonstrations against the adjustment imposed by the IMF towards the government of Lenin Moreno' (La Izquierda Diario, 2019)..
26 'Ecuadorean migrants protested in New York (United States) against the IMF. This time, they took over the office of the IMF special representative to the United Nations (Santana, 10 October 2019)' (Le Quang, Chavez, and Vizuete, 2020, p. 68).

> The relationship with the Indigenous 'other' also changed. They were no longer 'poor barefoot people' to be pitied, but rather brave men and women determined to fight in defence of the rights of all (Noriega and Criollo, 2020, p. 137).

Expressions such as 'our Indigenous people' that once had a possessive meaning and, far from showing respect, infantilised them, were superseded by 'our Indigenous brothers and sisters'. The change eroded the ethnic frontier between the *mestizo* and the Indian, which was constructed during the nineteenth-century project of assembling Latin American nations, based on an idea of progress borrowed from the countries of northern Europe and the United States (Burns, 1990).

1.5 SYMBOLIC UPRISING AND THE MYTH OF OCTOBER

Symbols build meaning. They give transcendence in time and space to an object, an action, a gesture, a word. They carry a load of information that goes beyond the rational; they touch on the emotive, on desire and move through the different levels of subjectivity: conscious, unconscious, subconscious. Symbolic language gives a mythical dimension to reality. Just as in art and religion, symbols are also created in politics that give a particular meaning to phenomena. In the accumulated struggle of the peoples of Ecuador, symbols from the Latin American and international left (red flags, burnt tyres, slogans, the wearing of hoods, etc.) converged with others from the Andean, Amazonian and coastal cosmovision – the ceremonial use of fire, spears, *aciales* (a kind of whip used to corral animals), machetes, face painting, medicines and the presence of *taytas* and *mamas*,[27] among others).

Just as for Sorel (2005) the general strike was the highest myth for modern emancipation, in our case rebel October became the most powerful symbol. It encapsulated what was new, from the disgust with ignominy to the pathos of indignation. 'It was in the [rebellion] that the people affirmed its existence' (Sorel, 2005, p. 351). But there were other reference points too.

---

27 *Tayta* and *mama*, literally father and mother, are the gendered titles given in Quichua tradition to certain mountains, regarded as deities. For example, Taita Chimborazo or Mama Tungurahua. There are tales of love affairs between some of these, giving rise to offspring, such as Guagua (Child) Pichincha.

October was an extraordinary episode, full of symbolic actions. The most remarkable was surely the mainstream media's reluctant broadcasting of the final negotiations, which were 'unprecedented in the history of Ecuador' (Stoessel, 2019). The transmission called into question the bloc in power and the state as a whole; it consolidated new political voices on the national stage, and demonstrated that if popular organizations are driven by the needs and ideas of the exploited classes, no negotiations will take place in commissions cobbled together by 'eminent figures', behind the backs of the people.

The decrees issued by CONAIE had a symbolic weight that translated into material force. The first was the declaration of a state of emergency in the Indigenous territories, which made possible the detention, *en masse*, of members of the repressive forces in the conflict zones, who in some cases were ordered to shout slogans in favour of the rebellion. The right saw this as an example of 'absolute self-determination', which undermined the power of the President of the Republic to decree a state of emergency (*El Comercio*, 2019). In fact, it was the right of the exploited classes to *potestas*, the authentic basis of popular sovereignty. In opposition to this, the Minister of Defence, Oswaldo Jarrín, ignoring constitutional principles, said:

> There is no such thing as Indigenous territories, the territory belongs to the Ecuadorean state and the only person who can make a declaration on behalf of the Ecuadorean state is the President of the Republic, in accordance with the constitution and laws of Ecuador. Here there is no other minority that can lay claim to the powers of the national state.

CONAIE's second decree declared three days of national mourning for the death of Edgar Yucailla, who was given a mass burial in his native Sablog, in the heart of the Province of Chimborazo (*Ecuavisa*, 2019). The same thing happened with the funeral of comrade Inocencio Tucumbi, whose wake in Quito saw a huge turnout and was broadcast live and reported on by at least a hundred national and international media outlets. The ceremony was one of the few occasions in human history where the forces of repression have been ordered to take responsibility for extrajudicial executions. After the verdict of the Indigenous justice system, the ruling classes, through their institutions, were forced to make some reparation for the murder of a son of the people, through a popular resolution that the people who murdered him should be the ones to carry the coffin.[28]

As Jaime Bayly (2019) regretfully observed, the demonstrators gave orders to the forces of repression and they obeyed. It showed that democracy is not suffrage: it is the power of the people. Luis Salvador, Vice President of the Chambers of Industry of Guayaquil, following the same logic as former President Correa, argued that you have to win elections to take such action, asking 'How many elections have they won?' (Jairala, 2019). Such rhetoric legitimizes the restrictive, bourgeois conception of democracy.

In fact, it was the very character of the political system, the nature of the state and its ideological apparatus that was challenged; its ability to manoeuvre was undermined, making it impossible to apply the clientelist strategies typical of Latin American domination. Faced with a vacuum of power, it was the Casa de la Cultura Ecuatoriana cultural centre and the Arbolito Park in Quito that became the new centre of political life, based on the barricades and the heroism of the people throughout the country. October brought a critique of the concept that reduces democracy to a question of the market for votes, while ignoring the simple reality that the poor will never have the 25 million dollars needed for a presidential campaign, nor the 'connections' within the state organizations needed to make elections happen at the right time. What would have been the result if elections had been called during the rebellion? Of course, the ruling classes would never have recognized the validity of 30% of the population in the streets, nor of the 68% popular support for the protests, because that, unlike election expenses and political marketing – which the bourgeoisie defines as democracy – cannot be bought with money: it is about dignity and awareness.[29]

In a third decree, CONAIE called for a *minga*, a collective community effort, to clean up the protest area; this revealed both the dimension of the events (the bonfires, debris, sticks, burnt tyres, the residue of tear gas bombs, ammunition casings from lethal and 'non-lethal' weapons, layers of ash on the streets and pavements) as well as the capacity of the organized people to sweep away injustice, and the willingness of the people to rebuild after ending the opprobrium. At the same time, cabs,

---

28 'Eight motorcycle policemen were detained in the morning, near the Cultural Centre. The officers faced the Indigenous justice system for more than six hours, and its verdict ordered them to carry the body (covered with the Ecuadorean tricolour flag and the *wipala* Indigenous flag) of one of the demonstrators who died the night before, as it was transferred from the Eugenio Espejo Hospital morgue to the auditorium of the Ecuadorean Cultural Centre. Amid the people's indignation, the auditorium became 'a town square for recrimination' (*Plan V*, 2019).

buses and trucks were provided free of charge for the demonstrators to return to their communities.

Another symbolic action that raised the morale of those who were surrounded by the forces of repression in the conflict zone was the *cacerolazo*, or banging of pots and pans, on the night of 12 October: 'Empty pots and pans have been a symbol of popular discontent against governments' (Morán, 2019). The sound of the pots symbolised the protest against Decree No. 888 and the curfew (Morán, 2019), and combined with the way people challenged the legitimacy of state power by staying out in the street during the curfew (*El Universo*, 2019).

> We knew there would be a *cacerolazo* at 20.30 thanks to the citizens' call made on social media. It was an expression of opposition to Moreno's curfew. Thirty minutes before, hammering was heard, the origin of which was unknown. After the tension generated by the police, a stream of local people arrived at the gates of the Catholic university, PUCE, to support the brigades of students, doctors and volunteers. With their pots and pans in hand, the curfew decreed by Moreno was no longer in effect in the peace zone. Paradoxical as it may seem, it was the beating of the pots and pans that produced a sense of calm (Noriega and Criollo, 2020, p. 142).

Even in these situations, attacks by the repressive apparatuses of the state still happened – as was the case with Jhajaira Urresta (*El Comercio*, 2019). Such outrages teach us that, even if their protest is peaceful, repression looms over the people when they do not submit to the whims and petty games of the big economic groups.

Special mention should be made of the creative, playful and artistic exhibitions that took place in the context and after rebel October. Ángel Guaraca, national singer-songwriter of the Puruhá people, composed the song *Homenaje a la Resistencia* (Homage to the Resistance). Students and teachers of the Faculty of Arts of the Central University made a mosaic,

---

29   The structural incapacity of the state to listen to popular demands in an unfavourable economic context – unlike the unique and exceptional period of the thirty 'glorious' years of metropolitan capitalism (1945–1975) – means that satisfaction with elections – wrongly called 'satisfaction with democracy' – is on the decline, along with people's support for the electoral system itself (Latinobarómetro, 2019).

People see less and less point in voting, because 'no matter how one votes, it will not make things better' (*Latinobarómetro*, 2019). A change of government becomes of little importance for more and more people, because in the daily life of working people, both in the countryside and the city, this fact does not result in any change of direction (*Latinobarómetro*, 2019).

visual works and cantatas referring to the rebel days. There was the Universidad de las Artes with the collective performance '*Supongamos*', or 'Supposing'; the hip-hop and rap music of Warmi Rap with their song '*Warmi Hatari*'; Los Nin with their song '*Ricchary*'; Warmi Taki with '*Que No Pare el Paro*', or 'Don't Stop the Stoppage'; Rapdikal with '*Las jornadas de Octubre*', and several groups and soloists such as Clandestinos, Skan, Don Leonard, Real Cultura Clika, Carla Espín, Diana, Jota al Cuadrado, Mugrel Sidorenko, Tonik, Pu MC, Poeta Under, Davrap, Trapos MC, Rima Rina Warmi, Abraham MC.

The re-adaptation of the iconic song, '*Aguanta*' or 'Hold On', by the band Sal y Mileto; the metal band Coraje from Quito; the neo-ancestral techno performance '*Meztizo*' by Stalin Pacheco from Cuenca; the theatre and puppet company El Revuelque, with the play '*Extracotidiano, el tiempo de los enlunados*'; the engravings of the visual artists of Guayaquil; the Museo del Paro, or Museum of the Strike, organized by Fábrika Zurda and the Movimiento de Barrios en Lucha (Movement of Neighbourhoods in Struggle), which toured several localities, with photographs and artefacts that enhance political memory; Catalan hip-hop artist Pablo Hasel composed the song '*En Chile, Ecuador, Haití o donde sea*' ('In Chile, Ecuador, Haiti or wherever'); the group Chilla Jatun from Bolivia with their song dedicated to the protest '*Justica para vivir*' ('Justice to live'); solidarity messages from Rubén Albarrán, lead singer of Café Tacuba; the *murga* group, La Muñeca, from Uruguay, in their version of the Latin American struggle adapting the popular Argentine–Bolivian tune '*Carnaval*'; Chilean artist Mon Laferte's position on the emergence of the Latin American struggle; the displays of affection from the popular Quechua-Peruvian comedian 'Cholo' Juanito; the work of the icon of Ecuadorean popular theatre, Carlos Michelena; the contributions of the anarchist singer-songwriter 'Chamo' Jaime Guevara; the satire of Hugo the 'Owl'; the collages from the coast by the sculptor Tony Balseca; the hospitality for the demonstrators from the artist Adriana Oña; the intervention in the park El Arbolito by Darío Caisa with the work 'Evict the road' in homage to the fallen in the rebellion; the poetry and music of Xavier Silva Cárdenas, 'Compa Xavucho'; the scatological protest paintings of Pancho Dueñas; the graffiti of Alejo Cruz and several urban artists; the images captured by dozens of photographers and visual artists; the songs of Victor Jara interpreted by rock legend Roger Waters; the immense creativity of hundreds of anonymous young people who, with their visual elaborations, comments, memes and posts stripped bare the actually existing power and raised the morale of the fighters of the rebellion.

There was also the theatrical spirit expressed in the new year celebrations of 31 December, when the tradition of burning an effigy of the year past was carried out with subsidized gasoline, as a result of the people's victory and the dignity people had shown in October; the poetic, satirical and prose writing of the Ecuadorean rebel minstrels; the urgent research undertaken on the rebellion and the large number of students who have oriented their research towards understanding what happened in October; the debates held in universities, neighbourhoods and other organized spaces, and the unforgettable anthem of rebel October, taken from the emblematic song: '*Movimiento Indígena*' by Charijayac.

The symbolic expressions of protests were not isolated initiatives or internet messages from small groups. They were the other face of the accumulation of forces by the popular camp, whose effectiveness had been demonstrated in the course of struggle. Mass mobilization was the central feature of the negotiations and confrontations with the state and the ruling class, and the key to understanding the direction taken by the October rebellion. It is in that framework that the significance of the performances, the tweets and the online activity has to be understood; otherwise they will be reduced to areas of self-indulgence and social immobility.

October was an overwhelming demonstration of human community, of mutual protection of the members of the extended family as suggested by the teacher Paco Salvador: the realisation of the *muyundi yawar kanchik* of the Kichwa peoples, of the 'We are all brothers and sisters'. Nevertheless, with malice aforethought, the retired colonel and Assembly member Fausto Cobo said 'the mobilizations cost at least 20 million dollars' (*DemocraciaTV*, 2019). He was wrong – they cost much more. If we add together the solidarity, the hours of voluntary labour, the work of organization and the creativity of the people in rebellion, the popular contribution of the exploited classes to the struggle was monumental, huge, greater than all the money in the world – in a word, humanity.

1.6 LUMPENBOURGEOIS CULTURE AND THE EXCESSES OF POPULAR RAGE

A large part of the repertoire of political action by the popular sectors during the October rebellion was a reaction against state violence. The people do not have the means to organize violence, only to defend themselves against it. The evidence is in the innumerable and systematic acts of police terrorism.

> Today I and my brother were kidnapped and tortured by Policia Ecuador. To explain: my brother and I have been delivering humanitarian aid, transporting bowls of water with bicarbonate, to help people affected by tear gas. Today, at around 5.30 in the afternoon we came back to my car a block away from the Catholic University, because the police repression had already begun in the area, and were going to leave. We were sitting in the car, with the engine off, when a group of police on motorbikes came up and surrounded us, and began to smash the windows of my car. One of them pointed a shotgun at my face and threatened to shoot if I did not get out of the car. They dragged me and my brother out of the car and a group of policemen began to hit us on the ground and kick us. If we raised our heads a bit they kicked us and shouted to us not to look up. After beating us around the head and on the back they pushed us into a patrol car and drove round Quito for around two hours. We were never charged, or told why we had been detained (Testimony of an arrest at the Alliance of Human Rights Organizations in 2019).
>
> I lifted my head and felt the impact in my face – they shot me in the face, just like that. Everything went black and I felt dizzy. I remembered where the door was and I crawled towards it and pushed the boy through. Then I crawled to the door and managed to get under it. They examined me later and I fell into a kind of limbo – I couldn't feel anything. I found out I had been shot when the doctor told me I had been lucky and that they had got thirty pellets out of my face when they operated. Really? I said, and he said there were still another fifty in my face. They fired point blank and the

pellets didn't open (Testimony of an arrest at the Alliance of Human Rights Organizations in 2019).

The actions of the police make clear the dehumanization of the repressive forces. What was the crime here? To limit the circulation of capitalism's commodities?[30] Does this justify beating, torturing, isolating, cruelly mistreating and denigrating people? (*Plan V*, 2019; Alliance of Human Rights Organizations, 2019). Anything to defend the accumulation of capital and the enrichment of a few.

If we compare these actions with the work of the Community, Indigenous and People's Guards, the differences become very clear. Beyond the fact that people became animated in the heat of battle, how many testimonies do we have of police trying to calm their comrades? Very few, in fact, and they were seen as indiscipline, as opposed to the many examples on the demonstrators' side.

Among the events recorded are the four uprisings in prisons around the country, in the Provisional Detention Centre in Quito, Latacunga prison, the Social Rehabilitation Centre in Cañar and the escape of 80 prisoners from the Portoviejo Detention Centre in Manabí (*DemocraciaTV* 2019); the alleged sexual assaults on policewomen in Pujilí and Calderón;[31] the stones thrown indiscriminately at cars and the arbitrary 'tolls' taken; the attacks on 42 Red Cross ambulances (after a private ambulance was videoed supplying the police)[32] and the possibly self-organized arson at the Comptroller's offices, even though the images in the public domain show police firing on demonstrators from the terraces and air vents of the building (Jairala, 2019).

We were struck by the occurrence, above all, of looting because most of this took place in Guayaquil, though they were also reported in Santo Domingo de las Tsáchilas, Ambato and Quito – Guayaquil had also experienced them during the police revolt of 2010. This can be explained because for forty years the city has been the preserve of the right, between 1978 and 1992 by its populist version (PRE, CFP, APRE, FRA)[33] and its modern version between 1992 and 2019. Throughout this time, the city has been

---

30 In the circuits of capital, the only interest in the circulation of people is in a labour force that has to go to work. One more factor of production.

31 No sexual assaults are registered by Human Rights Watch (HRW, 2020). But independently of the truth of the declarations of the police, which were probably designed to discredit the social mobilisations, we oppose any form of sexual aggression, unlike the state.

32 The Report on October by the Legislative Commission includes an account by an agent who organized some Health Ministry workers to dress her as a doctor so that she could pass unnoticed in the demonstrations.

33 Partido Roldosista Ecuatoriano, Concentración de Fuerzas Populares, Acción Popular Revolucionaria Ecuatoriana and Frente Radical Alfarista.

shaped by different fractions of the bourgeoisie, and particularly in the modern period of Social-Christian government,[34] through the consolidation of the 'urban regeneration project'.[35]

The looting was the result of the poverty and privation experienced particularly by the youth of the marginal barrios 'who tried to resolve their issues of welfare and the scarcity by non-traditional means like looting, which has traditionally happened during mass mobilizations in the port city' (Chiliquinga, 2019). Some 300 small and medium businesses were affected. But there is a clear difference from the mass mobilizations. While in other cities the protests had a political character and the looting was limited to a small minority, in Guayaquil the opposite was true.[36] Here the events were characterized as 'vandalism' by the mass media and elite of the city, since most looting took place in the commercial centre dominated and controlled by those elites; if that is the case, who was responsible? CONAIE? Communism?

Far from the obtuse point of view of the conservative representatives (who cling to repression as a solution to social problems and support the APP [Stop, Beat, Shoot] strategy designed by the Social-Christian politician Alfonso 'el Pocho' Harb), and as distinct from the simplistic ideas of some leaders of the institutional left,[37] our position is that the looting was the consequence of the precarious living conditions faced by many. In particular, that means unemployment, the growth of the lumpenproletariat, the proliferation of the neoliberal principle 'save yourself first', the breakdown of the organizational structures of society, as well as the absence of a left, anti-capitalist project.

Was there an evil plot to create chaos on the coast and start a revolution in the mountains? No, it was a popular initiative; as one journalist wrote, 'Nobody organizes the youngsters who set out to rob' (Jairala, 2019).

The cases we have cited show that spontaneous and uncoordinated action by the exploited classes goes nowhere and does not change people's living conditions. The excesses of social

---

34   Partido Social Cristiano, Madera de Guerrero.

35   The Social-Christian administration implemented a project to rationalize the development of capitalism in Guayaquil and its surrounding areas (Samborondón, Daule and Durán) and in the River Guayas Basin. In the central urban area this was called 'regeneration'. It included an economic stimulus and institutional reengineering, with the aim of perfecting the model of domination, building hegemony and governability, eliminating political conflict and raising the rate of profit for the groups in power, by overcoming the chaos of previous populist administrations.

36   On 3 October there were 150 imprisoned in Guayaquil and 118 in Quito. The charge, in the first case was of looting and in the second of 'crimes', testifying to the criminalisation of social struggles.

rage were indicative of the limits of so-called 'self-organization' and of the lack of a national political leadership, able to cohere the partial struggles in a programme to fight for power – which means more than just disputing the government – uniting workers, men and women, to change their conditions of life.

2 PROBLEMS OF THE REBELLION

The transcendence of October makes sense of a number of apparently unconnected political, economic, social and institutional phenomena dating back to before the uprising. At the same time it points to possible events in its aftermath. The rebellion was a moment of historical synthesis, a laboratory it would have been impossible to imagine simply by intellectual analysis and without reference to the concrete reality.

October laid bare the specific tendencies in the class struggle, the confrontation with actually existing power in Ecuador and allows us to identify the successes and the problems of the popular camp. Far from a triumphalist account, we need to establish what were the external and internal difficulties faced by the popular camp in the course of the rebellion.

The first, external, factor was the strengthening of the repressive apparatus. The other, internal, factors were opportunist practices, the lack of cohesion of the popular sector, the weight of a trade unionist or corporatist mentality, the democratic illusion and short-term political thinking.

2.1 A REPRESSIVE APPARATUS RENOVATED IN THE BOOM

The ruling class learns from history and from its own mistakes. Failed revolutions, according to Engels, perfect the state machine. The Latin American crisis of the nineties forced the elite to rethink their social models and to rewrite the official discourse responsible for the collapse in a context of generalized uprisings across the continent.

The elements that needed to be reassessed included: the chaotic project of private accumulation, the displacement and weakening of the state, the increase in poverty, the absence of welfare policies, the aristocratic nature of the modern republics.

---

37 Here is an analysis by one sector of the institutional left that describes the looting as the product of a conspiracy by criminals, ignoring the structural conditions that produced it. 'Acts of vandalism by criminals, mainly in Guayaquil, but also in other cities, took advantage of the situation to loot warehouses and supermarkets. The Latin King gang was active in looting. These events were used by the government, the bourgeois parties and the mass media as an opportunity to blame Indigenous peoples, workers and the youth who fought the austerity measures. They constructed a whole framework to be able to discredit the protests' (Miranda, 2019, pp. 20–21).

The Ecuador of the nineties lacked a hegemonic project capable of winning the consent of the dominated. The modernisation and subordination of the forces of repression to the state and liberal democracy – something which had positively served the needs of the reproduction of capital since the return of the party system – proved insufficient to prevent episodes of insubordination, like that of Frank Vargas in Taura in 1987, that of the middle- and higher-ranking officers with Lucio Gutiérrez in 2000, or of the police revolt on 30 September 2010.

The current Ecuadorean state is not the same as it was in the past; it has become stronger. Part of it is the result of the neo-constitutional project promoted by the 'progressive' governments. In recent years, strengthening the state implied building supremacy, through both consensus and coercion, in the context of a reordering of the economy, raising the profits of capitalists, satisfying some basic demands of the masses and expanding the middle class. Today some of these aspects have failed to develop – the hegemonic cultural project, the satisfaction of basic demands – but the repressive structure has been strengthened.

If we imagine the scenario in which the October rebellion had erupted under the old Ecuadorean state, it would almost certainly have achieved more and in less time. One of the problems faced by the mobilizations was the strength of a renovated state as a result of the modernisation of the repressive apparatus and the reopening of military relations with the USA (Ramos 2019). That modernized apparatus was set in motion during the recession.

As we explained in Chapter Two, the Ecuadorean people faced a strategic offensive by the state, which increased exponentially the number of injured and of extrajudicial executions, as well as the number of arrests. In a word the state set up, as a politico-military mechanism to silence and crush the will of the demonstrators, death and physical injury, to the eyes in particular. But because of the size of the mobilization, the state was not able to determine the terms of the outcome at will; in fact the final negotiations occurred against a background of burning barricades. Nevertheless, despite the level of institutional and extra-institutional violence, the state did not press as hard on the accelerator as it could have done.

2.2 THE DECADENT AND OPPORTUNISTIC ETHOS OF THE PARTY SYSTEM

For Sun Tzu, in a battle it is vitally important to know your enemy as well as yourself if there is to be any chance of victory.

But October exposed the difficulties involved in both senses; internal errors were as significant as the power of the state. The range of popular demands was condensed in the struggle for the withdrawal of Decree No. 833, which covered various clauses in the Letter of Intent signed with the IMF.

To carry forward the struggle required going beyond the practices of the institutional left, for example its tendency to see the apparent flexibility of bourgeois democratic institutions as the key to achieving its demands. According to this approach, improving living conditions depends on using the mechanisms of dissent built into the liberal institutions, through citizens' initiatives, binding consultations, collecting signatures, popular consultations, intersectoral discussions, negotiating forums, arbitration tribunals, raising constitutional objections, etc. These activities dilute the exercise of politics into legal calculations, relegating direct mass action and ignoring the political autonomy of the working class.

This discourse of the left is restricted by the network of state institutions in the mistaken belief that liberal democracy is a horizontal model that creates a plurality of political relationships (Miliband, 1988). In reality, political and economic relations are vertical and ultimately tyrannical. The historical conquests of the people have been won by the intensification of the class struggle. Two years of 'dialogue' with the government, apart from ending some criminalization and recomposing social forces, achieved only an enormous waste of time.

In October, social democracy and the institutional left colluded against the anti-capitalist left and the uprising. They attempted to torpedo the rebellion, accusing the movement of vandalism and the demonstrators of being infiltrators. The overwhelming rejection they received forced them to 'escape' from the public's wrath (*El Universo*, 2019). Three factors explain this behaviour:

1. The rebellion was not expressed as an electoral platform, which meant that figures who in the past have used struggles as a springboard to being elected to public or private posts, sheltering behind the rhetoric of the defence of rights, were marginalised. October did not facilitate pre-candidacies for the institutional left, which led to denunciations by those who have dedicated their lives to parliamentarism.
2. A half-asleep party system, institutional politics and the democratic credo have produced a profound respect

for bourgeois property, which the rebellion set out to confront directly. The representatives of social democracy tried, unsuccessfully, to diminish the insurrectionary impulse behind October.

3   What should we call October? A rebellion? An insurrection? October with a capital O? An explosion that defies reason? A pendulum over the abyss? The intensity of the events produced sensations like fear – logically so, since few people have lived through a revolution directly. But recalling Siddartha, sadness can become suffering and sickness, and fear become terror. It is what was experienced by the middle strata embedded in the institutional left. The feeling of defencelessness in the face of one of the highest points in the class struggle in Ecuador pushed them to adopt conservative, cowardly, opportunist positions.

The intensification and prolonging of the rebellion was directly proportional to the growing discomfort of the institutional left. It used different arguments to create anxiety, the supposed bribing of leaders, the threat of raids on the humanitarian areas, complaints about the logistical problems in the supply centres, objections to the escalation of the struggle, denunciations of the lack of political direction, warnings of supposed external infiltration, pressure to seek an agreed outcome, the creation of parallel assemblies, and the unofficial naming of spokespeople – all actions deigned to distort the popular rebellion and minimize the anti-capitalist tendency at its heart.

The rebellion represented a logistical challenge that went beyond all previous struggles. The numbers of those involved in the taking of Quito were far higher than in previous risings, and the country was completely paralysed for eleven days. The first days of the occupation of the capital were especially difficult, though the problems were addressed by self-organization, popular initiatives and the moving solidarity of the people, especially from the people of Quito and its suburbs. The leading figures who, in this atmosphere of conflict, tried to use the opportunity to undermine the rebellion and discredit the anti-capitalist leaders of the popular camp expressed the ethos of a decadent and opportunistic party system.

There is nothing new about pointing out the different ideological tendencies in the popular movement; they have always existed. The evidence has been there since the beginnings of the left in Ecuador and the world. But it is essential that the anti-capitalist tendency impose itself on the social-democratic and institutional left elements.

2.3 POLITICAL SHORT-TERMISM, DEMOCRATIC ILLUSIONS AND THE ABSENCE OF ANY PERSPECTIVE FOR POWER

Another of the problems in October was the absence of a broader reading of reality that would integrate the question of power into the political narrative, and therefore prevent short-term views from getting in the way of the long-term strategic project. This can result in the absence of an autonomous political line, in a Manichean understanding of what is going on, and in confusion when making crucial decisions.

The popular camp, given its subjective limitations, inclines towards an understanding of reality shaped by the logic of the state. What should or should not be done is defined in relation to the rule of law. The latter is on the one hand a positive expression of social relations, but it also tends to be tailored to the needs of the strongest social class, the bourgeoisie. In October, the pressures within the social movements to 'negotiate a way out of the crisis' or to enter into 'dialogue to resolve the conflict' generated uncertainty among the masses. The unilateral attempts by some individuals to negotiate with the state showed the need to think about the programme of the left not only in terms of legality, but above all in terms of legitimacy.

October confirmed the proper hierarchy of concepts: legitimacy; the validation of an act by the social consent of the majority, in practice takes precedence over legality. The latter holds sway as long as the population, consciously or unconsciously, obeys the legal order; the exception comes in periods of disruption, as in the events of October.

The dilemma between legality and legitimacy, short-term and long-term politics, institutional reformism and revolutionary rupture, unionism and the perspective of power was not resolved through a kernel of autonomous and class-based thinking. The most immediate concerns prevailed. October lacked a vision that could see beyond the immediate sphere of political events, with a perspective of power, due to the speed at which the events took on tectonic dimensions, as well as the absence, in the popular camp, of more critical political reflection, which would have made it possible to overcome the fictions of modern democracy.

The Manichean opposition between Correism and anti-Correism (the supporters and opponents of former president Rafael Correa), promoted during the events of October, and its practical economic correlate, statism and neoliberalism, or what Žižek called 'Anglo-Saxon neoliberalism and authoritarian capitalism with 'Asian values' (2016, p. 16), demonstrate the need to broaden the left perspective, so as not to be caught between two variants based on the needs of capital reproduction and which are outside the orbit of revolutionary rupture. The construction of a post-capitalist society, in the Latin American situation, forces us to criticise the hope of finding 'life after neoliberalism' (Borón, 2008), of the governments that defined themselves as progressive – an unfulfilled hope, as it happens – which resulted in the Keynesian solution of the centrist State. If we do not learn to look outside this dichotomy (Correism/anti-Correism, statism/neoliberalism), the responses of the popular camp will never be able to advance towards an anti-capitalist project.

The agenda of the social movements in recent years has emphasised issues such as governance, rights, local development, gender and participation. They have left out the problem of power. It is time for leftist reflection and debate in the popular camp to free itself from the short-term view. As Antonio Gramsci (1999) put it, we need to transcend from small politics – the administration of the prevailing type of society, parliamentary politics, the politics of the day and of trifles – to big politics – the totality of society, the problem of power, the destruction of the prevailing type of society.

3   THE QUESTION OF VIOLENCE

According to the dominant bourgeois narrative, in October violence was the responsibility of only one of the contending parties. The terms people and 'violence', Indigenous and 'vandals', social movements and 'delinquents' were used indistinctly. A clean slate was made of the earlier and aggressive actions – including Decree No. 883 – that provoked a reaction in defence.

By the same logic, October was reduced to an essentialist and conspiratorial explanation: the organized people are naturally violent; instigators, infiltrators, terrorists and Taliban-like extremists put together a plot to overthrow the system. The great majority of Ecuadoreans were attacked on two fronts: through a series of economic, structural adjustments designed to raise the rate of profit for the capitalists and make the living conditions of the working class even more precarious; and through the strategy of the state to break, by means of violence, the will of millions of people who opposed those measures. The people react to the violence of the ruling classes.

In this way, the state does not act as a peacemaker, but as a guarantor of terror. This is a principle of the modern world order. Recent governments have moved systematically to bolster the state monopoly of violence; to modernize the armed forces, the police and national security system; and to increase the influence of the US State Department in domestic affairs.

The people's response, on the other hand, came out of historical memory and the accumulated experience of struggle, especially during the periods of confrontation with neo-developmentalism and neoliberalism, especially in the year 2019 itself. This section will examine the violent response of the state to mass protest, the dispute over the legitimacy of violence, the condemnation of the rebellion and the effects of the struggle overflowing its boundaries.

3.1 THE STATE'S VIOLENT RESPONSE TO PROTEST

One explanation for the people's response to the escalating repression by the state was the attempt, on three occasions, to wipe out the protests in Quito, analogous to the events of Bloody Sunday in Russia in 1905. The first was the ambush, on 9 October, in the San Juan neighbourhood of Quito. On that day a gigantic march skirted the historic centre to avoid confrontation with the police. The response of the police was violent, to the point that an armoured car broke through the middle of the demonstration on Benalcázar Street.[38]

The second was the police operation, on the night of 9 October, against the main protest assembly zone in Quito, which involved a violent attack on the peace and reception areas, and ended with the death of Segundo Inocencio Tucumbi Vega, a leader of the Organization of Indigenous Peoples of Jatun Juigua (OPIJJ), an affiliate of the MICC (the Indigenous and Campesino Movement of Cotopaxi, of which Leonidas Iza was then president). The third was the failure to respect the 'truce' requested by the police and army, when they were overwhelmed

---

38 Regarding this event, Herrera (2019) argued that 'although confrontations with the police were avoided throughout the march and discipline was maintained thanks to the "Indigenous guards", in the afternoon police repression unleashed confrontation again'.

by the popular resistance. This was a smokescreen that gave the security forces time to be re-supplied by helicopter. Then, as reported by CNN in Spanish, an indiscriminate attack against the demonstrators took place on the afternoon of 11 October.[39] From that moment 'until a little before 02.40am the following day, the bombs did not stop, amid fears of an imminent armed attack on the movement's headquarters in the Ecuadorean House of Culture' (Alianza de Organizaciones por los Derechos Humanos, 2019, p. 69). In the furore of the events, the same source reports that 'the police looked rather more aggressive in their movements than what we had seen in the morning', as a result of which 'the same people we saw facing police violence in the morning, are now looking for stones to throw'.

What was the turning point here? The exploited classes could see that the state does not respect the people's wish to protest, the constitutional right to resistance, the humanitarian peace zones and even the truce proposed by itself. The state does not respect the peace it demands from the people; therefore, its discourse is hypocritical and one-sided. Confrontation with the repressive apparatus became the only option, unleashing what Walter Benjamin calls divine violence: 'a popular uprising whose force is a violent response to the symbolic and systemic violence of capital' (Sierra, 2019).

The events, however, cannot be understood without the organized intervention and the will to struggle of the vanguard of the people. One of the elements that launched this dynamic is summarized in a fragment of the call for the 14 October strike, issued by CONAIE:

> We will not sell out, not for a plate of lentils, and not even for millions! The dignity of the people is not for sale and is achieved, in the present as in the struggles of the past, thanks to a series of decisive actions by the social movements and by constant mobilization. The call for the Progressive Day of Struggle is based on the unified declaration of the Indigenous uprising, the national strike of the

---

[39] On '11 October, one day after the public funeral of Inocencio Tucumbi, held in the auditorium of the Casa de la Cultura, a large group of Indigenous women together with women from the city held a march from El Arbolito Park to the main entrance of the National Assembly, where they staged a symbolic act of raising and showing their empty hands, sitting down and remaining there in peace: "We are women, we are not criminals", they shouted at the security forces, in the midst of an apparent truce. However, at around 17:00, the National Police of Ecuador began a new wave of repression, without any reason and quite disproportionately, firing tear gas indiscriminately against thousands of people who were gathered at the time, putting all of them at risk' (*Plan V*, 2019).

trade union confederations and the people's strike of the popular organizations. We demand, in this way, respect for the programme of struggle drawn up from the heart of the people's organizations.

This is not an intransigent position. It is the understanding of politics from an anti-capitalist position. The systematic plundering of the poor is called public policy, but their actions of struggle are considered 'radical'. Such an approach is only coherent because it seizes the problem by the roots and not by the branches.

3.2 THE PARADOX OF VIOLENCE: BETWEEN THE MANUAL OF GOOD MANNERS AND DIGNITY

The Minister of the Interior, María Paula Romo (*El Comercio*, 2019), argues that there are many reasons why the population protest, including how they are affected by public policies. If we follow the minister's argument, we see that 'the population' is a generic term that conceals a reality: the rich do not go out to protest because they do not need to (Luisa Delgadillo in Jairala, 2019). They pursue their interests behind the scenes, through lobbying and enticement, using their economic and family connections, their symbolic and social capital. Doing so is considered legal because the concept of corruption excludes the private sphere and focuses on the public sphere. Public policy, the cause of protest mentioned by Romo, is therefore applied in an asymmetrical and differentiated manner: while it favours the upper classes, it annihilates the middle and lower classes. So, as a result of this syllogism, we discover the paradox of state action: what if it only serves the rich? Then a padlock is put on popular demands and needs, which causes a loss of legitimacy of the state; and thus the mask of the 'public good' falls, and the action of those at the bottom grows.

To get out of the quagmire of not being heard, while following useless bureaucratic procedures, the exploited classes are pushed into a zone that the powerful identify as 'acts of vandalism and organized violence' (National Police in *Plan V*, 2019). According to their narrative, protests should be limited to good citizen behaviour – demonstrating with the Manual of Civility and Good Manners in one hand – but as this is a stupid and useless method, then they choose to criminalize the protests and this reinforces the social outburst (Adrián Bonilla in *DemocraciaTV*, 2019).

At this point the causal order of events – of cause and effect – is reversed. The arguments are standardized and presented as follows. First: 'In all cases the police used only dissuasive force. The police never used lethal force in any context' (Romo in Morán, 2019), despite lacking both the 'appropriate uniforms for much more serious incidents' and 'dissuasive equipment' (Romo, 2019). Second: the forces of repression acted with 'clemency',[40] even though the UN asked for access to investigate a possible disproportionate use of force (*El Comercio*, 2019).[41] Third: there is no systematic use of violence; an armed body that exists only to administer violence, produces, 'sporadically', 'abuses', 'excesses' or 'isolated incidents' and 'it is very difficult to judge the police for a single event. It shouldn't be done. It's not fair' (Romo, 2019). Fourth: the police and armed forces defend themselves;[42] those who have weapons defend themselves from those who do not. Fifth: it is insinuated that people 'put themselves in danger', because the demonstrators know that the police are going to use force, so they are committing suicide! Sixth, when things get complicated, they say that 'according to the circumstances, we always try to comply with the law' (Romo, 2019). Finally, the conclusion is that it is imperative to administer violence.

> I do not know of any incidents of this gravity, of this level of violence, of this magnitude, in which nobody is wounded. So, it is not a question of professionalism [of the security forces]: it is a question of the level of violence, of the number of people, of the chaotic part of the situation and of the organized part, and the pressure they are under (Romo, 2019).

> I don't know how you can teach a policeman to control a hundred people, I don't know how 300 policemen can control 3,500 [people], without shooting (Romo, 2019).

---

40 'I always give as an example the takeover of the governorships because we never evicted a single governorate: most of the takeovers of the governorships were negotiated by me. What was the negotiation? If there is no violence, we are not going to evict them'. (Romo, 2019)

41 The United Nations (in *El Comercio*, 2019) mentioned that 'victims and witnesses denounced the repeated use by security forces of tear gas and pellets fired at close range against demonstrators, causing hundreds of injuries and probably some of the deaths, the mission concluded'.

42 'The military, like any citizen in the national territory, have the right to self-defence'. (Jarrín, Minister of Defense, in the National Assembly, 2019, p. 67)

43 The population of Quito and Guayaquil agrees with the resignation of the repression ministers at 78%, 87% in Quito. (Opinion Profiles in *Kolectivoz*, 2019)

Cynicism and hypocrisy are part of the act. In this regard, some points are worth repeating. First, the growth of the popular struggle was a response to the mounting repression and not the other way around. An article in *El Comercio* (2019), for example, reports that the police checkpoint on the 24 de Mayo Avenue in Quito was burned after the death of Marco Oto. The people's reaction was not a result of 'military training': you just need to observe the anti-riot tactics of the security forces, in the midst of a rain of projectiles, to know what to do. Second, it does not matter how 'professional' or well-trained the policemen are, nor how many human rights courses they take, it is impossible for them not to repress the poor. Third, it is absurd to claim that the deaths and injuries on the side of the people occurred 'in the context of the protests', while the injuries among the forces of repression were due to 'terrorist attacks':

> Witnesses saw my brother fall in the middle of the demonstration. It was not an assault. In a video you see that Edison stops and bends down to pick up something that had fallen. Then the policemen knock him down and start beating him. One approaches and shoots him. The rubber bullet hit him behind his ear. We do not have the autopsy report or the ballistics report. At the hospital they gave us a copy, but when we filed our complaint at the Police Conduct Unit they took it away because they said it was evidence (Patricia, Edison Mosquera's sister in *El Comercio*, 2019).

This is not an attempt to hide what happened or to create myths about it. Behind these different narratives lies a dispute over legitimacy in the use of violence. 55% of the population in Guayaquil and 66% in Quito said that the armed forces and the police were very violent, 28% said they were quite violent and 17% that they were only slightly or not violent: among the medium- and high-income sectors, the percentage who thought their actions were violent fell to 34% (Opinion Profiles in *Kolectivoz*, 2019).[43]

Approval of the use of violence is proportional to socio-economic status: those belonging to the better-off strata tend to justify the action of the forces of repression, while the popular sectors condemn it. The legitimacy of the monopoly of violence is not universal, but depends on the class you belong to; the state has lost consent to its monopoly on the use of violence. As a consequence, in the weeks following the October rebellion, in some cities such as Otavalo and Latacunga the armed forces and the police were prevented from participating in parades for local holidays (El Norte, 2019), which showed how people had lost trust in the military institutions.[44]

Given this, the public medal-giving ceremonies held to decorate police officers after the events of October caused outrage (Jhajaira Urresta in *El Comercio*, 2019), despite the fact that media outlets such as *El Comercio* had been publishing glowing reports to boost the image of the institution for months. The state's administration of violence has been put in question. What was the strategy of the state's repressive apparatus in response to this gradual loss of popularity? To threaten more repression, with the argument that deterrence means 'being ready to use the means you have' (Fausto Cobo in *TVC El Comercio TV*, 2019).

'The worst thing a government can do is to threaten something and not follow through with the threat [...] They announced that the military was ready to use all the weapons at its disposal, and yet not a shot was fired' (José Ayala Lasso, ex-Chancellor, in Bedón, 2019). The threat to 'use all the weapons available' was only surpassed in brutality by the Minister of Defence, Oswaldo Jarrín. He was eloquent in expressing the tautological argument that the legitimacy of the repressive forces is ensured by their exercise of repression:

> The only radicalisation there will be is if they try to take over the transmitters that are already under military control. Then they will meet with the strongest possible use of force, which is appropriate because we are protecting, in the first place, private property, we are protecting the media and their communication signals, we are protecting vital interests and we will not allow this to happen ... Similarly, any other move against a sensitive point or strategic installation will be repelled with maximum force ... At such a moment,

---

[44] It is for this reason that previous governments insisted on rebuilding the legitimacy of the armed forces, through channels that allow overcoming the negative institutional image. According to the Latinobarómetro Corporation (2004), the Ecuadorean Police was perceived by the population as the third most corrupt at the Latin American level (Pontón and Rivera, 2016, p. 218), a statistic similar to that of 2005 which, according to the ENACPOL survey, the national police was, together with the judicial function, one of the worst perceived and evaluated institutions in the country, due to the discredit arising from corruption. This situation changed during the Correa administration, when the project of reassembling the state, which took into account the construction of hegemony and domination, under the horizon of the interests of the ruling classes, repositioned the repressive forces.

there will not be any kind of dialogue or allowances made ... We need to differentiate between acts of vandalism ..., which are dealt with by the police, and rebellion ... which entails an act of defence, and the radical use of force. We are not talking about non-lethal weapons, which are used to control public order, and maintain the peace.... It will no longer be only non-lethal weapons, the full strength of the armed forces will be used ... which means real force (Oswaldo Jarrín, Minister of Defence in *Teleamazonas*, 2019) [emphasis added].

Patricio Carrillo, Commander of the National Police, said that 'once this option [chemical agents] has been exhausted we move on to the next one which is the use of rubber bullets [...] which can have a greater effect than was intended'. To the question, 'Can a rubber bullet cause death?', he answered, 'Yes it can, because everything depends on how it's used' (in FM *Mundo* Live, 2020). The lethal use of 'non-lethal' weaponry.

3.3 ARTHUR FLECK, POPULAR ANGER AND AN UNBEARABLE SITUATION

In relation to violence, there is agreement between liberals and the institutionalist left: both are politically opposed to it. However, in practice, as they exercise power, there is a difference: the former use it, the latter do not. The ruling classes always condemn violence, even while they make daily use of it. They brand the popular camp as violent, while they are the ones responsible for numerous extrajudicial executions with lethal and 'non-lethal' weapons. But this condemnation is also extrapolated, and is shamefully repeated by the institutionalist left.

Foucault (2016) argues that in modernity there are three things that break with the established norms of behaviour. The first is madness which affronts reason, understood as the subjective state of 'normal' human beings; the second is sexual dissidence, because it alters heteronormative codes; and the third is theft, which, by affecting private property, challenges the foundation of the bourgeois establishment. In capitalist modernity, the three factors are conceived as forms of transgression that must be punished, monitored, segregated or confined.

According to the ruling-class narrative, what happened during the October rebellion can be reduced to theft (in the flower and broccoli plantations) and vandalism (both public and private). This is a moral judgement that stymies debate and condemns the effects of violent acts by one of the parties, without taking into account the causes that led to them. Far from this moralising approach, typical of a certain, instrumental version of history, the violence unleashed in October should be understood through a reading of previous events. Its roots lie in the precarious living conditions of the majority of the Ecuadorean people, and the accumulated experience of class struggle over at least the last two decades.

Why has violence been a common denominator in the popular uprisings that have occurred since mid-2019 in Haiti, Ecuador, Chile, Bolivia, Lebanon, Iraq, Colombia, Hong Kong, Spain and other countries? There are several possible answers to this question.

Hobbes's theory of the social contract argues that violence originates in the warrior instincts of people, which must be repressed by the state (Hobbes, 2005). The fascist explanation is that violence is the result of disorder in society, caused by an absence of the monopolisation of politics in the state (Schmitt, 2014). The republican argument is that it is the consequence of an 'overflow' of un-channelled demands in the absence of 'true' democracy.

In all these cases, popular violence is rejected, without questioning the violent nature of the state itself, thereby legitimising the need to ensure order and progress in civil society, through the rationality condensed in the state (Hegel, 2010) or through self-government understood as the construction of a liberal society (Tocqueville, 1963).

In the Marxist perspective, violence is not part of human nature. It is a historical phenomenon that channels a voice that the nature of the institutions of restrictive democracy is incapable of absorbing. In other words, violence is not a choice, but the result of an accumulation of unbearable situations; it acquires a political character because it interferes with the prevailing social order, through the massive participation of the population. According to Enrique Terán, the first Secretary General of the Ecuadorean Socialist Party (PSE): 'Violence used against those who oppress entire masses of workers, violence in favour of millions of exploited human beings, can never, ever be bad, this violence is sacred'. (Terán in Larco and Espinosa, 2012). Evidently, some later socialist 'co-thinkers' did not assimilate the lessons of their predecessor.

In the context of the October rebellion, violent disrespect for property was the expression of a historical subject that had been excluded from society's key decision-making processes; deciding whether or not economic policy is steered by the IMF is not something that, in practice, can be decided by the 'democratic' system, due to its restricted and class-based character, which precludes the participation and interests of the masses. The definition of what is just or unjust, a violent or a legitimate act, is determined by a certain ideological interpretation corresponding to a specific class interest. We can pose some questions that show the different concepts and their uses:

- What is revealed by the protest actions in the flower, broccoli and dairy farms in the provinces of Cotopaxi, Pichincha and Imbabura, which were organized by the workers, their families and neighbouring communities?
- Why is it that for the majority of the population the occupation of public spaces is far from being understood as senseless violence, as seen in the collective effort to turn cobblestones into barricades?
- Why has the people's resort to stones and home-made devices been seen as a just response to the enormous violence perpetrated by the state, which uses sophisticated weapons designed by the arms industry?
- Why are the collective efforts to build burning roadblocks on the highways, to erect barricades in front of the riot squad, the giant human chains to carry supplies (water, stones, debris, food, cobblestones) to the young people on the front line of the struggle, the mass participation in sustaining the various logistical needs (health, children, food, sound, etc.) seen in a diametrically opposite way by the ruling class and the people?

To answer one of these questions: Flower farms are one of the most profitable industries in Ecuador, due to the comparative advantages enjoyed on the international market, the low capital costs and the cheap and abundant supply of labour. This booming business includes hundreds of factories spread across the best land of the high Andean valleys, particularly in the north of the provinces of Pichincha and Cotopaxi; however, the labour conditions of the workers are in stark contrast: precarious wages, strenuous work, lack of legal guarantees, illness, lack of job security and child exploitation are constant features. In addition, the economy of poor peasant communities close to the plantations is also badly affected. We cannot say that all the looting took place because of the pent-up resentment of the workers and communities against the flower industry, but most of it did. If the situation of the flower and broccoli workers and the neighbouring communities were different from the actually existing reality, would there have been a similar level of response?

In the movie *Joker*, masterfully played by Joaquin Phoenix, there is an under-layer that can help to explain the seemingly unjustified violence. If a person like Arthur Fleck – the main character – has been systematically abused at home, denigrated at work, excluded from public health, harassed in the media, assaulted by the elites, and is in a desperate economic situation – an experience shared with a significant proportion of the population that faces poverty and exclusion in a context of grotesque accumulation of wealth by the few – then the response can hardly not involve violence.

The people's anger has material causes. If the ruling class wants to spare itself the effects, then let it solve the causes. Otherwise, there will be more Octobers in the future.

4 PENDING TASKS AND PROSPECTS FOR EMANCIPATION

It was not the protest that divided society: it was already divided. It is that division that triggered the events described above. The ruling class wants to maintain its privileges by appropriating the labour of others, but complains about the class struggle that comes along with such socio-economic inequality. They want the benefits, but not the consequences. Even Patricio Alarcón, President of the Chamber of Commerce of Quito and a prominent representative of the Ecuadorean bourgeoisie, recognized that the October uprising was much more than a political game: 'There is considerable discontent in society' (on *DemocraciaTV*, 2019). This 'considerable' discomfort is an indicator of the immediate consequences of the process of capital accumulation and the increasingly precarious living conditions, which turned into protest, and then rebellion.

Historically, much of modern bourgeois property was obtained at times that included moments of intense social conflict. Why do those property owners now defend the rights obtained, but not the right that engendered them? Because on this occasion the use of that right which creates rights – the use of protest – is beyond their control, and that directly affects their economic and political interests.

This section looks at the perspectives opened up by the October rebellion for the emancipation of the exploited in Ecuador, as well as the pending tasks for those who are committed to the transformation of Ecuador. The possibility of advancing depends on tasks that have not been completed, or which were simply never undertaken. If we don't pay attention to certain aspects, and identify others that have been ignored, we will never move beyond October.

All of this goes well beyond the electoral path, and the aspirations of the institutional left, which seeks to channel the achievements of October into the race for the fiction of governmental 'power'.[45] The reality is much more complex. The lessons for the popular camp and the anti-capitalist left must take into account the most urgent needs and tasks of the period; they must not be confined to the illusion of the party system, which neglects essential imperatives such as unity among the sectors of the anti-capitalist left, the need for growth of the social and organizational fabric, urgent awareness of the dangers of a counterrevolutionary preventive move, and developing the strength of the popular sectors.

4.1   UNITY OF THE ANTI-CAPITALIST LEFT

October bordered on the epic. It was an event impregnated with rebellion, a synthesis of voluntary work on a mass scale and of the fathomless capacity of the people for destruction and construction. It was a moment that moved the human spirit, and generated opposing emotions among the polarized social classes. But this feat, in spite of everything, was still far from reaching the depth of radicalisation needed for the subversive cause. This was not yet a revolution. What does history demand for the efforts of the working class to result in a society built in its own image and likeness? Among other things, the vanity and the sectarian spirit of the left, and of humanity, must be shrunk to nothing, so that after being shipwrecked on their own trifles they return to sanity and become part of a collective will to power.

The German Marxist, Walter Benjamin, spoke of 'moments of danger'. He was referring to the explosions that can halt

---

45   'How are they going to convert the enormous political energy produced by the October mobilizations into electoral results that will allow them to transform the state from within and build their historic project of the Plurinational State?' (Dávalos, 2020). 'Along this path, the political struggle will be expressed in 2021 in the general elections, when a new government and a new National Assembly will be elected. This is a fact that the political forces of the left, the organizations and the Indigenous movement cannot ignore; on the contrary, the main task will be to build a political alternative to confront the neoliberal right and the supporters of Correa' (Almeida, 2019, p. 89).

the careering course of a history characterized by barbaric modern progress. These were the revolutionary periods. In the case of Ecuador, they forced the various fractions of the elite to close ranks and form a class bloc, in opposition to the people's camp.

We can see this, for example, in the united response of the ruling class during the fall of presidents, the rise of workers', Indigenous and people's struggles and, of course, during the October rebellion. The splits between the different fractions of capital (commercial, financial, industrial and bureaucratic) and their political representatives (PSC, PRE, CREO, AP, ID) vanish when the people put at risk the stability of actually existing power itself (economic, state and ideological). In other words, those tight-lipped characters – the banana lords, the mini-monarchs of agribusiness, the banking elites, the ladies of the Guayaquil Benevolence Board, the careerist bureaucrats, the pipe-smoking patricians, the military gorillas and the golden-cassocked clergy – all unite at moments of risk, when facing the rise of the popular struggle. Regardless of the differences in the extent of their property and their political identities, they band together in a single cohort, bringing together right-wing populists, conservative bankers, social-democratic technocrats, the bureaucratic bourgeoisie and modernising liberals.

Why does the left not adopt a similar *esprit de corps* to confront its political antagonists? Why does it not emulate, from an ontologically different starting point to the ruling class, the capacity to build a bloc of the exploited? October encourages the popular camp to rethink the question of unity, an element that rebalances the correlation of forces against the bourgeoisie. This is expressed at two different levels: first, the unity of the popular camp, that is, the need to consolidate the social base for the transformation of Ecuador (workers, peasants, Indigenous communities and popular sectors, excluding the rich peasants and the Indigenous bourgeoisie); second, bringing together the political forces and identities that are committed to the ideas of the anti-capitalist left.

Does this mean unity at any cost? No; it is not an excuse to abort the long-term political strategy, but to achieve unity of action that goes from less to more, and maintains the disruptive character of the project. This has a double implication which, due to its complexity, may seem contradictory: that the dimension of power be inscribed, as Marx put it, in 'the merciless critique of all that exists', and that the debates not be over-ideologized.

On the contrary, they must be grounded in a concrete praxis, which overcomes the sectarian and dogmatic barriers that have characterized the left in Ecuador.

Unity should not undermine the strategic perspective, unlike the multiculturalist approach, which promotes the idea of tolerating differences, while ignoring social and economic inequality. Unity among sectors of the left rests on an equality of interests, within an anti-capitalist project. A serious approach to the problem of left unity has to be based on actions that go beyond the immediate situation, especially if that is one of elections.

The criteria for unity must not get bogged down in the fiction of 'reaching' power through the party system, thereby squandering the dreams of October in an electoral nightmare, as the institutionalist left proposes: 'If October turned indignation into mobilization, I believe that this year we have the obligation to turn that mobilization into a political [electoral] alternative' (Atarihuana, 2020). In the same way, the political 'gap' cannot be reduced to an opposition between conservatism and progressivism, the right and the supposed left (Zibechi, 2019), neoliberalism and statism. Whatever kind of government they incline towards, the protests in the region are phenomena that correspond to a specific moment in the cycle of capital accumulation. Latin America cannot be characterized by the succession of governments declaring themselves to be of the right or of the left, or by the alleged 'return' of either of these, because the situation across the region is not homogeneous.

The process of capital accumulation is global. The strategies of the popular movement must not become atomized by merely local concerns. The problem of working-class unity must go beyond the needs of a single country. It is necessary to build pan-American unitary platforms to confront the offensive of neoliberal capitalism (or statist centrism), based on defence of the principle of political class independence. In that way, whatever the government of the moment, it will be possible to guarantee the organizational autonomy of the popular movement on a permanent basis.

October awakened huge expectations among ordinary people, across different points of view and different kinds of organization. It is necessary to bring together these concerns, questions and dreams (to draw all these currents into an organized space); to correct the historical errors of the left; and to steer these utopias towards a programme that is both realistic and impossible, in order to build a different society.

4.2 EXPANDING THE SOCIAL AND ORGANIZATIONAL NETWORK

Based on what has been said about the various actors in the October rebellion, we need to consider the state of the social and organizational fabric, especially in areas where it has been weakened in recent years (the working class, the peasantry) and which it is important to incorporate (neighbourhood organizations, women, youth). Any attempt to raise the level of social mobilization and achieve better living conditions requires broadening the organizations that represent the people. This implies, particularly, the need to organize: a working class concentrated in the urban industrial belts, whose unionization rate currently is no more than 4%, and especially the strategic agro-industrial proletariat; the precarious workers living in poor urban neighbourhoods of the major cities; the unorganized peasantry, in both the coastal and highland regions; the sectors of the youth that are open to organizing themselves in poor neighbourhoods, schools and universities; and the women of the popular sector.

It's worth pointing out that this objective of expanding the organizational fabric goes against the grain of some experiences of the left in Ecuador, which have disregarded the principle of mass action as the essence of political praxis in modernity (Madrid, 2018a). In these traditions, although the principle of force has been included as a part of political practice, it has lacked a comprehensive mass strategy. However, modern politics has society as its principal arena for action. It is not possible to act politically outside the public framework, where the forms of power are manifest, visibly or latently. In this sense, the concept of revolution and counter-revolution in modernity gives political conflict a permanent relationship with the multitudes, the masses, the majority.

Following Gramsci, modern political action is not an individual adventure, but the consequence of a collective strategy. Without the growth of social movements, it is impossible to build a new reality. Even in the bloodbath of Vietnam, the importance of mass political strategy was never minimized, but was rather made a central pillar of the strategy for power.

The strategy of the ruling class has been reproduced, ideologically, among the popular classes, which affects their relationship with revolutionary praxis. Examples include: the links between the urban poor of Guayaquil with the Social Christian Party, between a sector of the Indigenous movement with the NGOs, or of the trade unions with a legalistic perspective. Can mass political action, with a class emphasis, counteract the common sense ideas implanted in the sectors that need to become the social base of the struggle in Ecuador? These sectors, paradoxically, have actually strengthened the grip of the ruling class by supporting the Social Christians' modernizing project, the ideas of multicultural local development, or the legalism of much trade union practice.

To clarify these questions, we must start from the fact that the working class is not revolutionary by definition; it is not tangentially anti-capitalist, unless there is a specific orientation within the trade union, Indigenous and popular organizations. The idea that the working class is by nature revolutionary derives from a romantic, mechanical and essentialist of concept (Madrid, 2018a). The people do not have an immanent leftist proclivity, an idea that has led to painful historical experiences. As examples: the role played by the sectors of the working class most impoverished by the crisis in the United States in bringing Donald Trump to the presidency, the electoral support – with the exception of Paris – for the candidacy of Marine Le Pen in France, the defeat of the peace referendum in Colombia in areas such as Caquetá, the broad support for Nebot's administration in Guayaquil, the electoral support for Hitler's access to power in Germany, the labour–management pact of European trade unionism in the welfare state, the support of the urban periphery for Bolsonaro, or the participation of the Indigenous Misquito people in the anti-Sandinista contras during the period of Ronald Reagan.

The masses are a contested space. In the popular organizations, discourses are reproduced (despite the fact that they have certain components of struggle on their agenda, create certain moments of tension with the state and achieve benefits for their base) that do not pose a rupture with the project of domination, and can even strengthen it. How can an agenda of struggle be articulated in relation to the process of long-term transformation and yet not to immediate demands of a proto-bourgeois character? The answer: because of the structural link between a short-, medium- and long-term anti-capitalist platform, which flourishes in step with popular organization.

One of the most important lessons of the October rebellion is the broadening of the socio-organizational fabric. The project of anti-capitalist transformation is a chimera without an increase in the percentage of the working class that is organized and active in class unionism – especially in the strategic agro-industry; without the organization of the unemployed proletariat of the marginal urban zones of the main cities and of the peasantry, above all, of the Coast; without a strengthened anti-capitalist line in the Indigenous movement; and without the inclusion of the youth and women of the popular movement.

4.3 PREVENTIVE COUNTERREVOLUTION AND MCCARTHYIST POLITICS

We agree with Sierra (2019) when he points out that 'the big losers in these days of struggle were: the State, the Government, the Social-Christians – spearhead of the traditional right – the Correists – spearhead of the progressive right – and the hegemonic media'. However, for the State this was not the final battle, but one more stage in the project of perfecting the machinery of the counter-revolution; it only suffered a partial defeat. The support received by all the elites allowed it to lubricate the power bloc essential to the process of political domination in Ecuador. From then on, the neo-fascist policy of repression was relaunched, which in recent years has acquired its own muscle. Having lost the initiative, the most reactionary sectors argued that during October 'the Ecuadorean State as such was on the defensive' because 'it had lost the capacity to dissuade' (Cobo in *DemocraciaTV*, 2019). On that basis they launched some new strategies.

The first was the Orwellian strengthening of the intelligence structure, to confront the so-called 'violent groupings' with an 'ideological background on the extreme left' (El Comercio, 2019); the existence of 'a planned insurgency, sabotage and terrorism' (Cobo in DemocraciaTV, 2019) to 'attack the strategic infrastructure and [...] the institutions of the State' (Romo on DemocraciaTV, 2019); and warn that we are living a 'process of half peace' (Mario Pazmiño, former Director of the Intelligence Service in DemocraciaTV, 2019).

The second is the aspiration to modify the current laws that prevent the armed forces and the police from shooting (Cobo on DemocraciaTV, 2019). The intention is to legally raise the level of violence and brutality without having to account to anyone; so that the 'exceptionality' referred to in the state of exception becomes an outdated notion. Despite everything, the evidence shows that the recurrent appeal to terror and physical violence have become normal patterns of state behaviour. In addition to extrajudicial executions, among other still illegal actions, we must remember the use of ambulances – humanitarian symbols of health services – to disguise the delivery of supplies to repressive forces, in clear disregard for the Geneva Conventions (1949). The powers increased the use of military jargon in October, but were incapable of respecting minimum humanitarian standards.

The third was the criminalization of people under the pretext of fighting 'impunity', using judicial documents drawn up arbitrarily without due process. This occurred when the Prosecutor's Office accused the protesters detained during the fire in the Comptroller's Office of acting in a 'premeditated and organized manner', despite the fact that, according to García (2019), they were held on the terrace because 'they could not get out as they were burning the floors from the bottom up'. Of course, the state agency had to reformulate its charges and finally declared the process null and void due to lack of evidence. Another proof of arbitrariness are the arrests plagued with inconsistencies of former Alianza País members such as the Prefect of Pichincha, Paola Pabón,[46] as well as Christian González and Virgilio Hernández.[47] These repressive and selective actions were based on criminal legislation they had elaborated themselves and on the persecution by the Correísta government of 'social movements, especially Indigenous and workers, to the point of fragmenting them and polarizing the society permanently'. (Herrera, 2019). Thus, in this period there were 247 cases of political persecution of the popular movement, 59% with criminal charges.

The fourth was to purge the military leadership due to its 'inefficiency' in repression, since it was widely known that a sector of the army command 'prohibited the use of lethal weapons, against the orders of the Minister of Defence' (Bedón, 2019). Additionally, 'disciplinary offences' were noted in the midst of a protest on García Avilés Street in Guayaquil on Wednesday 9 October when a group of military personnel intervened and physically confronted police motorcyclists to stop the violence against the protesters.

Finally, Minister Romo (2019) sustained the thesis that 'the military does not start the war; it is the politicians who start it'. It highlights the continuation of politics by other means: bringing together the two poles where the ruling classes defend their interests. And Minister Jarrín clarified that, 'on this occasion',

---

[46] Among those persecuted were members of the National Assembly, local authorities, neighbourhood leaders and the Director of Radio Pichincha (one of the few national media to broadcast what was happening). There were arrests, homes raided and people who went into hiding or into exile.

[47] 48% of people in Quito and Guayaquil think this was a case of politically motivated persecution. 52% think it has legal grounds. *(Perfiles de Opinión en Kolectivoz, 2019)*

it was not part of the plan of the repressive forces to create an internal enemy, which his co-thinker, the Minister of Government, corroborated and radicalized saying that, if the state faces 'another scenario, this is part of what must be updated' (Romo, 2019). The internal enemy is the organized people.

This repertoire is part of a strategy – inscribed in a moment of advancing world conflict – that holds communism – the most critical expression in capitalist civilization – responsible for the modern crisis. This is nothing more than the re-issue of the formulas constructed in the last century, evading responsibility for the crisis of civilization with a cure that simply worsens the disease: capitalism is cured with more capitalism. McCarthyism – an anti-communist political tradition formulated by US imperialism, which persecuted tendencies that distanced themselves from capitalism – has taken hold in the most reactionary right-wing circles. It instils hatred toward all those it considers its adversaries: revolutionary syndicalism, popular ecologism, class feminism, counter-hegemonic subalternity, contested art, militant Marxism, sexual dissidence, autonomous popular organizations, the revolutionary left, and even 'progressive' tendencies.

The advance of fascism and US white supremacy are dogmas that equate socialism with darkness and diversity with decadence. Other hemispheric reactions that have demonized the left and the popular camp are: the reorganization of the Brazilian far right, which proposes the 'elimination of cultural Marxism'; the Chilean neoliberal advance, the hate speech in Bolivia, Uribism in Colombia and the Mexican narco-state. Also: the advance of popular and nationalist parties in Europe, the affirmation of authoritarian states in Asia, the advance of Islamic fascism in the Muslim world (a fact that finds resonance in Africa), the encouragement of colonialist occupation in the world, the revival of the arms race, and the weakening of multilateralism. They herald the capitalist ideological offensive, in a period of preventive counterrevolution.

4.4   CONFRONTING THE ACTUALLY EXISTING POWER

The conflict reached its limits because of the intensity of the popular struggle, rooted in a deep sense of dignity. However, if repealing a government decree costs so much effort, what will it take to defeat capitalism, what is the level of force that the people will need to build a different society? In the words of the trade union bureaucrat Valentín Pacho (2019), 'the popular insurrection, with its painful cost, was aborted by the absence of the political vanguard', a vanguard that he had done nothing to create in his own country, as was confirmed by the television presenter Jorge Ortiz (in DemocraciaTV, 2019):

> In Ecuador there is not even a radical left party, a Communist Party, a Revolutionary Socialist Party. Here that left has ended up […] as a few social leaders […] who are the left of these countries, of Ecuador, a country where there is no consistent, ideological left party […] not this turbulent, loud-mouthed left based on publicity, and based around a group of leaders that has politically set these countries back.

From the deep divide that separates us ideologically from the positions described there, we believe that they reveal a condition: the bulk of the left does not affect the state of things. It is harmless. The left as a project must be recreated, for it does not exist as the negation of capital, but only as a mechanism to validate the democratic illusion.

One of the major limitations of October was not the fact that President Moreno remained in office, since, even if he had been overthrown, the discussion would at most have been limited to the fate of the government and not to questioning the actually existing power. If the left does not take on the responsibility of taking criticism beyond appearance – for example beyond the empty rhetoric that blames all the country's problems on the fiscal crisis and ignores the modern structural crisis – the transformations will not go beyond their historical antecedents. Even if several of them have been glorious, they have not allowed the emergence of a society built in the image and likeness of the working class.

October dissected reality. It allowed us to see, in its objective dimensions, the truth that was in dispute. The bourgeoisie complied with the dominant inter-class dynamics: violence surgically designed by the state. The exploited were able to win by accumulating their forces and contesting the truth of the oppressors. The autonomous organization of the people, too, had faced its opponents, not only the openly capitalist characters, but also the 'democratic' figures sponsored by the institutionalist left, that argued that bourgeois social organization is 'the only army of Ecuador'; 'the rest is farce' (Paco Moncayo in DemocraciaTV, 2019).

October confirms the lessons learned during other struggles: it is impossible to defeat capitalism without building the necessary worker-peasant-Indigenous-popular alliance, without distancing itself from the institutions, without the self-determination of the peoples, without breaking the bourgeois democratic illusion, without questioning the nature of the state and of the actually existing power, without seeing Life as the relationship between the different forms of existence beyond the human species, without recreating a subject integrating diverse types of non-capitalist subjectivities, without trusting that the material force of transformation lies in the working class, without giving back to politics its two fundamental axioms: contradiction and universality. ★

Demonstrators outside the House of Culture arming themselves with shields to protect them against the tear gas cannisters fired at them at point blank range Quito, 6 October 2019 (Photo: Alejandro Ramírez Anderson).

Demonstration in Quito on its way to the National Assembly Quito, 10 October 2019 (Photo: Andres Leon / Kaucha).

A ceremony in memory of the murdered leader Inocencio Tucumbi, a member of MICC, 10 October 2019 (Photo: Luis Herrera / Audiovisual Cooperative).

'The light of all lights, it is said, is beyond the darkness', Bhagavad Gita (Photo: Hamilton Lopéz).

Young people with wooden shields on their way to the front line of the struggle in Quito (Photo: Axel Naranjo).

Barricade of demonstrators from the city and the country, in El Arbolito park, Quito, 8 October 2019 (Photo: Axel Naranjo).

Mobilization of the Front of Organisations in Struggle and other social movements in Buenos Aires, Argentina (Photo: Alez Muñoz Teran).

Sit down protest outside the Ecuadorean Embassy in Mexico City, 10 October 2019 (Photo: Victor Romero).

Sit down demonstration by Ecuadorean and Latin American migrant women in Lisbon, Portugal, 9 October 2019 (Photo: Nuno Alonso/Carla Badillo Coronado).

Ecuadorean women and the Latin American Bloc outside the Ecuadorean Embassy in Berlin, 9 October 2019 (Photo: Charlotte Christa Achneber Merizalde).

The struggle of the people is not about elections, Communist consciousness, in the working class

Capital, profit, let them die along with the bourgeoisie.

Popular slogans of the October rebellion

The snake's progress never goes backwards only forward, forward, forward

Tayta Alejo, Andean folk song

Epilogue:
Our day-to-day October

Shortly before this book was published, a micro-organism invisible to the human eye occupied the dark present. Although the dystopian markets insisted that the Coronavirus disrupted the 'best of all possible worlds' we saw how a health crisis set off an explosion. Like a game of dominoes, COVID-19 pushed forward the weak tiles of the capitalist economy, giving way to a dance of mud and blood that, as Nikolai Kondratieff showed, moves in cycles; a brief boom heralds the arrival of a crisis. A chain reaction followed; industry collapsed, together with wages, company shares, the financial heart of the stock exchanges, the price of black oil, the rate of profit, the illusion that the crisis of 2008 had been overcome, the far-fetched idea of the dematerialisation of the economy, and finally the dogma that the cure for capitalism was more capitalism.

The rapid spread of the virus was only possible because of the dynamics of the global capitalist market that transported the pathogen on goods and humans, and which the logic of capital refused to stop in time. Despite the knowledge of the mechanics if its propagation, cities like Bergamo, Guayaquil, New York, Sao Paulo, Madrid or Wuhan were not closed down. It is no coincidence that the places in the world most affected by the pandemic shared similar characteristics: they were areas of commercial and industrial exchange with dense populations. And in addition, they were places of enormous social inequality which, because of the pressure from economic powers and their denial, failed to implement lockdown measures at the right moment – for that reason 'the capitalist centres should be considered the principal pathogenic focuses'(Wallace, 2020, p. 41). 'Capital had no room to manoeuvre, because its only ethics are accumulation. According to United Nations projections, in the coming months 300,000 people could die of hunger every day' (Clarin 2020). The pursuit of capitalist profits is so urgent and pressing that 'the selection of a virus that could kill a billion people is considered an acceptable risk' (Wallace 2020 p.42).

Despite this there are even greater horrors. Amid one of the most serious economic crises capitalism has ever faced, potentially even greater than the Crash of 1929, with historic levels of unemployment and economic contraction and with a tendency for the situation to worsen, there are those who celebrate their appearance in the Forbes Rich List, and who have passed from multimillionaires to multi-billionaires. The social and economic inequalities are so huge that fewer and fewer people believe that those who have more care about those who have nothing, even if their fortunes are measured in digits followed by several zeroes. The class struggle is more real than ever but those who are emerging victorious from it, for the moment, prefer not to speak about it. As the US magnate Warren Buffett put it; 'There certainly is a class war, but it's my class, the rich, who are waging this war, and we are winning it' (Buffett in the New York Times, 2016).

The hunger, sickness and death of the poor does not concern capital; on the contrary, they see it as an opportunity to make money. Industrialists across the world howl about returning to 'the new normality' which is in fact the old formula of bourgeois stupidity; sacrificing part of the 'factors of production' (in their language) to continue defending value, because there is always a surplus of labour that can replace the workers who have succumbed to the pandemic. Furthermore, on the basis of seizing an opportunity, they plan to deregulate and make labour more precarious, the dream of a sick line of people who are cheered by the possession of things and who know that business is done with money. For them the fastest route and one that is always open – in compliance with imperialism – is unscrupulous indebtedness. The spectre of the eternal debt and the 'letters of intent' have become part of the daily humiliation.

Given the course of events, it is a minority that still has blind faith in the state as an impartial and efficient arbiter of human affairs, or who consider capitalism the saviour of society. Most of us think the opposite. Who would defend the mean against the will of the majority? Who profess a fundamentalist practice? We identify with the thinking of the exploited; we are of them and share our lives with them.

If you want to find the causes of October uprising, the answer is in the logic of the capitalism that governs our country (and the world) and which gives everything to a few families and leaves the crumbs for the majority of working men and women of the city and the country. Wealth, derived from the exploitation of human beings and the depredation of nature, has allowed tuna fleet owners, oil and mining companies, the owners of banana and cacao plantations, the broccoli and flower growers, the coffee farmers, the forestry enterprises, the rubber and palm oil tappers, agro exporters, industrialists, landowners, and the pharmaceutical companies and bankers to accumulate capital and increasingly enrich themselves alone.

When an exhausted people organize, struggle and make legitimate use of their constitutional right to resist, the spokespersons of power through the capitalist communications media employ (as they always have and always will) every kind of epithet to undermine the legitimacy of popular anger. The prosecutors, judges, the military apparatus and the machinery of repression pursue, jail, criminalize, threaten, injure, stigmatize and kill them. In a word, they use force to dissuade them from any actions directed against the powerful.

It is crucial to reaffirm the authenticity and legitimacy of the right to confront power. 'Give us your ideas,' they say. We can do that, but the first step must be the 'sacrifice' of the wealth of a few who live 'well' (if that is what obscene luxury consumption and high spending is). That is the only way to respect the character and life of the nine-tenths of society who produce its wealth. The solution is to think of human society as a whole and not to consider only what is in private bank accounts. To paraphrase Perdo Jorge Vera, we must stop the dog dancing for silver and gold.

The task is to invite the exploited men and women to participate in common action in defence of life. Visceral and byzantine confrontations serve no purpose. We must learn to identify the origins and modes of reproduction of class, oligarchical, patriarchal, discursive, repressive and racist cultural and symbolic domination. Electoral dreams and illusions contribute little; power lies with money, resources, the media and institutions. The fiction of universal suffrage is paralysing, distorting our horizons and our ultimate objective – a society for each and all where the concept of exploitation, dispossession, theft and accumulation are no more than sad memories of what our grandfathers and grandmothers, our mothers and fathers once had to deal with in order to offer us a life of dignity.

Fortunately, the October rebellion is engraved in the memory of our people; it is matter, heart and spirit. It is myth and faith in our liberation. It is the most important continuation of the struggle of the Ecuadorean people. It is an icon, the continuing symbol of the sons and daughters of the first risings, of the grandchildren of the national strikes, of Aztra, of La Gloriosa, of 15th November, events that reverberate through all the actions taken to build a different society. For the defence of Pachamama and a community life, it is where all the great utopias merge.

Marx said, 'You cannot destroy with pinpricks what must be smashed with hammer blows'. The crisis will not be overcome with the pinpricks of the institutional left, who speak out against neoliberal capitalism while they cosy up to members of the State. Beyond its minor differences, the bourgeois mode of production and civilization generate death, just as their prodigal son the nation-state does, whether it is regulated or not, monetarist or welfarist, fascist or multicultural, liberal or republican, representative or participatory, mono-national or plurinational, democratic or a police state. All its versions leave scars.

The only hammer blow that is possible and necessary, it seems, comes from Rosa Luxemburg and Dolores Cacuango, from the testimony of the rebellion of the peoples of the world, from the men and women dedicated to turning into reality the dream of bringing us together in embraces, *mingas* and barricades, from those who 'inhabited a thousand homelands and none', as the Chilean writer Luis Sepúlveda, who recently died of COVID-19, put it. The light at the end of the tunnel comes from the affirmation, the object of faith, sought after without delay – Indoamerican communism or barbarism. ★

Bibliography

Books in English

Burns, Bradford E. 1980. *The Poverty of Progress,* University of California Press.

Foucault, Michel, 1981. *The Order of Discourse.* kit.ntnu.no/sites/www.kit.ntnu.no/files/Foucault_The%20Order%20of%20Discourse.pdf

Gramsci, Antonio, 2011. Prison Notebooks, Columbia University Press.

Gramsci, Antonio, 1971. *The Modern Prince,* International Publishers, New York, marxists.org/archive/gramsci/prison_notebooks/modern_prince/index.htm

Haug, Frigga, 2001. *The Mass Strike in Rosa Luxemburg's Writings,* rosalux.de/en/publication/id/43671/mass-strike

Hegel, Frederich, *The German Constitution (1798–1802),* marxists.org/reference/archive/hegel/works/gc/index.htm

Hobbes, Thomas, 1651. *Leviathan,* web.archive.org/web/20030218000757/http://oregonstate.edu/instruct/phl302/texts/hobbes/leviathan-contents.html

Luxemburg, Rosa, 1906. *The Mass Strike.* marxists.org/archive/luxemburg/download/mass-str.pdf

José Carlos Mariátegui, 1928. *Seven Interpretative Essays on Peruvian Reality,* marxists.org/archive/mariateg/works/7-interpretive-essays/index.htm

Miliband, Ralph, 1988. *The state in capitalist society,* legalform.files.wordpress.com/2019/04/miliband-state-in-capitalist-society.pdf

Schmitt, Carl, 1985. *Political Theology,* MIT Press.

Schmitt, Carl, 1996. *The concept of the political,* University of Chicago Press.

Sorel, Georges, 2004. *Reflections of Violence,* Dover Publications.

Thompson, E. P., 1978. *The Poverty of Theory,* files.libcom.org/files/poverty_of_theory_and_other_essays_ep_thompson.pdf

Tocqueville, Alexis de. 1835. *Democracy in America,* xroads.virginia.edu/~Hyper/DETOC/home.html

Wallace, Rob. 2020. *Agribusiness would risk millions of deaths,* sniadecki.wordpress.com/2020/03/23/coronavirus-wallace-en/.

Žižek, Slavoj. 2016. *Refugees, Terror and Other Troubles with the Neighbors: Against the Double Blackmail,* Penguin.

Books in Spanish

Acosta, Alberto y John Cajas. 2019a. *Insistimos: subsidios en clave integral.* lalineadefuego.info/2019/10/22/insistimossubsidios-en-clave-integral-por-alberto-acosta-y-john-cajas-guijarro/

Acosta, Alberto y John Cajas. 2019. *Propuestas hacia un horizonte más democrático.* lalineadefuego.info/2019/10/18/propuestashacia-un-horizonte-mas-democratico-por-alberto-acosta-y-john-cajas-guijarro/

Alarcón, Jorge. 2019. *La rebelión de octubre y la participación juvenil.* ecuadortoday.media/2019/10/23/la-rebelion-de-octubre-y-la-participacion-juvenil/

Almeida, Alejandro. 2019. 'Apuntes sobre el Movimiento Indígena'. En *Revista Política* 34, 69–90. Quito: ERE.

Álvarez, Silvia. 2019. 'El paro popular e indígena de 2019 en Ecuador. Una crónica etnografiada desde la Costa'. *Periferia, revista de recerca i formació en antropologia,* 24(2), pp. 289–303. doi.org/10.5565/rev/periferia.711

Andino, Marco. 2020. 'Las organizaciones campesinas indígenas de la Sierra Centro en el levantamiento de octubre'. En *Octubre*, 42–50. Quito: El Árbol de Papel.

Arana, Silvia. 2019. *Ecuador: El movimiento indígena ha dicho basta y ha echado a andar.* alainet.org/es/articulo/202620

Atarihuana, Giovanni. 2020. *Izquierda y derecha. Giovanni Atarihuana y Pablo Lucio Paredes reaccionan a las medidas económicas.* youtube.com/watch?v=soRnlloyJDw

Báez, Jonathan. 2019a. coyunturaisip.wordpress.com/2019/10/10/entre-subsidios-y-privatizaciones-el-ingreso-delos-hogares-mas-pobres-debe-subir-masque-el-incremento-delsalario-basico-unificado-del-ultimo-ano-tan-solo-para-cubrir-el-aumento-de-10-centavos-de-p/

Báez, Jonathan. 2019b. *La regresividad del IVA y las alternativas de los impuestos progresivos, el control a la evasión y elusión fiscal.* alainet.org/es/articulo/202332

Báez, Jonathan. 2019c. *Élites económicas en Ecuador, remisión y contribución progresiva.* lalineadefuego.info/2019/10/30/elites-economicas-en-ecuador-remision-y-contribucion-progresiva-por-jonathan-baez/

Báez, Jonathan. 2020. 'Captura empresarial del poder: preludio del Paro Nacional'. En Franklin Ramírez (Coord.). *Octubre y el derecho a la resistencia: revuelta popular y neoliberalismo autoritario en Ecuador,* 195–219. Buenos Aires: CLACSO.

Banco Central del Ecuador. 2016. *Estadísticas económicas. Información Estadística Mensual,* No. 1977, bce.fin.ec/index.php/component/k2/item/776, consultado en noviembre de 2016.

Becker, Marc y Silvia Tutillo. 2009. *Historia agraria y social de Cayambe.* Quito: FLACSO, Sede Ecuador: Ediciones Abya Yala

Bedón, José. 2019. *Fascismo neoliberal mediático.* rebelion.org/noticia.php?id=261775&titular=fascismo-neoliberal-medi%E1tico-

Bayly, Jaime. 2019a. *01 Crisis en Ecuador 10oct2019 Jaime Beyly.* youtube.com/watch?v=RXIwV8eIa8w

Bayly, Jaime. 2019b. *02 Crisis en Ecuador 11OCT2019 Jaime Beyly.* youtube.com/watch?v=RXIwV8eIa8w

Bonfil Batalla, Guillermo. 1990. *México profundo. Una civilización negada.* México D.F.: Grijalbo

Borja, María, Basantes, Ana Basantes y Mayuri Castro. 2019. *Las versiones del paro nacional contrapuestas en la Asamblea.* GK.city/2019/11/25/versiones-paro-nacional-en-ecuador

Borja, María. 2019. *La prensa herida.* GK.city/2019/10/14/prensa-atacada-paro/

Borja, María. 2019a. *Los delitos investigados tras el paronacional,* GK.city/2019/11/05/delitos-investigados-paro-nacional

Borón, Atilio. 2008. *Socialismo del siglo XXI: ¿Hay vida después del neoliberalismo?* Buenos Aires: Ediciones Luxemburgo.

Borón, Atilio. 2019. *Un Octubre que fue Febrero.* alainet.org/es/articulo/202673

Boscán, Andersson. 2019. *Café la Posta: ¿Ha sido un año loco es nuestra impresión?* youtube.com/watch?v=BaMJLg1HxAg

Campaña, Isaías. 2019a. *¿Sector privado motor de la economía?* alainet.org/es/articulo/198966

Campaña, Isaías. 2019b. *¿Ecuador sin proyecto nacional?* alainet.org/es/articulo/202701

Cantuña, Fabián. 2015. *La política fiscal como instrumento de estabilidad y crecimiento bajo un esquema de dolarización.Caso Ecuador. Período 2000–2012* (tesis de maestría). Quito:Universidad Andina Simón Bolívar.

Carrillo, Daniela. 2009. *La industria de alimentos y bebidas en el Ecuador.* Quito: Universidad Andina Simón Bolívar. uasb.edu.ec/UserFiles/381/File/ALIMENTOS.pdf

Castro, Apawki y Andrés Tapia. 2019. *Ataques, vulneraciones y cerco mediático al movimiento indígena durante el paro nacional.* alainet.org/es/articulo/203809

Cedeño, César. 2018. *El nuevo Ministro de Defensa tiene un currículum impresionante y gestiones espeluznantes.* GK.city/2018/05/01/quien-es-oswaldo-jarrin

Chancosa, Blanca. 2020. 'Octubre como un anuncia. Octubre continúa'. En *Octubre*, 24–32. Quito: El árbol de papel.

Chiliquinga, Javier. 2019. *El movimiento indígena durante la derogación del 883.* lalineadefuego.info/2019/10/22/el-movimientoindigena-durante-la-derogacion-del-883-javier-chiliquinga-amaya/

Chiriboga, Andrés y Leonardo Arias. 2020. 'La ruta al 'paquetazo' y el retorno de la economía fondomonetarista al Ecuador'. En Franklin Ramírez (Coord.). *Octubre y*

Coronel, Valeria. 2020. 'Crisis de la política de regateo y renovación del movimiento popular ecuatoriano'. En Franklin Ramírez (Coord.). *Octubre y el derecho a la resistencia: revuelta popular y neoliberalismo autoritario en Ecuador*, 169–193. Buenos Aires: CLACSO.

Coronel, Valeria. 2020. 'Crisis de la política de regateo y renovación del movimiento popular ecuatoriano'. En Franklin Ramírez (Coord.). *Octubre y el derecho a la resistencia: revuelta popular y neoliberalismo autoritario en Ecuador*, 309–. Buenos Aires: CLACSO.

Correa, Rafael. 2019a. *Mashi Rafael habla claro sobre los dirigentes de la Conaie*. youtube.com/watch?v=7A_Lsu6QP6o

Correa, Rafael. 2019b. Rafael Correa – La disputa por América Latina. youtube.com/watch?v=64U9gJhPeoY

Cuvi, Juan, Érika Arteaga, Jorge Cueva y Xavier Maldonado. 2019. *El agotamiento de un modelo de controlsocial*. lalineadefuego.info/2019/10/22/el-agotamiento-de-un-modelo-de-control-social/

Dávalos, Pablo. 2020a. *Confesiones. Los eventos de octubre y la ley de Crecimiento Económico*. http://pablo-davalos.blogspot.com/

Dávalos, Pablo. 2020b. *Diez tesis sobre la coyuntura política del Ecuador: las consecuencias de la rebelión de octubre*. http://pablodavalos.blogspot.com/

Dávalos, Pablo. 2020c. *Hoja de Ruta EN VIVO Pablo Dávalos Perspectivaseconómicas y las mentiras del Gobierno*. youtube.com/watch?v=KDaeMi7RPZo

Díaz, Isabel y Adriana Mejía. 2020. 'Las elites en octubre: deciudadanos indignados a propietarios alarmados'. En Franklin Ramírez (Coord.). *Octubre y el derecho a la resistencia: revuelta popular y neoliberalismo autoritario en Ecuador*, 271–285. Buenos Aires: CLACSO.

Espinel, Belén. 2015. *Plan Nacional de Seguridad Integral ¿discurso o posibilidad? Análisis del caso de la Policía Nacional dentro del Plan Nacional de Seguridad Integral propuesto por el Estado ecuatoriano* (tesis de maestría). Quito: Universidad Andina Simón Bolívar.

Espinosa Apolo, Manuel. 2010. *Los mestizos ecuatorianos y las señas de identidad cultural*. Quito: Tramasocial.

Figueroa, Santiago. 2017. *Plan de Negocios 'Proyecto Inmobiliario Sakura'* (tesis de maestría). Quito: Universidad San Francisco de Quito.

Freidenberg, Flavia y Manuel Alcántara Sáenz. 2001. *Los dueños del poder. Los prtidos políticos en el Ecuador (1978–2000)*. Quito:

FLACSO, Sede Ecuador. García, Jacobo y Eduardo Soria. 2020. 'Las fracturas de Octubre'. En Franklin Ramírez (coord.). *Octubre y el derecho a la resistencia: revuelta popular y neoliberalismo autoritario en Ecuador*, 393–410. Buenos Aires: CLACSO.

García, Ramiro. 2019. *Café la Posta: ¿Cuál es la situación del Ecuador?* youtube.com/watch?v=quRjanTnT6M

Guamán, Adoración. 2020. 'Fin de Estado de derecho y la protesta popular'. En Franklin Ramírez (coord.). *Octubre y el derecho a la resistencia: revuelta popular y neoliberalismo autoritario en Ecuador*, 149–168. Buenos Aires: CLACSO.

Guanche, Julio. 2019. 'A los ricos no les gusta / Que los pobres se reúnan'. En Julio Guanche, Cristina Vega, Jorge Estrella y Decio Machado. *Ecuador: el comienzo del fin del gobierno de Lenin Moreno. Dossier*. sinpermiso.info/textos/ecuador-elcomienzo-del-fin-del-gobierno-de-lenin-moreno-dossier

Herrera, Stalin. 2019. 'El movimiento indígena y la insurrección de los zánganos'. lalineadefuego.info/2019/10/22/el-movimiento-indigena-y-la-insurreccion-de-los-zanganos-por-stalin-herrera/

Larco C., Carolina y León Espinosa O. (Introducción y selección) (2012). *El pensamiento político de los movimientos sociales*. Quito: Ministerio Coordinador de la Política y Gobiernos Autónomos Descentralizados.

Le Quang, Matthieu, Nila Chávez y Daniel Vizuete. 2020. 'El Octubre plebeyo: cronología de doce días de movilización social'. En Franklin Ramírez (coord.). *Octubre y el derecho a la resistencia: revuelta popular y neoliberalismo autoritario en Ecuador*, 53–83. Buenos Aires: CLACSO.

León, Carlos. 2020. 'Desdolarización y desendeudamiento externo (Una relación de causa y efecto)'. En *Octubre*, 205–239. Quito: El Árbol de Papel.

Luque, Arturo; Carlos Poveda y Juan Hernández. 2020. 'Análisis del levantamiento indígena de 2019 en Ecuador: entre la respuesta legal y el lawfare'. En *Nullius* 1(1), 18–45. revistas.utm.edu.ec/index.php/revistanillius/article/view/2334

Machado, Decio. 2019a. 'Lo más interesante en el reciente proceso de luchas populares en Ecuador son sus nuevos liderazgos' (entrevista). ecuadortoday.media/2019/10/15/decio-machado-lo-mas-interesante-en-el-reciente-proceso-deluchas-populares-en-ecuador-son-sus-nuevos-liderazgos/

Machado, Decio. 2019b. 'País de lucha'. En Julio Guanche, Cristina Vega, Jorge Estrella y Decio Machado. *Ecuador: el comienzo del fin del gobierno de Lenin Moreno. Dossier*. sinpermiso.info/textos/ecuador-el-comienzo-del-fin-del-gobierno-de-leninmoreno-dossier

Madrid, Andrés. 2018. *En busca de la chispa en la pradera. El sujeto revolucionario en el pensamiento de la intelectualidad orgánica de la izquierda en el Ecuador 1975–1986*. Quito: Nacional Universidad Andina Simón Bolívar.

Madrid, Tito. 2017. *La clase obrera de Regreso. Mercado, Condiciones y Conflictos de trabajo en Ecuador 1988–2015* (tesis de licenciatura). Quito: Universidad Central del Ecuador.

Madrid, Tito. 2018. 'La política agraria en Ecuador (1965–2015)'. En *Revista Economía* 112 (70), 89–120. Quito.

Miranda, Pablo. 2019. 'El levantamiento indígena popular, victoriasobre el neoliberalismo'. En *Revista Política* 34, 9–68. Quito: ERE.

Morán, Susana. 2019a. *La protesta y la represión invisibilizadas por el cerco informativo oficial*.

planv.com.ec/historias/sociedad/la-protesta-y-la-represion-invisibilizadas-el-cercoinformativo-oficial

Morán, Susana. 2019b. *Las horas de terror en Quito*. planv.com.ec/historias/sociedad/horas-terror-quito

Morán, Susana. 2019c. *Paro: las cifras y la información no cuadran*. planv.com.ec/historias/sociedad/paro-cifras-y-la-informacion-no-cuadran

Moreano, Alejandro. 2020. 'La simbólica del Paro de Octubre'. En *Octubre*, 75–89. Quito: El árbol de papel.

Nebot, Jaime. 2019a. *Entrevista en La Posta*. youtube.com/watch?v=Qvag4rdEols

Nebot, Jaime. 2019b. *Ex Alcalde Jaime Nebot sobre las manifestaciones*. En: Así Amaneció, 09 de octubre. youtube.com/watch?v=Rs1oCcbF6rI

Noriega, Jahiren y Gonzalo Criollo. 2020. 'Solo el pueblo salva al pueblo: centros de acopio y acogida humanitaria como corazón de la resistencia'. En Franklin Ramírez (coord.). *Octubre y el derecho a la resistencia: revuelta popular y neoliberalismo autoritario en Ecuador*, 127–146. Buenos Aires: CLACSO.

Ordóñez, Cristian. 2016. *Las Fuerzas Armadas en el período de la Revolución Ciudadana (2007–2016)* (tesis de maestría). Quito: Universidad Andina Simón Bolívar.

Pacho, Valentín. 2019. *Ecuador, insurrección abortada. Faltó la vanguardia política*. rebelion.org/noticia.php?id=261750&titular=falt%F3-la-vanguardia-pol%EDtica-

Paz y Miño, Juan. 2015. *Historia de los impuestos en Ecuador*. Quito: SRI / PUCE / THE.

Paz y Miño, Juan. 2019. Ecuador: ¿Cómo entender la movilización indígena y popular? alainet.org/es/articulo/203006

Pontón, Daniel y Freddy Rivera. 2016. 'Postneoliberalismo y policía: caso de Ecuador 2007–2013'. En *Desafíos*, 28 (2), 213–253.

Ramírez, Franklin. 2019. *Las masas en octubre Ecuador y las colisiones de clase*. nuso.org/articulo/las-masas-en-octubre

Ramírez, Franklin. 2020. 'Paro pluri–nacional, movilización del cuidado y lucha política. Los signos abiertos de Octubre'. En Franklin Ramírez (coord.). *Octubre y el derecho a la resistencia: revuelta popular y neoliberalismo autoritario en Ecuador*, 11–44. Buenos Aires: CLACSO.

Ramos, María. 2019. *El nuevo viejo rol de los militares ecuatorianos en la política*. alainet.org/es/articulo/202622

Romero, Iván. 2010. *Cambios en la política de defensa nacional del libro blanco hacia la nueva agenda de seguridad interna y externa* (tesis de maestría). Quito: Universidad Andina Simón Bolívar.

Romo, María Paula. 2019a. *María Paula Romo Ministra de Gobierno – Coyuntura Nacional | ASI AMANECIÓ | 18 OCTUBRE 2019*. youtube.com/watch?v=fqUlidZXA3k

Romo, María. 2019b. 'El diálogo no significa que vamos a hacer exactamente todo lo que nos digan'. GK.city/2019/11/18/ministra-gobierno-paro-nacional

Ruiz, Miguel y Manuela García. 2019. *Una victoria sui generis*. alainet.org/es/articulo/202668

Ruiz, Miguel y Pablo Iturralde. 2013. *Estado, petróleo y patrón de acumulación en Ecuador*. Quito: CDES.

Saltos, Napoleón. 2019. *De paquetazos y resistencias: no son medidas, es un modelo*. ecuadortoday.media/2019/10/07/de-paquetazos-y-resistencias-no-son-medidas-es-un-modelo/

Santi, Marlon. 2020. 'La agenda no era un golpe, sino cambios trascendentales'. En *Octubre*, 33–41. Quito: El árbol de papel.

SENPLADES. 2009. *Plan Nacional de Desarrollo 2007–2010. Planificación para la revolución ciudadana*. Quito: SENPLADES.

SENPLADES. 2013. *Plan Nacional del Buen Vivir*. Quito: SENPLADES Sierra Natalia. 2019. *La victoria de los pueblos del Ecuador: Octubre 2019*. ecuadortoday.media/2019/10/17/la-victoria-de-los-pueblos-del-ecuador-octubre-2019/

Silva, María. 2019a. *Más de 12 000 personas perdieron su trabajo en el sector textil en el último año*. elcomercio.com/actualidad/personas-sector-textil-inec.html

Silva, María. 2019b. *Proyecto de ley propone cobrar contribución a 10 403 empresas*. elcomercio.com/actualidad/proyecto-ley-contribucion-empresas-ecuador.html

Stoessel, Soledad y Rodrigo Iturriza. 2020. 'Repliegue sectorial y representación universal: formas del diálogo durante el Octubre plebeyo en Ecuador'. En Franklin Ramírez (coord.). *Octubre y el derecho a la resistencia: revuelta popular y neoliberalismo autoritario en Ecuador*, 249–269. Buenos Aires: CLACSO.

Stoessel, Soledad. 2019. 'Fue una negociación pública inédita en la historia de Ecuador' (entrevista), ecuadortoday.media/2019/10/16/ fue-una-negociacion-publica-inedita-en-la-historia-de-ecuador/

Tamayo, Eduardo y Helga Serrano. 2019. *Ecuador: Toque de queda y la gente resiste*, alainet.org/es/articulo/202627

Tamayo, Eduardo. 2019. *Revuelta popular tumbó el paquetazo del FMI… pero las heridas quedan*. alainet.org/es/articulo/202649

Tapia, Evelyn. 2019. *PIB de Ecuador se contraerá este 2019*. elcomercio.com/actualidad/pib-ecuador-paro-banco-central.html

Unda, Mario. 2020. *Ecuador: Enseñanzas y desafíos a la luz de octubre*. sinpermiso.info/textos/ecuador-ensenanzas-y-desafios-a-la-luz-de-octubre

Vaca, Fermín. 2019. *Así festejó el David indígena la derrota de Goliat*. planv.com.ec/historias/politica/asi-festejo-el-david-indigena-la-derrota-goliat

Varela, Marcelo. 2020. 'La estigmatización de las pérdidas económicas por la movilización social'. En Camila Parodi y Nicolás Sticotti (eds.). *Ecuador la insurrección de octubre*, 94–99. Buenos Aires: CLACSO.

Vega, Gustavo. 2020. 'El pandemonio de once días. Reflexiones desde la historia, la antropología y la psiquiatría'. En Centro Ecuatoriano de Estudios Internacionales y Escuela de Relaciones Internacionales – UIDE. *Boletín Panorama Global* 7, 4–9. Quito: CEEI / UIDE.

Velasco, Fernando. 1979. *Reforma agraria y movimiento Campesino indígena de la Sierra*. Quito: El Conejo.

Vélez, Roger. 2019. *Ministra de Gobierno entregó a la Asamblea informe preliminar sobre protestas*. elcomercio.com/actualidad/ministra-gobierno-asamblea-informe-paro.html

Villavicencio, Fernando. 2020a. *Café la Posta: Nuevos casos de corrupción*. youtube.com/watch?v=SqAVAm1tNkg

Villavicencio, Fernando. 2020b. *Nuevas revelaciones*. youtube.com/watch?v=PJ-XZzObayc

Villavicencio, Renato. 2019. *El día después de la negociación ¿Victoria popular?* rebelion.org/docs/261574.pdf

Vogliano, Soledad y Apawki Castro. 2020. 'Ecuador: estallido tras una década de silencio' en: Revista *Catarsis*, número 2. Buenos Aires: Catarsis por doquier.

Weisbrot, Mark y Andrés Arauz. 2019. *Obstáculos al crecimiento: El programa del FMI en Ecuador*. Washington: CEPR.

Zapata, Juan. 2019. 'Daños por 214 300 dólares en ECU 911 de Ecuador durante las protestas'. lavanguardia.com/internacional/20191016/471030277809/danos-por-214300-dolares-en-ecu-911-de-ecuador-durante-las-protestas.html

Zavaleta Mercado, René. 2013. *Ensayos 1975–1984, Obras Completas II*. La Paz: Plural.

Zibechi, Raúl. 2019. *¿De qué ha servido la revuelta en Ecuador?* ecuadortoday.media/2019/10/18/de-que-ha-servido-la-revuelta-en-ecuador

In a number of cities around the country *cacerolazos* (the banging of pots as a protest) were called. Women and their children join one of them (Photo: Karen Toro).

A group of young urban men carry the Ecuadorean flag during the days of struggle (Photo: Alejandro Ramírez Anderson).

Troops fill the streets of Quito, ready to launch repression. They are carrying Mossberg 12 bore shotguns (Photo: Karen Toro).

Unity between the Indigenous and the popular sectors of city and country
(Photo: Daniel Andrade).

All out on the streets, stop production and close the roads on Tuesday 15 October!

Dialogue between workers and Indigenous peoples, and struggle against the government and the rich!

A campaign of struggle without Lassos, Nebots, Morenos and Correas!

Just how the peoples of Ecuador fight: saying-doing, saying-doing, saying-doing, dammit!

When we mould our words, we will fill them with our actions!

'Mama Rosa Elvira and Tayta José María: your struggle against the huasipungo servitude bears fruit in our struggle against capitalism'.

Appendix
Platform for the 'Campaign of Escalating Struggle'

This text was published by CONAIE *on its website on 26 September 2019, six days before Decree 883 which triggered the uprising. It reflects the positions adopted by the main Indigenous movement at its annual assembly in Rukullakta in August that year, and the decision to break off negotiations with the government of President Lenin Moreno. As this book explains, these positions already adopted by* CONAIE *became one of the key ingredients of the rebellion in October.*

No to extractivism, the elimination of labour rights and neo-liberalism

1   DIALOGUE ONLY BETWEEN EQUALS

The resolutions reached at the Annual Assembly of CONAIE (23 August 2019), which are in line with the decisions adopted by other social movements, open the way to raise an agenda of struggle that breaks with passivity and overcomes the dispersion of the many fragmented struggles throughout the country.

The declaration of a break with the government is based on the following:

a   The talks were unsuccessful and basically created the illusion of a democratic moment; hiding the gradual creation of a state project by the Social-Christians (heterodox neo-liberals) and other fractions of the ruling class (orthodox neo-liberals).
b   The agenda of the talks has been limited to the handing over of second-order public positions such as directorates, secretariats, etc.; a procedure that has blocked the demands of the organisations for benefits and rights for the majority of the people.

c   The easing of the criminalization of political struggle has only been partial: cases of criminalization of leaders,[1] and popular fighters continue, maintaining the policy of criminalization that has led to hundreds of comrades being imprisoned, prosecuted and even killed (such as the courageous Bosco Wisum, José Tendetza and Freddy Taish).
d   The main lesson of this period confirms a long-known fact: the government and bourgeois power are not disposed to give in unless there are forceful actions that support the demands of the people.

We broke off talks with the government because of the enormous benefits that the bourgeoisie continues to receive through the many policies to reactivate the economy, which do not depend only on 'corrupt officials' but are part of the core of the economic policy. It is clear that this government serves the ruling elites just like the previous ones, only without the 'left' trappings that its predecessor donned through social welfare policies.

In short, we are facing a transition from Correa's regulatory state interventions to a deregulatory state intervention. Both strategies are typical of a government of the rich, but in different contexts: the first at a time of economic boom (where the state had large oil revenues that made it possible to finance social programmes) and the second at a time of capitalist recession. But in the end, the transition does not change the central issue: both then and now, companies were assured of a very high rate of profit based on state intervention in the economy, and on the mechanisms that the state generates so that the crisis is paid for by workers, men and women, and not by the bosses.

In line with this, and based on the clauses stipulated in the Letter of Intent signed with the IMF and on the demands of the employers, which were mainly expressed in the Economic Reactivation Law[2] and the Law for the Promotion of Production, Attracting Investment and Generating Employment,[3] the government implemented a series of measures in favour of the employers:

---

[1] The case of Cristian Aguinda, of the Kichwa Pastaza people, accused by the Genefran company of the alleged crime of intimidation. Also, the leaders Marlon Vargas (Confeniae), Cristian Aguinda (Ponakisc), Antonio Vargas (Kichwa), under investigation for the alleged offence of paralysing public services in the Piatúa struggle.

[2] Approved on Wednesday, 27 December 2017 in the National Assembly, it was published on Friday, 29 December 2017 in the Official Gazette.

[3] Published in the Registro Oficial Suplemento 309 of 21 August, 2018.

a   Representatives of the bourgeoisie were given top jobs in the state:

   • Minister of Finance: Richard Martínez (former President of the Ecuadorean Business Committee).
   • Former Minister of Foreign Trade: Pablo Campana (linked to the NOBIS Business Group).
   • Former Minister of Labour and current Minister of the Environment: Raúl Ledesma (linked to agribusiness).

b   Tax breaks for large companies[4] (while a street trader has to pay his taxes on time):

   • Writing off tax debts worth a total of more than 4 billion dollars.
   • Big companies could be let off an amount that could reach, according to the SRI's (Inland Revenue) own estimates, US$2.355 billion, out of a total debt of US$4.4 billion.
   • Refunding of advance payments on income tax (the Eljuri group alone got a rebate of 30 million dollars, according to SRI figures).

c   The deregulation and casualization of labour through a wide range of measures, including: the flexible application of the 40-hour working week and the extension of the probationary period of the worker in a company;[5] the legitimisation of summary dismissals to eliminate trade unions; the legalisation of remote working and the exploitation of young people through internships and agreements with companies; the casualization of labour through apps like Uber, Cabify and Glovo, as well as in shopping centres and call centres; the persecution of

---

4   The Basic Law for the Promotion of Production, Attraction of Investment, Generation of Employment and Fiscal Stability and Balance provides for a period of 90 working days to benefit from a 100% write-off of interest, fines and surcharges, and applies to tax obligations administered and/or collected by the SRI (Inland Revenue).

5   The government together with employers within the so-called National Council for Work and Wages (CNTs) establishes three types of working hours: the ordinary one, of 40 hours in five days and 8 hours a day; the special one, which will be created with a written agreement and registration in the ministry, with 40 hours to be completed in up to 6 days and could be up to 12 hours a day. Also, the 90-day probation period is eliminated and a new form of contract, 'for entrepreneurship and new investments', allows for the possibility of using the option of redundancy and this not being considered untimely dismissal for a period of up to 3 years.

informal workers; the absolute lack of guaranteed labour rights in agribusiness, where there are no possibilities for union organization and the working day and salary are determined by the company on the basis the daily wage, as well as a permissive attitude to slave labour as shown in the Furukawa case.

All this is topped off with a policy of concealing the corruption (including lobbying) of big private companies, claiming that corruption is the preserve of public officials, while ensuring impunity in the trials of big businessmen such as Juan Eljuri[6] and Fidel Egas.[7]

In addition, the government has launched constant public campaigns to publicise the 'benefits' of mining and extractivism in the mainstream media, such as *El Comercio* and *Televistazo*, with the support of government institutions, while the plundering of Indigenous territories and unrest among the population continues, among which (and only as examples) we can mention the following:

a   The imposition of an oil concession in Block 28 in the province of Pastaza.[8]
b   The conflicts over the start of mining operations in the subtropical areas of the provinces of Cotopaxi and Bolívar, in Intag (on the border between the provinces of Imbabura and Pichincha) and in Río Blanco (Molleturo, province of Azuay).
c   The beginning of the extraction phase in the mining concessions in the Cordillera del Cóndor and the Shuar territory.[9]
d   The abuses committed by prawn farming companies in the Gulf of Guayaquil and on Puná Island against their workers and against the neighbouring communities who were previously stripped of their land.
e   The persecution of banana workers' leaders and the cover-up of abuses committed on the plantations.

Last but not least, we are observing how the state as a whole is part of the advance by conservative forces, fascism and the most reactionary common sense, preparing society for an even more pronounced turn towards the Social Christian right, the most brutal expression of which is the demonization of the struggle for women's rights. This neo-fascism has permeated public discourse and policies, criminalising and distorting the agenda of women's struggles, especially those of the poorer sectors, for fundamental rights such as abortion in the case of rape, the denunciation of femicide and, in general, the struggle against patriarchy and capitalism. This comes on top of a series of demonstrations with conservative demands: 'pro-life' marches led by the church, 'white marches' against violence, 'don't mess with my children' parades or marches organised by the Social-Christian movement.

Added to this is an apology for institutional violence and racism, with the spread of a discourse promoting law and order to increase the presence of the police and leave the country's serious social and economic problems unresolved,[10] as well as the dissemination of slogans against poor migrants in order to criminalise the presence of foreigners, especially Venezuelans.[11] All this illustrates a shift to the right with campaigns to discredit leftist ideas and the communist perspective, confusing it with regulatory intervention by the state.

In this context we are forced to conclude that, beyond the individual actions of more or less willing officials, there is no political will to tackle the underlying issues, and that the implementation of an orthodox neo-liberal programme is underway, supported by the Social-Christian right and neo-fascism.

---

6   Members of the Eljuri group were investigated in the Odebrecht case for their links with the national and international bank, Sai Bank. On 12 March 2018, Juan Pablo Eluri Vintimilla received notification of an acquittal ruling in his favour from the Public Prosecutor's Office.

7   Linked to the 'notario Cabrera' case and the laundering of illicit funds through the Banco Pichincha.

8   For example, on 7 September, in an act of blatant pro-extractivist propaganda by the government, during the opening of the school year in the province of Pastaza, at the Héroes del Cenepa School in the canton of Mera, the Block 28 consortium, made up of PetroAmazonas, ENAP Chile and Belaruse, handed out backpacks bearing the slogan 'Consorcio Bloque 28' to the students, in the presence of the governor of Pastaza and government authorities.

9   The Panantza-San Carlos and Mirador projects owned by the Chinese consortium CRCC-Tongguan Investement Company with almost 50,000 hectares under concession and the Fruta del Norte project owned by the Swedish-Canadian company Lundın Gold Corp with 75,000 hectares under concession.

10   The latest reforms to the Criminal Code legalise showing the faces of those caught and arrested 'in the act', which violates the presumption of innocence. During the 2015 strike, the majority of protesters were reported as being caught in the act.

This gives more legal basis to the police for the 'use of dissuasive force'. The police in the Saraguro case applied for this option to act against demonstrators.

11   The imposition of a visa requirement for Venezuelan citizens was condemned by human rights organisations worldwide. In the first week after the measure was introduced, Ecuador received nearly 2,000 applications for humanitarian visas.

2   THE CAMPAIGN OF ESCALATING STRUGGLE AND THE PEOPLE'S DEMANDS

In this situation, it is time to propose a plan of action that will make it possible to achieve the demands of our people, and prevent the steamroller of reforms from crushing the living conditions of poor households. The call for a Campaign of Escalating Struggle is a strategic slogan to keep the popular organisations on their feet, to win benefits for the majority and to motivate the people's organizations in every province to join in protest actions of ever greater intensity.

Our list of demands contains two types of demands: 1) a set of demands for the immediate term that are related to the most pressing needs of the people in each locality; 2) medium and long term goals to promote national demands and a structural critique of the neoliberal administration (orthodox or heterodox) of capital.

As such, the demands of the Indigenous movement, the trade union movement, popular organizations, the women's movement and the people in general come together to push for a programme of unity, which, among others, includes:

Opposition to the neoliberal agenda in its entirety:
Complete reversal of the letter of intent with the International Monetary Fund and an end to the attempts to privatise public companies under the guise of 'granting concessions'.

Opposition to extractive industries with a view to declaring the country free of mining for metals:
a   Cancellation of the licences to drill for oil in Block 28 and for mining which is already causing high levels of conflict in the subtropics, the south, the north-west and the southern Amazon region.
b   Investigation into the corruption of private companies in obtaining concessions and licences in extractive industries, and guarantees that favourable rulings obtained by communities in defence of their territorial rights and those of nature will be respected. Some of the landmark cases include:

- The historic ruling protecting the Piatúa river from the building of the Genefrán S.A. hydroelectric plant (Santa Clara, Pastaza province).
- The victory of the Huaorani people in the injunction that prevented oil exploitation in Block 22, which protects 180,000 hectares of Amazonian rainforest.

- The court ruling against mining activities in the territory of the Cofan people of Sinangoe.

c Implementation of the agreements between Petroamazonas and the community members involved in the Chontapunta strike.
d An end to the abuses by big prawn farmers in the Gulf of Guayaquil and Puná Island.

In defence of plurinationality:
An end to the restrictions and criminalization imposed on the exercise of Indigenous justice, community transport, and intercultural bilingual education.

Investigate the corruption of large private companies:
a An end to impunity and the prosecution of big businessmen involved in corruption cases, in particular the cases against Juan Eljuri and Fidel Egas.
b The inclusion in the definition of corruption of the strategic lobbying and marketing carried out by large foreign corporations and the country's richest tycoons.

Guarantee the right to decent work:
a The proposals for flexible working hours and flexible work contracts should be shelved.
b Stop and sanction the practice of sudden layoffs of unionised workers, and guarantee the right of association.
c Guarantee the conditions for organising trade unions in agro-industry, for those working remotely, on part-time contracts, internships, or under special agreements with companies, as well as among workers for apps and in shopping centres and call centres.
d Investigate and halt the persecution of informal workers by local governments (as is the case of the municipalities of Guayaquil, Quito and Cuenca).
e Fulfil the state's obligation to retired workers, equalise the monthly pension payment on retirement in cash and not through coupons or other non-monetary forms.
f Meet the demands of the Furukawa workers.
g Declare a state of emergency in the cultural sector and resolve the demands of the associations of artists and cultural workers. Recognize the trade union organisations of broccoli workers.

h   Investigate, sanction and end the persecution of the leaders of banana workers and the abuses committed on the banana plantations and in the agro-industry.
i   Guarantee job security for public and private sector workers.

In defence of small peasant farming:
a   Protection and incentives for family farms and peasant farmers.
b   Access to low-interest loans for small-scale peasant production, debt cancellation for small-scale producers.
c   Ecological plant and animal health policies that break with the large agro-toxic monopolies.
d   Guarantee the guardianship of native seeds by peasant and Indigenous communities, and the elimination of seed hoarding by a few big companies such as Agroquímica and Pronaca.
e   A comprehensive audit of water and fertile land grabbing by agribusiness companies.
f   Redistribution of water and land suitable for cultivation.

Implementation of the agenda for the recognition and guarantee of women's rights:
a   Decriminalization of abortion in cases of rape as a fundamental human right.
b   Comprehensive policy, not only judicial, against femicide, machismo and gender violence, with the allocation of a budget and implementation of the Comprehensive Law against Gender Violence.
c   An end to the campaign of misrepresentation and attacks on the rights of working class and low-income women.

Responses to the crisis affecting small producers and peasants:
a   In keeping with the cancellation of the tax debts of large companies, cancellation of the debts of poor households acquired for their subsistence with financial credit institutions and the SRI (Internal Revenue Service); no increase in the VAT rate above 12%.
b   Respect for the minimum price of dry maize, rice and milk.
c   A comprehensive solution to the problems caused by middlemen with agricultural products.

In defence of the right to education:

a Resolution of the serious teaching problems in the school system, especially in schools for the rural and urban poor, prior to the imposition of a university entrance exam.
b Expansion of quotas for admission to public universities, including budgetary allocations to strengthen the infrastructure of higher education and the introduction of affirmative action policies for the Indigenous and Afro-Ecuadorean peoples and nationalities.
c Restoration of the Intercultural Education System in a comprehensive manner; this implies the reopening of community schools and the expansion of budget allocations to ensure job stability for teachers.
d Permanent appointments and job stability for teachers in the public sector nationwide.

In defence of public health:

a End the millions of dollars in financial transfers to the private health system and strengthen the infrastructure of the public health system.
b Audit the private insurance companies and health service providers that enriched themselves with public funds during the period 2007–2019.
c Pay the state's debts to the State Social Security Institute (IESS) in order to boost investment in health infrastructure.
d Stop all negotiations and attempts to privatise the social security system.

In defence of community media:

a Strict compliance with the Basic Law on Communication with regard to the 34% percentage of the radio spectrum reserved for community media.
b Democratization of radio spectrum concessions of the corresponding percentage in the cities.

3   UNITY IN ACTION AND ITS CONSEQUENCES

The mobilization will make the demands of the people visible and will give a perspective to a dispersed citizenry, since in the last few months there have been a series of struggles that have not managed to coalesce around a national set of demands.

It is therefore necessary to regroup the forces of the social movements with practical actions in each territory and with different forms of struggle, in order to overcome the stubbornness of the ruling class and the government. The aim is to advance towards an action that can achieve major victories for the majority of workers, peasants, people, women, students, youth, artists, and the Indigenous peoples and nationalities of Ecuador.

As in previous times, the government is using its favourite instrument to quell the people's struggle: the practice of division and co-option, aggravated by the behaviour of some leaders who, given their precarious ideological education, are dragged along by the government's agenda or who consciously submit themselves slavishly to the agenda of social democracy and even of the right.

We do not sell ourselves for a plate of stew, nor for millions! The dignity of the people is not for sale and is only achieved, both in historical struggles and in the present, through constant mobilisation. Let us move from the Campaign of Escalating Struggle towards a united declaration of an Indigenous Uprising, a National Strike of the trade union confederations and a People's Strike of the popular organisations. ★

You

Poem dedicated to María Paula Romo, in the heat of the repression of the Uprising of October 2019. By Xavier Silva Cardenas 'Compa Xaavicho'.

You
Young woman
You who are no longer young
You who will now never be married
You no longer you
You not
You.

There goes the one who was here they will say
She who was once here but now not even that
She. The woman. The other.
Anything inappropriate.
The tongues will be tied
When people try to mention her
Their throats will pierce the walls
Her name will no longer be hers
Because without a name you are nothing.
You will not be born
Youwill never be
You will be nothing
You will not be
You are not.

And yet
I reveal her
Even though she is not nor will be
Nor was
So much rowing to end by not being
An insubstantial roaming
Scarcely having been
What happened to her they will say
And my sister will answer
I don't know.She has not been

Why would she?
But my parents will speak
My brothers and sisters will speak
Because my mothers will have felt
You
Who never was
You are where memory is
When memory burns and shines
But because you never were
They will speak
Because they were,are,will be
My brothers and sisters my parents my mothers
Did see you, yes
See you who are no longer
Because you are incarnate in the executors
Who are gone too
But hear her and do for you
Because you learned for this
To be and not be
To be not being
And to order that others bring into being
What should not be
You
Being face to face
You were there
Signed the order
Stopped speaking

Sent in armoured cars kicked
You were there
Teaching
Through their actions
It was their hand which is no longer
And you spread the gas
Despair for the bones of my people
Break the eyes of my small children
You drive the brutal motor cycle!
That broke my comrades in two!
You dispensed with your pestilence
The sacred word
Gathered in assembly!
And you surrounded them and kicked them

You called them 'whores'
You did not respect the skirts
That protect the Earth.
And you murdered my brother
Threw him from the bridge
The unborn, his own ,like you
They broke the skulls of my people
Your unborn
Cruelly
You were there with your knees
Your testicles,you punched their breasts
Happy in persecution
Ordering,shouting
Be without being,
Spit in your own face
On your own feet
Let the rifle butts
Blind their own future with blood
Spit on your own history
This is not your people
You
Young woman
You who are no longer even young
You will not be a woman
You who are not you
You who no longer are
You who do not
You
You who no longer exist

Barricade in El Arbolito park, 12 October 2019
(Photo: Vinicio Cóndor).

'Leave me with hope', Miguel Hernandez
(Photo: Luis Herrera/Audivisual Cooperative).

Cover artwork courtesy Tony Balseca

About the publishers

RESISTANCE BOOKS is a radical publisher of internationalist, ecosocialist and feminist books. Resistance Books publishes books in collaboration with the International Institute for Research and Education (iire.org), and the Fourth International (fourth.international/en). For further information, including a full list of titles available and how to order them, go to the Resistance Books website.

info@resistancebooks.org
www.resistancebooks.org

THE INTERNATIONAL INSTITUTE FOR RESEARCH AND EDUCATION is a centre for the development of critical thought and the exchange of experiences and ideas between people engaged in their struggles. Since 1982, when the Institute opened in Amsterdam, it has organized courses for progressive forces around the world which deal with all subjects related to the emancipation of the oppressed and exploited. The IIRE provides activists and academics opportunities for research and education in three locations: Amsterdam, Islamabad and Manila. The IIRE publishes Notebooks for Study and Research in several languages. They focus on contemporary political debates, as well as themes of historical and theoretical importance.

iire@iire.org
www.iire.org

www.ingramcontent.com/pod-product-compliance
Lightning Source LLC
Chambersburg PA
CBHW061819290426
44110CB00027B/2918